REBUILDING THE AMERICAN DREAM

RESTORING AMERICAN JOBS AND COMPETITIVENESS THROUGH INNOVATION AND ENTREPRENEURSHIP

Bob Skandalaris

with Ken Harrington

Pembrook
PUBLISHING

BLOOMFIELD HILLS, MICHIGAN

Pembrook Publishing, LLC
33 Bloomfield Hills Parkway, Suite 240
Bloomfield Hills, MI, 48304
http://www.pembrookpublishing.com

© 2006 by Pembrook Publishing, LLC
All rights reserved. Published 2006
Printed in the United States of America

12 11 10 09 08 07 06   1 2 3 4 5

ISBN-10 (cloth): 0-9771743-2-8
ISBN-13 (cloth): 978-0-9771743-2-4

Publisher's Cataloging-in-Publication Data
available at http://www.pembrookpublishing.com

Written by Amber Clark
Book interior designed and typeset by Graffolio
Cover designed by Dunn+Associates Design
Printed by Sheridan Books

ACKNOWLEDGEMENTS

I am greatly appreciative of the input provided by the following individuals, who took time out from their busy schedules to share their expertise in interviews. Their words of wisdom have added greatly to the content of this book.

Thomas Anderson, Director of the Automation Alley Technology Center

David Attis, Director of Policy Studies for the Council on Competitiveness

Steven Ballmer, CEO of Microsoft

Alan Bender, Co-founder and former Executive Vice President of T-Mobile

Jimmy Clark, Professor Emeritus, University of Kentucky

Maxine Clark, Founder and CEO of Build-a-Bear Workshop

Robert Clark, Howard Hughes Medical Institute Research Associate, University of Michigan Medical Center

James Clifton, Chairman and CEO of Gallup Research

William Danforth, Chancellor Emeritus, Washington University in St. Louis

Barton Hamilton, Robert Brookings Smith Distinguished Professor of Entrepreneurship, John M. Olin School of Business, Washington University in St. Louis

Randal Kaufman, Howard Hughes Medical Institute Investigator, University of Michigan Medical Center

Randall Kempner, Vice President of Regional Innovation for the Council on Competitiveness

Kei Koizumi, Director of the R&D Budget and Policy Program for the American Association for the Advancement of Science

Robert Kuk, Managing Partner, Allsop Venture Partners

Daniel Maher, Partner, Deloitte & Touche

Charles McManis, Thomas and Karole Green Professor of Law, and Director of the Center for Research on Innovation and Entrepreneurship at Washington University in St. Louis

Amy Millman, President of Springboard Enterprises

Lesa Mitchell, Vice President of Advancing Innovation, Kauffman Foundation

Christopher Morin, President and CEO of Noble International

Michael Pressler, Head Coach of the Men's Lacrosse Team at Duke University

Tina Seelig, Executive Director of the Stanford Technology Ventures Program

Richard Snyder, Chairman of Gateway Computers, CEO of Ardesta, and Chairman of Ann Arbor Spark

Jeffrey Tefft, Howard Hughes Medical Institute Assistant Manager, University of Michigan Medical Center

Albert Teich, Director of Science and Policy Programs for the American Association for the Advancement of Science

Anthony Tersigni, President and CEO of Ascension Health

Richard Wagoner, Jr., Chairman and CEO of General Motors

CONTENTS

◇◇

PREFACE

◇◇◇

Several people have asked me why I wanted to write a book. The answer is simple. By doing so, I was able to better educate myself about the challenges we, as a nation, face. In preparing for this book, I spoke to several experts to solicit their thoughts on innovation, entrepreneurship, research, education, governmental policies, and capital strategies. Simply put, their contribution to my learning process was invaluable. While some of my comments may seem negative to some, they are not meant to be so. Rather, I hope this book helps open people's minds to the challenges ahead.

The concept of the American Dream was an excellent marketing tool that helped to create America's image as the world leader in innovation and entrepreneurship. Immigrants like my grandparents came to America believing that by working hard, they could achieve a better life for themselves and their families. The world sought out the American Dream, and the best place to achieve that dream was in the United States.

This country's ascension to the most powerful nation on earth was fueled by its greatest asset, its people. Early Americans were optimistic and were not afraid to take risks. After all, they left their countries of origin with little or no assets to pursue the dream of a better life. What risk could be greater? They were willing to work hard, start at the bottom, and learn new ways to perform a task. They were innovators who adapted to change, and their resolve was incredible. In addition to building an economy and capitalistic system that is the envy of much of the free world, they also achieved considerable financial benefits as individuals.

While early Americans were willing to work hard, society required them to do so. There wasn't anyone who would feed or care for them unless they could support themselves and their families. Bartering enabled tradespeople and farmers to earn a reasonable living, and this survive-or-die environment provided a strong incentive to work. Over time, that has changed. Many of the ethnic communities that were so prevalent in early America began to disintegrate as immigrants assimilated into society. Government spending, redistribution of income, and the realization that wealth will not be achievable by everyone have eroded some of the incentives to work. As the middle class has grown in numbers and political importance, our society's values and expectations have changed accordingly. People now work not just to survive and climb the economic ladder, but to support themselves and to pursue life's pleasures.

Americans returned home from World War II victorious and determined to achieve a new version of the American Dream. For the first time, returning soldiers were able to pursue a college education that was subsidized by the U.S. government. Many who took advantage of this, like my parents, would not have been able to afford a college education otherwise. Driven to succeed, more educated than any previous generation, feeling proud to be Americans and possessing strong family values, they propelled America to world leadership. Yet the success of that generation was not without help. Communism sheltered China and the Soviet bloc from the rest of the world. Much of Europe and Asia were poverty stricken and damaged by World War II. The world looked to America for leadership and innovation, and we responded. Over time, Americans grew to believe they could meet any challenge that was presented to them; however, with each new generation, the growing middle class lifestyle became an expectation. Trade unions prospered, and companies became a security blanket that people believed would support them through retirement. This feeling of entitlement is a relatively new phenomenon in America, and one that has not been to our advantage.

In 1989, the Berlin Wall came down and changed the political and economic landscapes. Not only did the Soviet Union and its former satellites break apart and abandon communism in favor of capitalism, but China and India subsequently adopted a friendlier attitude towards capitalism as well. Asia and Europe finally overcame their World War II damage, and almost overnight, the world became a global marketplace. As a result, American companies lost market share, and the image of America as the sole owner of the American Dream changed. In the 1990s, poor Chinese farmers flocked to China's big cities to achieve a middle class lifestyle. Eastern Europeans, who were willing to work hard and for less money than Western Europeans, started taking their jobs. The same thing happened in China, only they began to take our jobs. Where were the Americans while this was happening? Trying to decide whether to respond and, if so, *how* to respond.

We now face the difficult task of adapting to significant competition from a growing cast of global suppliers. Innovation and entrepreneurship are a must for our long-term survival. This necessitates changing the way we educate our population, figuring out ways to respond to an accelerating rate of change, altering our self-perception that we are the world's best at everything, compensating our workforce on an incentive basis, and adjusting our governmental policies to a new world economy. Unfortunately, it is easier to change directions in a small boat than a large ship, and America is a very large ship.

Are we up to the challenge? I believe we are, but only if we accept that the lifestyle of the 1950s is a thing of the past. That golden era will not return. Hard work alone will not be enough to succeed. Corporations will never again be a place of lifetime employment. So we must create new jobs through innovation, because we cannot compete for old jobs when cheap labor gives other countries a distinct advantage. The consequences of an improper or inadequate response to this challenge are significant, especially for America's middle class.

Americans today are "softer" than our forefathers were, and we must toughen ourselves and embrace the belief that our survival is on the line. Risk taking must be rewarded, and educators must train young Americans to pursue areas like entrepreneurship, engineering, biology, medical research, and physical sciences where future jobs can be created through innovation.

Oil magnate John Paul Getty once said, "A man may fail many times, but he isn't a failure until he begins to blame somebody else." If we fail in our effort to meet this challenge, we have no one to blame but ourselves. We have the talent, the resources, the capital, and the foundation to succeed. Identifying the challenge is our first mandate. I hope this book helps its readers to clarify the current challenge we face.

The writing of this book included contributions from several individuals: First and foremost Ken Harrington, who, as the director of the Center for Entrepreneurial Studies at Washington University, works every day to foster future entrepreneurs. Also Amber Clark, who enthusiastically took my concepts (and some of her own) and diligently massaged them into a final product. Thank you, Amber. Without you, there would not be a book. To my partners over the years who have lived with my failures, cultural experiments, and naïve enthusiasm, I thank you for your support, patience, and tolerance. Likewise to Jill Jordan, who provided balance to my life during my period of entrepreneurial re-examination. To my wife Julie and my parents, who championed a "little boy" with a lot of dreams to chase those dreams, I say, you're the greatest and thanks for everything. Finally, thanks to my children, Kristin, Lee, and Andrew, who allow me to share my ideas, and who inspire me every day to do my part to create a better world for them.

—*Bob Skandalaris*

1

THE MIDDLE CLASS
AND THE AMERICAN DREAM

◇◇

A large and prosperous middle class is a hallmark of American life, something that most of us take for granted. The ability to lead a private life, in a safe community with a good school system, is something we hold very dear, and we expect the great majority of the population to be able to achieve it. We believe in meritocracy, in a system where poor immigrants can become millionaires, and where people are upwardly mobile. While we accept that not everyone will be rich, we believe that anyone who works hard and diligently should at least be able to live a secure, comfortable life. In the wealthiest, most prosperous nation on earth, this ought to be possible. Indeed, since the close of World War II it has been possible. Yet somehow, the middle class lifestyle is slipping away.

The middle class, which swelled to include a majority of the nation's families after World War II, has been shrinking since the 1970s, and the chasm that separates the haves from the have-nots is getting wider with each passing year. Despite the increase in college graduates and dual-income families, many baby boomers have struggled to match the standard of living their parents enjoyed. The jobs that provided a middle class lifestyle are increasingly being eliminated due to automation and outsourcing, making many boomers downwardly mobile. Their children are even worse off. Those without a college degree are being left behind, and those with college degrees are discovering that even for them, the good life is not guaranteed. A significant number of young college graduates have returned to living with their parents, unable to afford their own home, and those who have managed to buy a house are often deep in debt and living paycheck to paycheck. Their outward signs of affluence—new cars, the latest electronic gadgets, designer clothes—are being paid for with deferred financing, increasing credit card debt, and more hours at work away from their families.

The financial strain is starting to show. While aggregate statistics indicate the middle class is, on average, better off than a generation ago, people's real-life experiences contradict those statistics. Many married couples sense that even with two incomes in the household, they are not as financially secure as their parents, and those who are single or divorced are in an even more precarious position. Incomes may be rising, but not for everyone, and the cost of a middle class life has skyrocketed. During 1999, a time of great prosperity, almost 1.3 million Americans declared bankruptcy.[1] Yes, that's 1.3 million! Ninety percent were people who considered themselves to be middle class, and while recent changes in the bankruptcy laws have made it harder to declare bankruptcy, the middle class is clearly in trouble.

For some, the decline from prosperity to bankruptcy has been slow and not always apparent, obscured by the business cycle, changing political policies, and easy access to consumer credit. The overall trend, however, is clear and unassailable—employment is less secure, downward mobility is common, and the income and wealth gaps are getting larger. While the high-tech boom of the late 1990s brought prosperity back to some members of the middle class, many others continued to lose ground. After the boom was over, we experienced a jobless recovery where corporations' profits rose, but they still had little interest in hiring. Investors are getting richer while new graduates and the unemployed can't find well-paying jobs. Real wages have stagnated for people with modest incomes, and the costs of housing, education, and health care have skyrocketed.

To be blunt, the middle class lifestyle is fading fast.

The Rise of the Middle Class

What does it mean to be a member of the middle class? There is no official definition. Historically, the middle class comprised a relatively small group of professional individuals who earned their living from business savvy and mental labor, such as bankers, doctors, and attorneys. They existed as a small slice of the social strata between the wealthy titled and land-owning elite on one hand, and the vast majority of farmers, factory workers, and craftsmen who comprised the working class on the other. As the middle class has grown to encompass the majority of Americans, however, it has come to include a vast array of people with a wide range of occupations and incomes— everything from managers to educators to skilled factory workers. Over time, the middle class has come to be defined according to a set of expectations, rather than occupation or a particular level of income. Those expectations include the ability to:

- Find a stable job or career, one with progressive promotions and pay raises that provides a steadily increasing standard of living over time

- Own your own home in a safe neighborhood with a good school system

- Cover basic expenses such as mortgage payments, car payments, food, clothing, and health care, while still having some money left over for other non-essential items

- Find a new job in the event of a layoff, one that provides a comparable income

- Provide one's children with the education and advantages necessary to remain a member of the middle class

Members of the working class, by contrast, are people who can't quite fulfill these expectations. They permanently rent an apartment or live with relatives because they can't save up the money for a down payment on a house. If they do own a home, they often live in neighborhoods with higher rates of crime and less successful schools. Covering their basic expenses is always a struggle, and they have little left over for luxuries. Their jobs provide almost no chance of upward mobility, and in many cases they have been laid off and are now earning less than they used to. They also have little or nothing saved for retirement. These people are surviving, but they are certainly not prospering. Below the working class are the poor or lower class, people who are really not surviving at all, and who are forced or who choose to live off welfare and other government transfer payments. At the other end of the spectrum is the upper class, people who are independently wealthy and supplement their compensation with investment income. In general, anyone with a net worth of $1 million, not including their home, would qualify.

It is hard to put a precise number on the size of each group, but a recent *New York Times* poll found that 1 percent of Americans consider themselves to be upper class, 15 percent upper middle class, 42 percent middle class, 35 percent working class, and 7 percent lower class.[2] Yet this self-perception may be overly optimistic, as it would put the cutoff between a working class income and a middle class income at around $40,000 per household. In many parts of the country, buying a house, raising children, and paying for all the basic expenses of a middle class existence would be very difficult to do on $40,000 a year. The tide has turned against the middle class, and as the twenty-first century progresses, people in the middle are going to find it increasingly difficult to fulfill their middle class expectations.

So how, exactly, did we come by these great expectations? A large, prosperous middle class is so much a part of American life one easily forgets it is a relatively recent phenomenon. Yet just over a century ago, the overwhelming majority of Americans were working class, and the distribution of wealth was the most unequal it has ever been in this country's history. According to one estimate, the top 1 percent of the population controlled an incredible 50 percent of the nation's wealth in 1900. That left only half of the nation's wealth for the other 99 percent. No wonder so many people were either working class or living in poverty! When the nation was first founded, the top 1 percent owned only 15 percent of the wealth. By the start of the twentieth century, the distribution of wealth and income had changed radically.[3]

While America's increasing economic dominance during that period gave rise to a distinct middle class of managers and professionals, it was still relatively small. The foundations of the large and prosperous middle class that we are accustomed to today were laid with President Franklin D. Roosevelt's New Deal legislation in the 1930s. The New Deal is often characterized as a program to lift the country out of the Great Depression, but it was also engineered to raise the standard of living of average Americans and to create a more equitable balance between the interests of big business and labor. The Tennessee Valley Authority, for example, didn't just provide jobs; it provided low-cost hydroelectric power that improved the lives of many Americans. Similarly, the Federal Housing Authority was created to provide low-interest home loans, and Social Security was established to provide pensions to the elderly. By the start of Word War II, New Deal legislation had smoothed the way for upward mobility from the working class into the middle class.

With that foundation in place, an unusual combination of economic factors came together which led to a sharp increase in the size of the American middle class after World War II. Veterans

> A large, prosperous middle class is so much a part of American life one easily forgets it is a relatively recent phenomenon.

returned home to benefits such as the GI Bill and the VA mortgage, which made it possible for them to attend college and buy a home at an early age. This allowed them to build significant home equity as the value of their property skyrocketed over the next several decades. Another key factor was a sharp increase in well-paying jobs. As war-torn Europe and Asia struggled to recover economically, American industry found itself without any major competition. Operating in a vacuum, the nation's gross national product rose from $101 billion in 1940, to $294 billion in 1950, then to more than $526 billion in 1960.[4] As a result of all that growth, white collar management and administrative jobs became available in record numbers, allowing the working class to move into high-paying professional jobs with relative ease.

What really tipped the scales, however, was the rise of skilled factory workers to the middle class, as collective bargaining, labor shortages, and overtime pushed their real wages to unprecedented heights. For the first time, the majority of American families could be classified as middle class instead of working class. During the thirty years following the war, real wages climbed steadily, as did disposable income. In 1945, the average disposable income per person was just $1088 per year; by 1975 it was $5498.[5] The entry of an increasing number of women into the workforce gave families even more disposable income, and the middle class was soon ensconced on tree-lined streets in suburbia.

Prosperity, however, is a double-edged sword. It raises the expectations for the next generation, who naturally want to continue living in the manner to which they have become accustomed. Post-war parents told their children to go to school, get a good steady job, and buy a house early, but that turned out to be increasingly difficult. By the 1970s, the post-war boom was over, and the steady jobs had already started to disappear. The tide had turned, and one brief generation after the great expansion of the American middle class, it was already starting to contract, creating downward mobility and increasing polarization of wealth.

The Decline of the Middle Class

What happened to change the fate of the middle class after it had swelled to such unprecedented size and prosperity? The 1980s were admittedly difficult with multiple recessions and corporate downsizing, but the high-tech boom in the 1990s revitalized the economy and created incredible growth. In fact, over the past fifty years, family income (adjusted for inflation) has steadily increased, even for the bottom 20 percent. Admittedly, income for the top 5 percent is accelerating much more rapidly, but a rising tide appears to have lifted all boats.

If incomes have increased, why are middle class families struggling? The answer is that aggregate statistics are masking profound changes

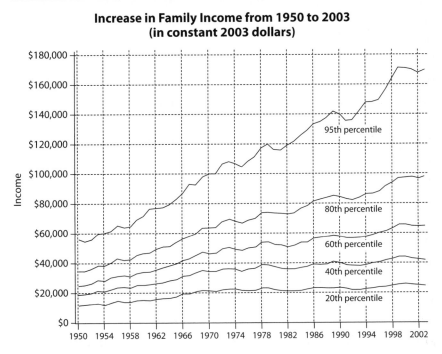

Increase in Family Income from 1950 to 2003 (in constant 2003 dollars)

Source: Data from the U.S. Census Bureau, "Historical Income Data, Table F-1 Income Limits for Each Fifth and Top 5 Percent of Families," http://www.census.gov/hhes/www/income/histinc/histinctb.html (accessed September 1, 2005).

in the overall distribution of income. A key part of this change is that semi-skilled factory and administrative jobs that require no more than a high school diploma have been rapidly disappearing due to automation, outsourcing, and industry consolidation.

In the 1960s, manufacturing and administrative support accounted for 56 percent of American jobs. Today, they account for only 39 percent.[6] Mechanics, data entry clerks, and many others who currently make around $30,000 to $35,000 a year are seeing their jobs streamlined or eliminated. The jobs that have replaced them are either highly specialized professional positions such as network administrators, operations managers, and registered nurses, or low-skill service jobs such as maids, orderlies, and wait staff. These jobs pay either towards the high end of the scale or the low end, rather than the middle, so while some Americans are moving towards the upper middle class, others are falling out of the middle class completely. Inevitably, recent college graduates with the required specialized skills take the well-paying high-tech jobs, while laid-off manufacturing and office workers move down the pay scale to less skilled positions. A survey conducted by the U.S. Bureau of Labor Statistics showed that of the manufacturing workers who lost their jobs during the last two decades of the twentieth century, only two-thirds had found new jobs, and a majority of those who did experienced a drop in pay of at least 15 percent.[7]

As a result, the distribution of income in the Untied States looks a lot different than it did thirty years ago. When the size of the middle class was at its peak, the distribution of income looked like a bell curve—the majority of people were clumped around the middle of the income distribution. Today, the peak in the middle of the income distribution is collapsing as semi-skilled jobs paying $17 an hour are being automated, consolidated, and outsourced. Instead, there is a new peak to the right of the median resulting from an increase in highly-specialized professional jobs that pay an average of $31 an hour, and another, larger peak to the left of the median resulting from an increase in relatively unskilled service jobs that pay about $11 an hour. Instead of one large middle class, we are now developing two

The Changing Middle Class Income Distribution

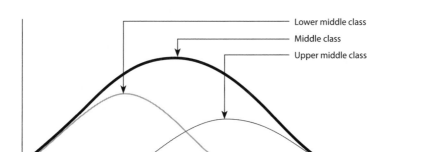

Lower middle class
Middle class
Upper middle class

increasingly distinct groups—an upper middle class, and a lower middle class.

The greater number of working mothers has increased the disparity, because the differences in household income are exaggerated when there are two incomes instead of one. A generation ago one-third of mothers worked while two-thirds were homemakers; today the situation is just the reverse. Furthermore, college graduates tend to marry other college graduates, and households with two professional incomes, such as an engineer and a teacher, have a huge advantage over households with two non-professional incomes, like a salesperson and a construction worker. Non-professionals who are single or divorced have fallen right out of the middle class, and if they have children, just staying above the poverty line is a struggle—while unemployment peaked at 6.3 percent in 2003, the poverty rate is rising and is now at 12.7 percent.[8]

This polarization can clearly be seen in the rate of increase in incomes. From 1950 to 1980, families in the bottom 80 percent of the income distribution saw their incomes rise at a significantly faster rate than that of the top 20 percent.

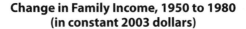

Change in Family Income, 1950 to 1980
(in constant 2003 dollars)

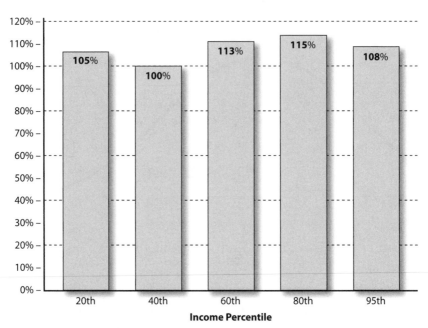

Source: Data from the U.S. Census Bureau, "Historical Income Data, Table F-1 Income Limits for Each Fifth and Top 5 Percent of Families," http://www.census.gov/hhes/www/income/histinc/histinctb. html (accessed September 1, 2005).

Starting around 1980, however, the rate of increase changed drastically as manufacturing and administrative jobs were lost and some families were forced to move down the income ladder, while married professionals surged ahead. The pattern throughout the 1980s and 1990s increasingly favored the top 20 percent and especially the top 5 percent, who generally possessed two incomes and specialized skills. Meanwhile, the gains for middle class and working class families were largely due to the addition of a second income and more hours spent working. Real hourly wages for 70 percent of American workers have stagnated or actually declined since 1970.[9]

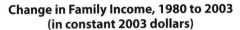

Change in Family Income, 1980 to 2003
(in constant 2003 dollars)

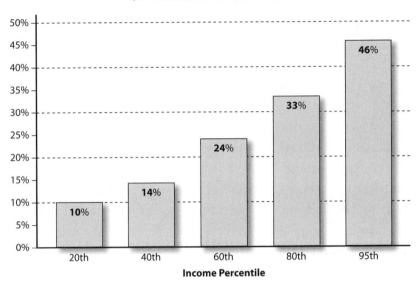

Source: Data from the U.S. Census Bureau, "Historical Income Data, Table F-1 Income Limits for Each Fifth and Top 5 Percent of Families," http://www.census.gov/hhes/www/income/histinc/histinctb. html (accessed September 1, 2005).

Thus, while aggregate statistics show that incomes have steadily increased over the past fifty years, averages hide the fact that the increasing upward mobility of skilled professionals has offset the downward mobility of the semi-skilled, who are sliding back into a working class existence.

Income alone does not determine financial stability, of course. The other side of the equation is expenses, and expenses are a big part of the reason why the middle class is more vulnerable to bankruptcy than it was a generation ago. Americans are spending more and saving less than ever before—our nation's average personal savings rate is now zero—and the popular explanation for this change is irresponsible spending habits. The average American, so the conventional wisdom goes, is spending way too much money indulging in café lattes, buying designer clothes, dining out at trendy restaurants, leasing the latest cars, and jetting off on expensive family vacations. They are financing this supposed radical increase in consumerism through easy credit and debt, and on the surface that certainly appears to be true. It is easy to believe that the middle class is going bankrupt by spending too much on unnecessary luxuries.

The actual data on consumer spending, however, tells a very different story. According to Elizabeth Warren and Amelia Warren Tyagi, authors of *The Two-Income Trap,* the average family of four spent 21 percent less on clothing, 22 percent less on food, and 44 percent less on major appliances in 2000 than they did in 1973.[10] They do spend about 23 percent more on electronics and home entertainment, and significantly more on services. In total, however, middle class families spend about the same percentage of household income on consumer goods as they did a generation ago. While professional couples in the upper middle class may be buying daily café lattes and McMansions, the same cannot be said of the middle class in general. Despite the fact that most married couples now have two incomes, total household discretionary income for those below the median has actually *dropped*. How is this possible?

According to Warren and Tyagi, the answer is that they have a lot more fixed expenses. In 1973, the median income for a typical family of four with a working father, stay-at-home mother, and two children was $38,700. (For purposes of comparison, all figures are given in year 2000 dollars).[11] A little over half of this amount went towards paying recurring, fixed expenses such as taxes, mortgage payments, car payments, child care, health care, and college tuition, leaving the family with $17,834 in discretionary income. By contrast, today's families have a lot more income, primarily due to women entering the workforce. A typical income for a family of four where both parents work was $67,800 in the year 2000, about 75 percent higher than a generation ago. Yet their fixed expenses have grown just as fast, actually leaving them with about $800 *less* in discretionary income than in 1973, for a number of reasons:[12]

- **Housing prices have gone up over 26 percent since 1984, and the cost of a home in a good school district rose 78 percent.** According to one study, an increase of 5 percent in fourth grade math and reading scores from one school district to the next results in a *$4000 increase* in home prices.

- **In-state tuition at public universities has doubled since 1980, representing 17 percent of the average middle class family's pre-tax income.** Worse, in fifteen states, pre-school tuition costs more than *twice as much* as state college tuition!

- **Personal expenditures on medical care as a percent of disposable income have grown from less than 10 percent in 1980 to over 18 percent.** Expenditures on legal and financial services are also taking up an increasing portion of people's income.

In total, a typical family earning the median income of $67,800 in 2000 used 75 percent of its income to pay fixed expenses, up from 54 percent in 1973.[13] Single-parent families and dual-parent families where one parent chooses to stay home fare much worse. Furthermore, because fixed expenses are long-term and are paid monthly, they can't easily be eliminated in the event of a job loss the way discretionary spending such as dining out can. Thus, families who go bankrupt generally do so because they can't meet their fixed expenses, not because of overzealous consumerism. While some would argue that middle class Americans want too much, like a trendy car and a big house, what is really killing middle class families is spending not on frivolous luxury items, but on critical, necessary ones like health care, education, and housing.

In the face of increasing expenses, the amount of money that it takes to remain a member of the middle class, and perhaps more importantly, to maintain one's children as members of the middle class, has consumed almost all of the second income that was added by the entry of mothers into the workforce and then some. No wonder middle class families are saving less, accumulating greater debt, and living from paycheck to paycheck. Not saving, however, has had critical consequences for the middle class. First, they have no safety net if they lose their job or suffer a medical crisis, which are the primary causes of bankruptcy. Second, they have no money available for investment, which is a key determinant of wealth. Thus, while the distribution of income has become increasingly unequal, the distribution of wealth

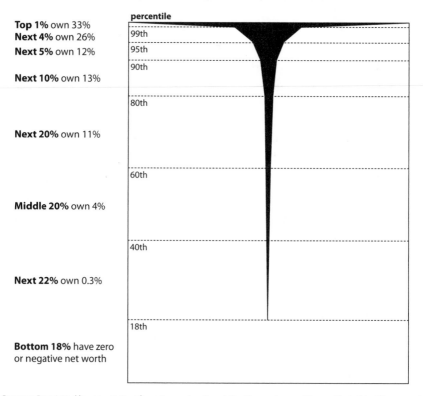

Distribution of Wealth in the United States, 2001

Top 1% own 33%
Next 4% own 26%
Next 5% own 12%

Next 10% own 13%

Next 20% own 11%

Middle 20% own 4%

Next 22% own 0.3%

Bottom 18% have zero
or negative net worth

percentile
99th
95th
90th
80th
60th
40th
18th

Source: Reprinted by permission from James Lardner, http://www.inequality.org/facts.html (accessed September 1, 2005). Data from Edward N. Wolff, "Changes in Household Wealth in the 1980s and 1990s in the U.S.," Jerome Levy Economics Institute, May 2004.

is even more unequal. The top 1 percent of Americans now own 33 percent of the wealth, and the top 10 percent own over 70 percent of the wealth. Meanwhile, the bottom 80 percent own less than 15 percent of the wealth, and the bottom 60 percent own less than 5 percent! This is not the kind of distribution you'd expect in a country with a large, prosperous middle class. Income and wealth disparity are at their highest level since the age of laissez-faire capitalism in the early 1900s, and are increasing.

"It's a pretty classic story of an economy that's leaving middle-income households behind," Jared Bernstein of the Economic Policy Institute told *USA Today* in August of 2005. "The gap between how this economy's doing and the living standards of the median family has never been larger."[14] Unemployment rates may be low and average incomes may be rising, but those are meaningless indicators when wealth is becoming more polarized. Some boats are rising while others are sinking, and that is decidedly undesirable in a democratic society that has become used to widespread prosperity. The increasing income and wealth disparity, along with the rising cost of key expenses such as housing, education, and health care, is profoundly changing the ability of middle class Americans to achieve and hold on to the American Dream.

The Loss of Middle Class Jobs

The middle class depends on employment income to survive, and thus the size and prosperity of the middle class is determined, first and foremost, by the availability of well-paying jobs. Since 2001, however, the U.S. economy has been struggling to create enough new jobs to replace the ones that it is losing, and this is not simply due to the aftermath of the dot-com bust. While the recession was short and the economy quickly recovered, the job market did not. In the past, job creation has gone hand-in-hand with economic growth, but recently that pattern has been broken. In 2003, gross domestic product (GDP) grew by 6 percent spurred by rapid gains in productivity, but job growth was a mere tenth of a percent. While the employment picture has improved somewhat since then, it is still anything but robust. Corporations have been reluctant to hire even though profits are up by almost 25 percent, and for the past several years job creation has consistently been lower than expected.[15] Fundamental changes are occurring that are causing significant losses not just of blue collar manufacturing and administrative support jobs, but of professional white collar jobs as well.

Ultimately, the fate of the middle class rests upon the American economy's ability to create new well-paying jobs faster than it loses them, and the situation we find ourselves in now is very different from the one we faced in the 1980s. Back then, corporate profits were weak, and most of the job losses were temporary. From 2001 to 2004, however, 1.6 million private sector jobs were lost, casualties of increasing foreign competition.[16] Most of them are never coming back, and the challenge for the United States is to figure out how

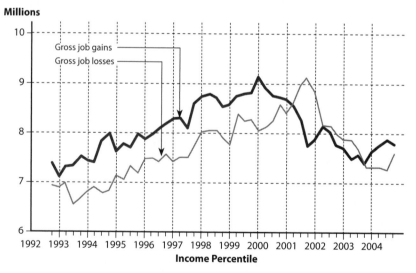

Private Sector Job Gains and Losses by Quarter, 1992–2004

Source: Chart from U.S. Bureau of Labor Statistics, "Private Sector Gross Job Gains and Gross Job Losses, Seasonally Adjusted, September 1992–September 2004," http://www.bls.gov/bdm/total_private.gif (accessed September 1, 2005).

to create well-paying new jobs to replace them in an increasingly global economy.

Automation

The largest contributor to job loss has actually been the automation of routine tasks that used to be performed by semi-skilled workers. American businesses invested heavily in information technology and other high-tech equipment during the 1990s, and while at first the gains from this investment were marginal, over time companies re-engineered their business processes to accommodate the new technology and started to see significant improvements in efficiency. In total, automation and other productivity gains from technology have been eliminating around 7 million jobs per year.[17] Foreign competition has placed a tremendous amount of pressure on American manufacturing to eliminate jobs, and now technology has allowed companies to cut their workforces and become more productive and efficient at the same time.

So far, automation has hit manufacturing and administrative jobs the hardest, which are exactly the type of mid-level jobs that have formed the backbone of the American middle class. Fortunately, the introduction of new technology doesn't always eliminate jobs.

> In total, automation and other productivity gains from technology have been eliminating around 7 million jobs per year.

Sometimes it simply enhances workers' output, making them more valuable and often leading to an increase in wages. It can also enable a company to lower prices which, if there is sufficient demand, actually leads companies to hire new workers. When competition is intense and demand is falling due to imports, however, companies look to technology as a way to boost profits by cutting their labor costs. In the 1980s, American corporations spent over $1 trillion on computers, robots, and other automated equipment, with each robot eliminating four jobs on average.[18] Now information technology is eliminating millions of white collar jobs as well.

Thanks to computerization and the Internet, receptionists have been replaced by answering machines, cashiers have been replaced by kiosks, and bank tellers have been replaced by ATM machines. All of these jobs still exist, but thanks to automation we need far fewer of them. As a result of investment in new technology, AT&T can handle 50 percent more calls with 40 percent fewer employees than it did in the 1980s.[19] An online bank like Netbank with 180 employees can handle assets that would require two thousand employees in a traditional bank.[20] Spread that across the entire American economy, and the impact is substantial. While the increased productivity is great for our competitiveness in the global economy, it is creating huge job losses. Since the 2001 recession, every one percent increase in productivity has eliminated 1.3 million jobs per year, and productivity gains have been running around 5 percent annually.[21]

It isn't just semi-skilled factory and administrative jobs that are being eliminated. Computers are automating various functions of professional jobs as well. CAD-CAM modeling software, for example, allows manufacturers to design new cars and aircraft with fewer engineers. Data mining software is reducing the need for business analysts; diagnostic software is reducing the need for doctors. One man even designed a software program that wrote 90 percent of the text of a romance novel! According to one estimate, over 90 million American jobs are vulnerable to automation.[22] That's roughly 75 percent of working Americans, which just happens to be the percentage who don't have a college degree. In other words, robots and computers are becoming capable of replacing anyone with a high school education, and over the long run they're generally cheaper as well. Incredibly low interest rates and falling prices for technology have made capital improvement a great investment, while rising heath care and benefit costs have made labor increasingly more expensive.

Industry Consolidation

Over time, automation frees up resources and allows some workers to migrate up the income ladder to new and better jobs, but only if they have the skills and education to do so. This type of evolution takes time and forces painful adjustments. What is problematic, however, is that automation alone isn't forcing all of the job losses—industry consolidation has a significant impact as well. Every firm has an optimal size at which it is most efficient. Thanks to mass production and mass marketing techniques, in most industries that size tends to be quite large, as the cost of activities like advertising, research, and development can be shared across many different plants. Being bigger tends to give companies increased economies of scale and scope, which means that they can operate more efficiently. Larger companies also have an advantage in lobbying for favorable legislation and negotiating better purchase agreements with suppliers, all of which is especially important in a global business environment where efficiency is critical.

The quickest way for a company to grow large is to acquire or merge with another company. Mergers and acquisitions are often the result of two companies that are trying to create efficiencies by becoming larger, but the combination generally just results in one big company that mirrors its former components and their weaknesses. It is much more difficult to communicate, coordinate operations, and maintain both consistency and flexibility in a large firm. Also, in the case of acquisitions, the acquiring firm generally increases its debt burden in order to finance the purchase of the other company, which makes it essential that they realize efficiencies and cut costs as quickly as possible.

One way to do this is to eliminate jobs, which is precisely what most merged and acquired companies do. A study by the U.S. Small Business Administration in the early 1990s showed that acquired businesses lose an average of 3.3 percent of their jobs as an immediate result of the acquisition, and another 4.4 percent of jobs within a few years after the acquisition. Businesses in the study that remained independent, on the other hand, created 0.7 percent new jobs over the same period. The impact on firms with over five hundred employees was much larger, as they lost 9.3 percent of jobs and were five times more likely to be acquired than small firms.[23] The job losses in manufacturing, retail trade, and financial companies due to mergers and acquisitions have been particularly devastating.

In theory, companies could gain many of the benefits of consolidation simply through partnerships, while avoiding a lot of the drawbacks. They could still perform joint research and development, purchasing, lobbying, and other activities through strategic alliances, while maintaining the flexibility, individual cultures, and payrolls of two smaller companies. Or they could form an entirely new company through a joint venture, which over time might create new jobs because it establishes a third company rather than collapsing two companies into one. Yet American executives, fueled by advice from investment bankers and lawyers, consistently seem to prefer the control of a full-blown acquisition, occasionally disguised as a so-called merger of equals. In the process, thousands of jobs are lost, and as foreign competition increases, the number of acquisitions is destined to increase as well.

Offshore Outsourcing

The most disturbing trend by far, however, has been offshore outsourcing. In the 1950s, American manufacturing and administrative workers had no problem competing with workers in China, India, Mexico, and other developing nations because their education, training, technology, and facilities made them vastly more productive, and the price of labor is determined chiefly by its productivity. For example, if Jane earns $10 an hour but is also ten times as productive as Jill, who earns $1 an hour, then they are equally valuable. In the past, American companies could afford to pay wages much higher than in other countries because technology and education made American workers vastly more productive. Over the past thirty years, however, that has changed.

The problem for American workers is not just that labor in developing countries is cheap, but rather that foreign direct investment is helping overseas labor to become rapidly more productive. This creates both a loss of American jobs and downward pressure on wages as less capital is available to pay American workers—every 1 percent loss of jobs due to imports or offshoring leads to a 0.5 percent drop in wages for the remaining workers.[24] Theoretically, as the productivity of workers in developing nations increases, their compensation should as well, bringing the worldwide supply and demand for labor back into balance. Unfortunately for American workers, the huge supply of labor in China, India, Mexico, and elsewhere in the developing world means that wages in those countries are rising very slowly, and thus American wages have a long way to fall before we reach a new equilibrium.

> **14 million of today's 57 million white collar jobs are capable of being offshored.**

There are limits to how many jobs can be outsourced, for many jobs require face-to-face contact with customers and fellow employees. As communications technology improves, however, those limits shift. Forrester Research has projected that at least 300,000 white collar jobs per year will be moving offshore through 2015, and a study done by researchers at the University of California at Berkeley estimates that 14 million of today's 57 million white collar jobs are capable of being offshored.[25] All indications are that outsourcing will continue to grow, and it is going to eliminate jobs higher and higher up the income ladder as technology becomes more sophisticated. The current projections indicate that jobs in the computer industry are likely to be hardest hit, with legal and business occupations following right behind. Clearly offshoring, which has had a devastating impact on America's factory workers, is going to have a significant impact on white collar jobs as well.

Manufacturing was always susceptible to offshoring because it produced tradeable goods that could be exported, while services generally required face-to-face contact. With communications technology, however, knowledge-based services could suddenly be traded, and most of what highly-paid, college-educated workers do nowadays involves information. This makes Americans extremely vulnerable to foreign knowledge workers. Employers can't offshore a job as a maid to India, but they can very easily offshore a job as a computer programmer to India. As the white collar job market becomes more global, the law of supply and demand dictates that white collar wages will be driven down, and the global supply of highly-educated workers is rapidly increasing. China, for example, has expanded the number of students allowed to enroll in college from 4 to 17 percent in an effort to become more competitive in science and technology. Yet about 30 percent of their recent graduates are unemployed.[26] This creates an increasing pool of cheap, highly educated workers in developing nations that has the potential to drive down wages for American white collar workers. As the cost of labor falls, the benefits of offshoring will increasingly accrue to corporate executives and investors, not employees.

Automation, industry consolidation, and outsourcing are dramatically impacting the American job market and are lowering the income levels that many middle class Americans can realistically achieve. This is hard to take, because the high standard of living enjoyed by America's middle class over the past fifty years has altered their expectations, with the result that they have come to take security and comfort for granted. Rather than working merely in order to survive, they now work to afford life's pleasures, and while adjusting one's spending and expectations upward is easy, adjusting them downward is traumatic. The middle class has clung to the idea that they can continue to raise their standard of living indefinitely, but the world has changed in many ways, and the forces working against them are considerable. Traditional middle class families with a household income of $34,000 to $55,000, who amongst them own a mere 4 percent of the total national wealth,[27] are fighting desperately to hang on to a middle class lifestyle in the face of many forces that are pushing them downward. With the continued loss of semi-skilled jobs in the range of $17 an hour, however, they're fighting a losing battle.

Then there are the college-educated members of the middle class, who are faced with a different set of challenges. Their education gives them a shot at the type of highly-paid professional jobs that are tickets to the upper middle class, but once a member, their position is precarious. Specialized knowledge takes time and money to achieve, and a software developer cannot easily become a geneticist as the demand for technical specialties changes. Not to mention the fact that as increasingly sophisticated communications technology makes outsourcing easier, college-educated professionals will be hard pressed to maintain their high salaries. In this environment no job is safe, and the loss of a job, a health crisis, or a divorce drastically reduces income in a way that makes upper middle class families almost as vulnerable to bankruptcy as lower middle class ones.

Entrepreneurship and the American Dream

The ongoing loss of semi-skilled jobs means that in order to maintain a middle class standard of living, American workers are going to need to improve their technical skills, become more flexible, and migrate towards jobs that require face-to-face interaction. A knowledge economy demands knowledge workers, people who are not only computer literate but who are creative and good at problem solving. The knowledge economy has placed a premium on having a college education, and the 75 percent of the American workforce that has not completed a four-year degree is being left out in the cold. In 1979, the earnings gap between a 30-year-old man with a high school diploma and one with a college degree was 17 percent; now it is over 50 percent.[28] Those without a college degree also bear the brunt of job losses. The unemployment rate for college-educated workers is currently only 3 percent, but it is 5 percent for those with a high school diploma, and 8 percent for those with less than a high school education.[29]

The semi-skilled jobs in the middle of the income distribution are disappearing, a fact that is clear from the U.S. Bureau of Labor Statistics' projections for the ten occupations with the most job growth over the next decade. As shown in the table below, only one of the jobs that does not require a college education—customer service representative—earns in the $20,000 to $35,000 range, and it is exactly the type of job that is increasingly being outsourced to India. All of the other semi-skilled or unskilled jobs earn less than $20,000. Furthermore, of the ten occupations with the most job growth, those

Occupations with the Largest Projected Job Growth

Occupation	2002 Jobs	2012 Jobs	Jobs Added	Change	Salary	Education
Post-secondary teachers	1,581,000	2,184,000	603,000	38%	$35,000 and over	Doctoral degree
General and operations managers	2,049,000	2,425,000	376,000	18%	$35,000 and over	Bachelor's degree
Registered nurses	2,284,000	2,908,000	623,000	27%	$35,000 and over	Associate degree
Customer service representatives	1,894,000	2,354,000	460,000	24%	$20,000 to $35,000	High school
Janitors and cleaners, except maids	2,267,000	2,681,000	414,000	18%	Less than $20,000	High school or lower
Nursing aides, orderlies, attendants	1,375,000	1,718,000	343,000	25%	Less than $20,000	High school or lower
Retail salespersons	4,076,000	4,672,000	596,000	15%	Less than $20,000	High school or lower
Cashiers, except gaming	3,432,000	3,886,000	454,000	13%	Less than $20,000	High school or lower
Food preparation workers	1,990,000	2,444,000	454,000	23%	Less than $20,000	High school or lower
Waiters and waitresses	2,097,000	2,464,000	367,000	18%	Less than $20,000	High school or lower

Source: Data from the U.S. Bureau of Labor Statistics, "Table 4, Occupations with the Largest Job Growth, 2002-2012," *Monthly Labor Review,* February 2004, Vol. 127, No.2, http://www.bls.gov/emp/emptab4.htm (accessed September 1, 2005).

which require post-secondary education are going to add only 1.6 million new jobs to the economy through 2012, while those that require only a high school education or less are going to add over 3 million. Clearly, even if those in the middle manage to get a college education, there will not be enough jobs to absorb them all. The majority of the growth is going to be at the bottom of the pyramid.

Middle class parents tend to believe that as long as their children get a college degree they are relatively safe, and in comparison to those without a college education that is certainly true. When compared to a generation ago, however, the jobs of even college graduates are far less secure than they used to be, and one out of five college graduates cannot find a job that requires a college education.[30] The rapid advances in communications technology such as fax-modems, cell phones, and the Internet have made it much quicker and easier to communicate with other highly educated people around the world, and this is where globalization and technology have come together to hit not just the average Joe, but the upper end of the middle class as well.

In a knowledge economy, the work highly educated people do is often on a project basis, either individually or in small teams. When mass producing automobiles, the question is whether one plant or another does the work more efficiently. When producing the design of a website, however, the question is whether one individual or another does the work more efficiently. Knowledge workers have to compete head-to-head with workers from all over the world, they cannot hide within a profitable company or industry, and the competition is fierce. Foreign knowledge workers are not only cheaper, they generally have a solid educational background and specific technical training as well. In the face of such competition, you have to be very, very good at what you do to make a comfortable, middle class living.

The uncomfortable truth is that the American Dream is increasingly migrating overseas. Fifty years ago, the kind of economic opportunity that the American Dream represented was something that people had to come to the West, and preferably the United States, to access.

It was not possible in China or Russia or India. Then on November 9th, 1989, all of that changed when the Berlin Wall fell and the Soviet empire subsequently collapsed. At the time, Americans celebrated our ideological triumph over communism as both a moral and an economic victory, one without any negative consequences. As the old saying goes, however, you should be careful what you wish for, because you just might get it. Most of these formerly communist countries realized that capitalism was the only rational way to organize a modern economy, and many of their citizens embraced it with zeal. The result went far beyond what most people had imagined. What we got was not a world full of independent capitalist economies trading cars for computers, but an increasingly integrated global economy full of 3 billion hungry new capitalists.

As Thomas Friedman has argued in *The World Is Flat,* America is now competing in a global environment that, thanks to communications technologies like the Internet, fiber optics, software applications, web browsing, and search capabilities, is more interconnected than ever before, and the consequences of this change are enormous. Globalization is leveling the economic playing field and obliterating the national comparative advantages of highly developed nations such as the United States—the very advantages which support our high wages and high standard of living. What's more, globalization has kicked into an entirely new gear during the past few years as companies have re-engineered their business processes to take full advantage of these new technologies. As a result, the economic landscape is "flattening," as Friedman would put it, at a startling pace, and the United States now faces an unprecedented level of economic competition from countries in Europe, Asia, and Latin America.[31]

What this means is that the turf war to host the American Dream has been expanded to include foreign soil and citizens outside of the United States. People in countries like India and China are no longer restricted by geography; their highly skilled workers don't have to come to the United States to achieve a better standard of living. Thanks to the Internet and fiber optics, they can now participate in the global economy from call centers in Bangalore, factories in Beijing, even dorm rooms in Moscow, and it doesn't stop there. Indian information technology companies, for example, now have the skills to compete head-to-head with American companies in high-tech innovation, a playing field America has long been used to dominating, and the Chinese are rapidly moving up the ladder as well. The open floodgates of capitalism and the flattening forces of communications technology have radically altered how work is done, where it is done, and by whom.

> The turf war to host the American Dream has been expanded to include foreign soil and citizens outside of the United States.

The question is, what does all of this mean for America? People frequently argue whether globalization is a threat or an opportunity; they often wonder if it has gotten out of control. Go to a cocktail party or a breakfast meeting and you will get any mixture of thoughts about what is happening and what should be done. All these ideas and thoughts are based upon each individual's perspective, education, age, job, personal wealth, influence points, and personality. These are all healthy concerns and need to be placed in some context as we ponder the economic future of America.

On one hand, the simple reality is that no country has benefited from globalization as much as the United States. Shareholders have benefited enormously as American corporations have expanded overseas and penetrated emerging markets. Consumers have benefited as well by buying cheap imports from China and elsewhere. American labor, however, has not done so well as jobs have been lost to automation, consolidation, and offshoring. Middle class wages have stagnated, and what gains have been made are largely due to the entry of women into the workforce. While the information technology boom of the 1990s benefited many knowledge workers, traditional middle class workers in manufacturing and administrative positions struggled, and in the past few years even highly paid service workers are now seeing their jobs offshored to India and elsewhere.

The only way for America to offset all of these job losses is to innovate, to constantly strive to create the new jobs and new industries of the future. After all, the United States economy lost millions of jobs every year during the 1990s; we just didn't notice because the economy was creating more jobs than it destroyed. Thus, innovation is critical to our economic future. In fact, it is the only hope Americans have of creating well-paying jobs. In a world where intense competition rapidly turns products into commodities, innovation is the only way to differentiate oneself, the only way to achieve and maintain an advantage over the competition. Fortunately, America has a long history of successful innovation. You might even say it's our national core competency, and that competency is going to play a critical role in the battle to preserve the American Dream.

The most important resource America possesses in this battle is our entrepreneurs, for they are the catalysts of innovation and economic growth. Entrepreneurs are champions who see opportunities and use limited resources such as capital, labor, and information to create enormously high value for customers, employees, and investors. They frequently serve as a bridge between scientific discovery and commercialization by forging connections and building new business models around breakthrough technologies and concepts. While scientists and engineers may be the ones who make the initial discoveries and inventions, it is entrepreneurs who take those discoveries and commercialize them. They promote defensive and offensive competitive responses that fuel the process of innovation, and are critical agents for change and economic growth.

Approximately one-third of the difference in economic performance among nations is attributable to the difference in their levels of entrepreneurial activity.[32] Across the globe, countries with high rates of entrepreneurial activity among both startups and established firms have gross domestic product growth rates around 5 percent, which is 2 percent higher than countries with moderate rates of entrepreneurial activity.[33] That's a big difference, especially when compounded over time. Without the innovation and entrepreneurship the United States has experienced over the past fifty years, our economy would be 40 percent smaller, and our standard of living 40 percent lower, than it is today.[34] Obviously, entrepreneurship is critical. Without it, the United States would not be the world's leading military and economic power.

The golden age of the American middle class was an accident of the post-war economy, and the days when high school graduates could get jobs on the assembly line or in the office typing pool, buy a house on tree-lined street in suburbia, and live happily ever after are gone for good. The American Dream is still possible to achieve, but doing so is going to require young Americans who respect the value of education, work hard to attain their goals, and are willing to accept less security and more risk. They must view success as something to be achieved rather than a birthright. The burden, however, does not rest entirely upon them. We as a society also have to create an environment that will support young Americans in achieving their dreams, a society that is committed to supporting innovation and entrepreneurship. Why? Because innovation is the key to maintaining our standard of living, and the entrepreneur is going to be a central figure in keeping the American Dream alive.

2

THE INNOVATION RACE

◇◇

Leonardo Da Vinci, the Renaissance painter, architect, engineer, mathematician, and philosopher, was perhaps the greatest genius the world has ever seen. Da Vinci conceived of a number of inventions—including a spring-driven car, hang glider, parachute, helicopter, machine gun, and a mechanical calculator—all in the late 1400s. Why were these never developed into working products? His drawings were clear and complete. The ideas were comprehensible. Why didn't he or other people move forward and apply his ideas?

One answer is that Da Vinci had little to gain personally by proceeding with his inventions. Rather, his motivation was driven by the desires of the benefactors of his time, which were the French monarchy, the Italian aristocracy, and the Catholic Church. These constituencies rewarded him for creating art or for using his talents in areas other than innovation. Da Vinci had little to gain by inventing and continuing to develop his ideas because the system of governance did not allow him to retain ownership in what he created.

In addition, there were no systems in place dedicated to nurturing and supporting innovation. Interestingly, Da Vinci's inventions were such that they should have had great appeal to the military, as many were items that would have been most useful in a war. However, representatives from France or one of the Italian city-states would have needed to provide funding for future development activities, and they did not. Without their permission and support, little could happen. In effect, Da Vinci was in an early stage startup with no source of funding and little hope of profiting from his inventions. The environment for creativity during this period was set and influenced by the monarch, aristocracy, and the Church, not the individual. His life might have differed greatly if he had been born after modern democracy, capitalism, and the rule of law had taken root.

The development of the steam engine several centuries later gives an indication of how much things had changed from Da Vinci's time. In 1698, an English military engineer named Thomas Savery patented the first version of the steam engine. He had based his creation on the pressure cooker, which was invented by Denis Papin a mere two decades earlier. Savery had been searching for a way to pump water out of coal mines, and his machine was constructed as a closed vessel filled with water into which steam was introduced under pressure. He used this invention to force water up and out of mine shafts.

In 1712, Savery worked with an English blacksmith named Thomas Newcomen to develop the atmospheric steam engine. The Newcomen version of the steam engine pumped steam into a cylinder, which was then condensed by cold water. This created a vacuum, and the resulting atmospheric pressure operated a piston that generated downward strokes. The main improvement was that the intensity of pressure was not limited by the pressure of the steam. Half a century later, Newcomen's design became the basis of James Watt's steam engine.

Watt made several improvements, patenting a design with a separate condenser connected to a cylinder by a valve. Unlike Newcomen's version, Watt's design remained cool while the cylinder was hot, and thus it became the dominant one used during the era of steam engines. In less than a century, Papin, Savery, Newcomen, and Watt changed the way machines were powered and the way work was done. The speed with which this occurred was in sharp contrast to the slow progress of medieval times.

As the evolution of democracy, capitalism, and the rule of law allowed individuals to benefit from their inventions, it spurred an era of innovation unprecedented in human civilization.

Americans owe our prosperity to innovation, to the wave after wave of new products, services, and systems that have transformed our very lives. Innovation is not just discovery of a new idea or the invention of a prototype, but rather its commercialization. It is not simply an idea but the practical application of an idea that is true innovation. Only when ideas are brought to society at large, changing existing systems, do they become revolutionary.

Innovation for the mass market, more than anything else, is what raises a nation's standard of living, creating widespread prosperity and a large middle class. At first, innovations tend to be affordable only for early adopters such as the wealthy or professional specialists— running water, electricity, and automobiles were at one time luxuries for the rich; sewing machines, cameras, and computers once appealed only to professional tailors, photographers, and scientists. It is when visionary entrepreneurs see the broader applications and make them accessible to the public at large that we suddenly get leaps forward in our standard of living, such as cheap water and sanitation, electricity, transportation, and communication; labor-saving devices like ovens, washing machines, and vacuum cleaners; life-saving medical tools like antibiotics, vaccines, and safer surgical techniques; not to mention all of the life-enhancing luxuries that soon become necessities, like store-bought designer clothes, televisions, and air travel.

Innovation creates more than new products; it also creates jobs, because as soon as there is a mass market there is a need for mass production. Henry Ford's introduction of the Model T not only made cars affordable to the average person, it created a new industry that provided employment for thousands of people. This process has happened repeatedly in the United States, most recently with the computer and telecommunications industries, and it is imperative that it continue. A high standard of living comes not only from affordable things to buy, but the wages to buy them with, and the more we innovate and create new businesses, the better off we become. In the United States, new ventures provide over 10.5 million new jobs annually, which accounts for about 8 percent of all American jobs.[1] Our economic prosperity can in many ways be traced to Americans' ability to innovate; it is a crucial element of our national economic competitiveness.

"Innovation is going to be the single most important factor in determining America's future economic success."

"Innovation is going to be the single most important factor in determining America's future economic success," declares David Attis, the director of policy studies for the Council on Competitiveness, a national organization whose mission is to drive economic growth and raise the standard of living for all Americans. "It is critical because it is the only thing that will allow the United States to succeed in global markets, and it is the only source of sustainable competitive advantage that most firms in the United States will have in the twenty-first century. In the past, both countries and companies were able to develop competitive advantage through better access to raw materials or because they were able to leverage large, low-cost workforces. But this is no longer the case. In the future, the only way that we will be able to differentiate our products and services and succeed in global commerce is by continually innovating at a faster pace."

The world is now engaged in an innovation race, a race to see which countries can create the breakthrough industries of the twenty-first century and reap the jobs and economic growth that innovation provides. Americans have led this race for so long that we now take our ability to keep winning it for granted. The last time there was a serious challenge to our science and technological superiority was when the Soviet Union launched Sputnik I in 1957. But while we have been coasting, the world has been catching up, and it is likely that we will actually be surpassed in key technological areas within the next few decades. This is, or should be, alarming, because the jobs and growth that innovation creates are critical to maintaining our prosperity, and the health of our future economy rests on the strength of today's entrepreneurship.

"At Microsoft, I see the innovation race unfolding right before my eyes, and that race is going to pose a lot of challenges for America over the next several decades," says Steve Ballmer, the CEO of Microsoft. "Globalization and high technology hold tremendous potential, but there's a lot that we all need to be concerned about in terms of our readiness for that transformation. In a sense all I think about, all Bill [Gates] thinks about, is how do we accelerate the pace of our innovation? How do we make sure we're investing enough at the right time? How do we reduce complexity and our internal processes so that we can decrease time to market, be more agile, and introduce more of our products? What are the new frontiers, and are we making bold, creative bets in those areas? Because if we aren't making those bets, if we aren't pushing the envelope in terms of innovation, then we're not going to remain the market leader for long."[2]

And neither will any other American company.

The Roots of the Innovation Race

The history of the world in many ways is the history of innovation. From the discovery of fire to the invention of the Internet, new ideas are a creative force that change our lives in important ways, particularly by fostering economic growth. According to the economist William Baumol, all meaningful economic growth has occurred over the last two centuries, a time of unprecedented innovation.[3] By modern standards, economic growth was practically non-existent before the tenth century, and even then progress was incredibly slow. As a result of the Enlightenment, however, scientific knowledge grew rapidly and eventually spurred a prodigious amount of innovation. These innovations jump-started the Industrial Revolution, first in Britain and then in America, and by the late 1800s, entrepreneurs like Cornelius

Vanderbilt, Andrew Carnegie, John D. Rockefeller, and many other legendary captains of industry had transformed the United States from an agrarian third world country into the leader in world manufacturing. One wonders, however, what exactly caused those entrepreneurs to blossom, and at that particular point in history? Was it just their personal initiative? Was it the economic climate? Was it that the world finally arrived at a point where technological developments combined to spawn commercial innovation and entrepreneurship? Perhaps more importantly, why did it happen, and how have the factors that influenced the growth of innovation changed since then?

The roots of America's economic success can be traced to the development of modern democracy and the rule of law, for when English barons forced King John to sign the Magna Carta in 1215, this was a momentous event not just politically, but economically. At the time, most of Europe was entrenched in feudal systems where the aristocracy was constantly wrangling for power, and where serfs and peasants generally had no civil or property rights. The average person had limited access to information, and while they occasionally invented things to make their lives easier, there was no incentive to commercialize those inventions. As democracy and the rule of law evolved, however, so did individual rights, which spurred the growth of innovation.

There were very few significant scientific or technological advances prior to the invention of the printing press in 1455. With this advancement, however, information was diffused on a much broader scale, allowing isolated ideas and inventions to spread and become revolutionary innovations. It also lead to widespread discourse that ushered in the Enlightenment, which among other things led to the Scientific Revolution and the evolution of a formal scientific research method and philosophy; the establishment of intellectual property rights including patents and copyrights; more sophisticated financial systems and instruments for providing risk capital; and educational systems that helped to develop the disciplines of science, medicine, law, philosophy, and eventually economics and business.

While democracy and the rule of law developed steadily in Europe throughout the Enlightenment, they entered a new phase in 1776. The Declaration of Independence firmly established individual rights, and while not yet treating all ethnic groups and genders equally, it provided the foundation for the continued expansion of individual freedoms in the New World. With the ratification of the U.S. Constitution in 1789, the desires of the revolutionary founding fathers were crystallized and documented as the basis for all future federal laws. The new form of government was a boon to free enterprise, giving Congress control over inter-state commerce and the power to collect taxes, defend the states, and protect property rights. Most importantly, the Constitution also preserved the rights of the individual through the Bill of Rights, and its refinement and evolution continues to this day.

Thus, the United States established laws protecting individual rights from the beginning and, after a period of instability during the thirteen-year interim between the American Revolution and the writing of the Constitution, it has preserved this philosophy ever since. That uncertain period and the next twenty years began a process of refining the rule of law and creating the start of a society that was steadily more inclusive in its approach. We began by including immigrants but excluding women, African Americans, Native Americans, and those who did not own land. Over the years and through the struggles of many individuals, however, property rights and freedoms were applied to more peoples and groups. This is not to say that America is perfect at this time—far from it. The point, however, is that the rule of law has been continually refined as the country has developed, and as more individuals have been allowed to participate, it has become one of the primary factors behind the growth of innovation and entrepreneurship in the United States.

As democracy, capitalism, and the rule of law were established in America and much of the Western world, innovation began to occur on a scale that had previously been impossible. Scientific knowledge reached a critical mass in the 1800s, spurring an unprecedented acceleration of innovation, entrepreneurship, and economic growth which transformed the United States from an insignificant former colony at the start of the nineteenth century into the world's leading industrial power by the start of the twentieth century. The source of this transformation was the gradual development of a number of supporting systems that together created an ideal environment for innovation, including a tradition of technological expertise, respect for intellectual property rights, a financial system capable of providing risk capital to entrepreneurs, a belief in the importance of education, and financial incentives to innovate. Add to this the fact that the United States was a land full of plentiful natural resources and a burgeoning domestic market that kept expanding westward throughout the century, and it created a country that was primed for innovation.

Innovation played a key role in the rise of the United States to global prominence, but economists in the early twentieth century paid it little attention. Instead, they attributed economic growth to increases in the three main factors of production—land, labor, and capital. They argued that the accumulation of these three factors allowed businesses to become more efficient and productive, which in turn created economic growth. Innovation, when it was mentioned, was considered to be a force which improved the productivity of labor rather than being recognized as important in its own right. As recently as the 1980s, traditional economic theory continued to ignore or downplay the role of innovation.

The economist Joseph Schumpeter was one of the first to recognize the importance of innovation and entrepreneurship to economic growth, and in doing so he was significantly ahead of his time. In his groundbreaking work, *Capitalism, Socialism and Democracy,* he introduced the concept of creative destruction—the idea that entrepreneurs foster progress through an ongoing series of revolutions that destroy old businesses and create new ones—and argued that innovation played a central role in the success of capitalism. Published in 1942 in the wake of the Great Depression, however, his theory failed to gain widespread support. His contemporary John Maynard Keynes attracted far more attention, and not until the latter decades of the twentieth century was the importance of Schumpeter's ideas fully appreciated.

By the 1970s, however, American manufacturing had fallen behind that of Japan, particularly in the automobile industry, and the country was struggling to respond. The Japanese were leading the way with innovative total quality management and just-in-time production techniques, while the American economy had stagnated. It took the development of the venture capital industry, the lowering of the capital gains and corporate tax rates, and the emergence of a powerful innovation center in Silicon Valley to revitalize the American economy. The emergence of high-tech industries in the 1990s, and the tremendous economic growth that America experienced as a result, finally showed just how important innovation is to a nation's economic prosperity. The innovative application of new technologies can create quantum leaps in productivity as well as entirely new industries, and produces a much higher rate of growth than the traditional land-labor-capital accumulation model.

> Innovation generates the productivity that economists estimate has accounted for half of U.S. GDP growth over the past fifty years. Innovation gives rise to new industries and markets; fuels wealth creation and profits; and generates high-value, higher-paying jobs. In a world in which many nations have embraced market economies and can compete on traditional cost and quality terms, it is innovation—the ability to create new value—that will confer a competitive edge in the 21st century.[4]
>
> —*Innovate America* report,
> Council on Competitiveness

Innovation fosters progress, and progress is a good thing. After all, I'd rather drive my car to work than a horse and carriage! In the process, however, it sometimes destroys existing businesses, jobs, and even entire industries. When Ford started producing Model Ts in 1908, a lot of people who made carriages, buggy whips, and other horse-drawn accessories were put out of work. Nevertheless, Schumpeter argued that the creative destruction resulting from disruptive innovation creates continuous progress, and eventually improves the standard of living for everyone. While it eliminates some jobs, it also creates new ones in more profitable industries, and he believed the net impact was positive. Yet many people fear or oppose the creative destruction caused by innovation, because it is volatile and unpredictable. In the process of creating a better world, innovation tears down and destroys the one in which we currently live, and that can force painful adjustments.

Today, innovation is happening faster than it has ever occurred in the history of the world, and that is making a lot of people uneasy. While technological innovations like email and cell phones have been welcome additions to our modern lifestyle for most, bigger changes, like genetic engineering and stem cell research, have raised concerns about the effect of progress on American values, and those concerns are growing as the rate of innovation and change accelerates. Eight times as much technological innovation occurred in the twentieth century as in all of previous history, and the last fifteen years of that century produced as much technological change as the previous eighty-five.[5] You only need to pick up the daily paper or turn on the television to hear the latest in this continuum of perpetual transformation.

As the rate of innovation has increased, the amount of technological and social change that occurs in the span of one lifetime is now much greater than it used to be, even more so because the average lifetime has gotten longer. When change happens too fast, we feel like it is destroying our life, assaulting our values. As a result, sometimes we forget all the good things that innovation has brought us and step on the brakes. This reaction is understandable, but it threatens to derail the innovative process, which is central to our economic prosperity. Without innovation and entrepreneurship, our economy will stagnate. Understanding this is crucial so that we do not kill the very process that we depend on for survival, because Americans are going to face a number of challenges in the twenty-first century that will require rapid innovation if we are going to have any hope of meeting them. These include:

- **Loss of middle class jobs**—In a global economy, the only way for the United States to compete with developing countries and maintain its standard of living is to pursue rapid growth. By doing so, we create jobs in new industries that allow us to replace the ones lost to imports and offshoring. A study by the U.S. Small Business Administration in 1998 showed that small firms with fewer than twenty employees accounted for half of the job growth in the United States, and large firms engaged in entrepreneurial activity also tend to create more jobs than average.[6] High rates of entrepreneurship are necessary just to have a society capable of creating enough well-paying jobs to support a large and prosperous middle class.

- **The baby boomer retirement crunch**—Starting in 2008, the first wave of the baby boomers is going to retire, which will place an incredible strain on the economy to support the Social Security and Medicare transfer payments that generation will require. Unless we want to raise taxes or defer the bill to future generations, the only way to fund the baby boomers' retirement and maintain our own standard of living is through rapid growth and the discovery of technologies that can lower the cost of health care.

- **The energy crisis**—The United States is extremely dependent on foreign oil, and the growth of newly capitalist economies is driving up demand for this dwindling resource. Oil prices are projected to rise through 2008 and remain high thereafter. Unless the United States wants to face a repeat of the 1970s stagflation induced by oil shortages, we are going to need to develop alternative energy sources. Potential worldwide food and water shortages will also demand innovative, technological solutions.

- **The War on Terror**—The War on Terror and homeland security spending are driving up the federal deficit at a time when we can least afford it due to the impending retirement crunch. The growth of the 1990s, in many ways, was supported by a significant reduction in military spending and reallocation of those funds to domestic concerns. If Americans want to both maintain a high standard of living and pursue an ongoing, pro-active military policy along with extensive homeland security, we are going to need high levels of growth to prevent the deficit from growing to such heights that foreign investors finally abandon the U.S. dollar as the currency of choice.

"Innovation is going to be key in facing all of the domestic challenges we have, whether it's health care, energy sources, or the War on Terror," says David Attis. "All of those problems are going to require innovation just to get more out of the resources we already have." Innovation is the only way for the United States to meet these challenges and retain our position as an economic superpower; it is also the only way we are going to be able to maintain our high standard of living. The only alternative to the faster rate of change is to have slower economic growth, since innovation and entrepreneurship are what spurs growth. In effect, we are on an innovation-entrepreneurship-growth treadmill, and getting off is too painful. Indeed, more countries are choosing to get onto the treadmill, and are forcing it to go faster and faster.

The Acceleration of Innovation

The pace of innovation has been accelerating for quite some time, but recently it has shifted into an entirely new gear. During the last twenty years, the rate of innovation has surged to an unprecedented level, as is evident by looking at the growth of U.S. patent applications and grants over time. Patent filings are an indication of new ideas that might be commercialized, and patent grants are confirmation by the patent agency that something truly new and novel has been discovered. In theory, patent applications should indicate that innovation and entrepreneurial activity are likely to follow as a result of a scientific

Increase in U.S. Patent Applications and Grants

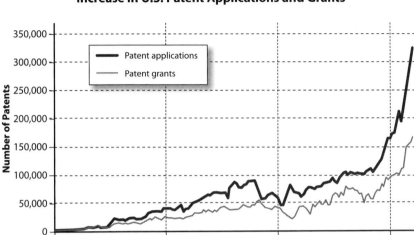

Source: Reprinted by permission from Ken Harrington, the Skandalaris Center for Entrepreneurial Studies. Data from the U.S. Patent Office.

discovery, and the sharp increase in patents starting in the 1980s demonstrates just how much the rate of innovation has accelerated over the past several decades.

What is causing this acceleration? Is the increase in innovation primarily driven by population growth? To a certain extent the answer is yes; people create and use technology, and the world's population is increasing rapidly. However, patent rates per person still show a sharp increase after 1980, so population alone does not explain the acceleration. There are several other main factors. One is the momentum that innovation itself creates, for as it gives rise to new possibilities and even more innovation, there is a multiplier effect as new technologies, products, and techniques become available. The greater the store of public knowledge, inventions, and technology there is to draw on, the more momentum drives innovation forward, faster and faster, resulting in an increasingly rapid growth of new technologies.

"Innovation has a way of building upon itself," says Steve Ballmer. "When Henry Ford designed the Model T and the first assembly line, for example, that was a truly breakthrough innovation. Ford taught the world how to make automobiles quickly, cheaply, and in very large numbers, and his efforts made cars affordable and put them within the reach of the average person. Yet as the Model T spread across America and throughout the world, it was still, if you really stop and think about it, only a hint of what the future of the automobile would be. It represented just the first few miles on the odometer of automotive innovation, and today, in terms of sheer volume, we are seeing more automotive innovation today than ever before, such as advanced navigation systems, safety sensors that trigger air bags and call the police, and hybrid vehicles.

"Over the past two decades, the information technology industry has really seen an evolution that is similar to the evolution in the auto industry. If you go back and think about good old MS DOS, it's kind of the Model T of software, and today we have information technology that's accessible to hundreds of millions of customers and runs mission critical systems in manufacturing companies, banks, hospitals, stock exchanges, governments, and organizations across the entire world. The commercialization of a number of information technology innovations—cell phones, personal computers, and the Internet—basically all came into broad distribution in the last ten years, and I think we're going to see even more information technology innovations in the decades to come. In fact, I believe the world is entering a whole new era of innovation, both in information technology and in general. The advances in high technology that we have experienced over the last few decades are converging, and they are going to reinforce and amplify all of the great innovations that have come before it."[7]

In addition to simple technological momentum, another dynamic that is spurring the growth of innovation is globalization, which is contributing several accelerating forces. One is the spread of capitalism, which is causing the free flow of information, capital, labor, and products around the world. Over the past thirty years, the number of capitalist economies in the world has quadrupled,[8] and the existence of capitalist economies in a greater percentage of the world is resulting in an acceleration of innovation as more people become entrepreneurs, both out of necessity and opportunity. By offering the opportunity for individuals to profit from their ideas and inventions, capitalism provides an incentive to innovate that has driven the global rate of innovation to new levels.

Much of the power of capitalism stems from specialization, the fact that by concentrating on a particular activity, we become more efficient, allowing us to produce more at a lower cost. This, in addition to innovation, is the magic that creates the ever-expanding economic pie. What globalization allows is an even greater degree of specialization than national economies can provide. Through privatization of industries, the reduction of barriers to trade, and the liberalization of capital markets, resources are being allocated more efficiently than ever before in formerly communist countries, and the power of capital and technology is being used to unlock the potential of dead assets. As a result of these changes, the National Intelligence Council predicts that by 2020, the world economy will be 80 percent larger, and average income 50 percent higher, than it is today.[9] That's a huge difference, one that will be spurred primarily by greater innovation and entrepreneurship. China, India, and a number of other countries seeking a better future through innovation-driven growth will provide both new markets and new competition as well. The implication for the rate of innovation is obvious: it is accelerating, and as capitalism spreads, it will continue to do so.

"The spread of capitalism has increased demand, which in discussing the negative aspects of globalization is something we sometimes forget," says Dr. Barton Hamilton, a professor of entrepreneurship at Washington University in St. Louis. "It's a function of what kind of access companies have to different markets. As there's more access to Chinese, Indian, and other emerging markets, there's increased demand for products. Before you just had the American, European, and Japanese markets, but now you have potential markets in India, China, and other places as well, and that increases the premium on innovation."

Another aspect of globalization that is contributing to the acceleration of innovation is the worldwide proliferation of productivity-enhancing communication tools enabled by the Internet and fiber optics. While the information technology industry itself has been fertile ground for entrepreneurial activity, the movement to information-based organizations has also opened up new opportunities in mature industries, allowing us to move money, coordinate activities, and exchange information in faster and more efficient ways. More information was produced in the last thirty years than in the previous five thousand, and the amount of information currently being produced is doubling every two years and is accelerating.[10] While the Internet was over-hyped, there is no denying that it has changed the pace of business, allowing competitors to understand and replicate rivals' actions more quickly. This adds an accelerator to innovation and entrepreneurship, with the result that activities and value are added for lower cost and at different points around the globe.

This point was driven home when contributing author Ken Harrington visited a hospital emergency room with his daughter. While they were waiting, a hospital staff person asked if he would like something to drink. One of the choices was apple juice, and they brought out the usual hospital plastic cup with an aluminum foil top. As Ken tore off the top, he noted the juice was made from ingredients that came from nine different countries across the globe. He reflected that commodity markets were not only acting more efficiently and globally, but also that the process of optimizing buying, coordinating shipping, managing imports, tracking quality, and producing these cups had probably changed massively over the last ten years.

When I heard this story, I remembered a conversation I had a couple of years ago with the executives of a company that has manufacturing facilities in China. While they had relocated manufacturing to China and built a new factory there, they felt threatened by the SARS epidemic and were uncertain about its duration and impact. In a very short period of time, they had assessed the critical criteria for a number of countries, contacted the economic development groups, and completed a full-blown contingency plan to move operations to an Eastern European country that was to be admitted to the European Union. They were ready to pull the trigger and move from China to the new location if the threat increased.

After this conversation I remember thinking, how could you have done all of that fifteen years ago? How would you have communicated, organized the information, contacted the right people, and negotiated the agreements in such an efficient manner? Globalization and high-tech communications have completely changed the speed at which we do business, which is forcing us to innovate faster just to keep up with the competition. While the "New Economy" of the dot-com era was a bust, that does not dismiss the importance of the high-tech industry and its impact on innovation and entrepreneurship.

"The speed and amount of competition has certainly multiplied as a consequence of globalization and communications technology," says Hamilton. "It has substantially lowered costs of inputs to production such as labor and capital, which has allowed innovations that in the past might have been too costly to develop and bring to market. As a result, the cost barriers to innovation have been substantially lowered, and increased competition by firms in other countries has basically increased the premium on innovation for everybody. In addition, the ability of companies to decrease their costs through outsourcing and by using global talent has decreased the cost of bringing new, innovative ideas to market as well, and as a consequence, there's more innovation."

The combination of the spread of capitalism and the Internet has greatly reduced barriers to entry in many businesses. In some cases, this has opened doors for entrepreneurs by giving them the ability to access niche markets and create targeted, specialized products at a far lower cost than previously. Some entrepreneurs have staked out little monopolies in these small but profitable niche markets.

For more mainstream products, however, falling communication and transportation costs have intensified competition and significantly reduced the time it takes for an innovation to become a commodity. Product lifetimes are getting shorter as new products are being introduced ever more quickly. In the late 1800s, it took over thirty years on average for a competing product to be introduced in response to a new innovation; now it takes less than five years, and the lag continues to shorten. This has massive implications for American businesses. Products and services are being commoditized more quickly than ever before, which means that American companies must innovate faster in order to stay ahead of the competition in China, India, Ireland, Indonesia, Brazil, and dozens of other countries. High technology has created a world where knowledge is becoming exponentially more valuable, and the Internet has created a world where knowledge and capital can be transferred cheaply and easily.

"We're going to see a wave of change in technology, how it helps connect us, how it helps us to collaborate," says Steve Ballmer. "Just as the last twenty-five years were about empowering the individual, these next twenty-five years will involve a wave of innovation that centers on empowering the interactions between individuals, groups, and organizations. As more and more of our interactions are mediated and involve the use of technology, I see tremendous opportunity to harness the connectivity of the Internet and workstation in the way we live, the way we work, and the way we interact. The degree to which people can be socialized for the increasing globalization in our economy is incredible, with the way technology really lets the world sort of melt away, if you will, at our fingertips. As a result, the businesses of tomorrow are going to be much more global than the businesses of today. The technology allows it, demands it even. The ways in which people interact with suppliers and customers and constituents will keep requiring more global awareness, and the power of technology to be a tool for really participating in global society is almost limitless."[11]

The rules of the game have changed, and as capitalism has emerged as the best method of managing a modern economy, more and more countries have concluded that they must innovate or die. The changes wrought by globalization and high technology are creating a challenging new environment unlike any Americans have faced before.

The Chinese Dream

Perhaps the best example of how the American Dream has spread to other countries is to look at what is happening in China, a country that is generating increasing interest and concern in the debate over our economic future. Over the past twenty-five years, China has slowly moved towards a more market-oriented economy, and it openly embraced capitalism starting in 1998 when Deng Xiaoping declared that it was "glorious to be rich." At the 2003 World Economic Forum, it was reported that nearly 60 percent of world export growth now comes from China, fueled both by foreign investment and Chinese entrepreneurship.[12] China now has the second-largest economy behind the United States in terms of purchasing power, and it is growing at a rate of 8 percent per year, far faster than the U.S. economy.[13] At that rate, it is destined to surpass us as the world's largest economy within two decades. In short, the United States has never faced an economic rival like the one it now faces in China.

One of the things that makes China so much of a threat is its massive domestic market of 1.3 billion consumers, a trump card which gives it an enormous amount of bargaining power on the world stage. American multinational firms, faced with saturated markets at home, practically salivate at the thought of accessing China's untapped markets. The Chinese government knows this, and has used it to wring significant concessions from American multinationals, which are seemingly desperate to access China at any cost. Rather than accept American exports, China has encouraged American manufacturers to set up shop in China with the lure of tax breaks, cheap labor, and fewer regulations as an incentive. The heart of its strategy, however, has been to require foreign companies to joint venture with domestic Chinese firms, and to demand a high degree of technology transfer. In exchange for access to the world's largest unsaturated market, American multinationals are trading away the keys to American competitive advantage—our advanced technology and business expertise.

China now has the second-largest economy behind the United States in terms of purchasing power.

I got a taste of this when, in March of 2004, we sent members of the executive team of Noble International, North America's largest laser welding company, to China. Noble is on the cutting edge of innovation in the laser industry—it is the world leader in developing curvilinear welding techniques and multi-dimensional tubular products. This leadership has allowed Noble to grow rapidly and, like the executives of so many other American companies, we had gone to China to explore the possibility of building a plant there. We were impressed by their tremendous manufacturing and engineering capabilities, and the Chinese, for their part, were extremely interested in acquiring our laser-welding technology.

The longer we stayed in China, however, the more uneasy we became. Basic management strategy dictates that while you should outsource those functions that others can do more efficiently than you do, you should always keep your core competencies in house. Noble's core competency is our cutting-edge, laser-welding technology; it is what we do better than anyone in the world. We went to China prepared to share some of our more seasoned tools and techniques, but the Chinese wanted more than this. What they wanted was our very latest technology, and not just the tools but the processes—which are the very heart of Noble's competitive advantage. Moreover, they wanted us to transfer this technology to them, with little guarantee of protection, in an environment that is notorious for counterfeiting and piracy.

It did not take us long to decide that we were not going to build a plant in China, and since we possessed cutting-edge technology and laser-welding techniques that few other companies could match, we had this power. We could forgo the cost savings of manufacturing in China, secure in the knowledge that our main customers would still buy our products, because they are unique. That is the power of being an industry leader in innovation. Unfortunately, many other American suppliers do not have this power. Without a unique, innovative core competency, they must compete based on cost, and are faced with the choice of either beating the Chinese or joining them. Beating the Chinese on cost, however, is downright impossible thanks to their endless supply of cheap and highly motivated labor. As a result, many American suppliers are practically being forced to move their operations to China if they want to stay in business—a decidedly unenviable position.

Meanwhile, many American multinational companies have acquiesced to Chinese demands and agreed to transfer their technology, and even relocate research and development to China as well. As Oded Shenkar, author of *The Chinese Century,* points out, American multinationals have struck this bargain because they assume that Chinese firms can not challenge them in high-tech industries, as they lack recognizable brands, a well-developed research and development base, and their financial system is dangerously close to insolvent.[14] Yet the pundits have failed to take into account the fact that China is rapidly becoming the center of an increasingly integrated Asian economy, and is trading access to the Chinese market for the research and development, business consulting, and financial services available in Japan and the four "Asian tigers" (South Korea, Hong Kong, Taiwan, and Singapore). China is investing heavily in education and technology infrastructure, and its businesses are leveraging their massive earnings from labor-intensive industries to break into high technology industries—technology products are China's fastest growing exports. While China lags far behind in service industries, the United States is going to face increasing competition from places like India and Ireland, which are specializing in services to avoid competing with China's manufacturing prowess.

China is not going to be content to remain a low-cost, low-tech manufacturer. Margins at the low end are thin, and like Japan and the Asian tigers before it, China is already moving up-market into higher quality, higher margin products, and branching out into more technology-intensive products as well. What makes China different, Shenkar warns, is that its massive population will enable it to do so without abandoning the low-end, labor-intensive markets. The coastal cities with highly skilled and educated workers will move up the ladder to challenge the United States and other highly developed nations in technology-intensive industries, while the rural areas specialize in heavy manufacturing and labor-intensive industries. The resulting economies of scale and scope are transforming China into the world's manufacturer of choice—a role that the United States used to occupy and which allowed it to achieve superpower status. China has the breadth and the depth to expand into a wide variety of industries, from low-tech textiles and assembly to high-tech computer and digital electronics manufacturing. Its advantage as a low-cost producer comes not just from low wages, which average $0.69 per hour in China vs. $21.33 per hour in the United States, but from an expanding network of supporting suppliers and high-tech manufacturing.[15]

American multinationals and discount retailers such as Wal-Mart see Chinese manufacturing as a huge opportunity, and they are procuring an increasing number of components, subassemblies, and finished products from Chinese firms. For smaller companies, however, Chinese manufacturing is more of a threat than an opportunity. Many smaller American firms serve as local suppliers to larger companies, and they are finding that they have to match Chinese prices that are generally 30 to 50 percent lower than what they can manage. This is driving small American suppliers out of business. In addition to supplying parts and raw materials, Chinese firms are also a direct source of competition for labor-intensive manufactured goods such as toys, clothing, and furniture, which under free trade agreements are imported into the United States at very low cost. While large American multinationals may have the marketing clout to compete with low-cost Chinese imports, smaller firms simply do not have the same resources.

China currently has over two million privately owned companies, and while most of them are still small, the Chinese government is providing significant incentives for growth and consolidation. As more privately-held Chinese firms expand and start selling globally, they are going to provide serious competition for American firms, driving them out of the market on price. Unlike the Japanese and Koreans, who usually took several years to gain sizeable market share in the United States, Chinese competitors are penetrating the American market swiftly with their dramatically lower prices. It is simply not possible for American companies to compete with Chinese manufacturing based on price, and small American firms are finding that they must either outsource work and relocate to China themselves, or go out of business.

Meanwhile, American multinationals are moving some of their manufacturing and an increasing amount of their research and development to China. There are significant synergies in co-locating manufacturing with research and development, and as manufacturing migrates overseas, R&D is destined to follow. Chinese leadership understands that in the twenty-first century, technology, innovation, and entrepreneurship are going to be key drivers of economic growth, not to mention geopolitical influence, and they are doing everything they can to encourage it. They are turning their lack of late-twentieth century technology infrastructure and expertise into an advantage by skipping straight to the next-generation technology, ramping up the number of scientists and engineers graduating from their universities, and doing their best to lure back students and professors who have studied and worked overseas. As a result, an increasing number of American multinational corporations are opening research centers overseas. As Chinese companies export more and more to the United

States, they are also using their American dollars to buy American companies. Following Lenovo's successful bid to purchase IBM's personal computer unit in December of 2004, there are now bids from Chinese companies to buy both Maytag and Unocal.

The effect this will have on American business, jobs, and the economy over the next few decades is going to be significant. Increasing competitive pressure from China is going to force an ongoing loss of American jobs as, in search of greater productivity, American firms increasingly automate activities and outsource portions of their business to outside firms that can perform them more efficiently. Offshoring and plant relocations will cut further into what remains of American manufacturing. Yet even if American companies refused to offshore jobs and relocate plants, many of those same jobs would then be lost to trade displacement, as cheaper foreign products drive down the demand for American goods. So far job losses from foreign competition have primarily affected blue collar workers in manufacturing industries, but as China moves up the ladder and drives global competitors up-market and into services, an increasing number of white collar jobs are being lost as well.

> There are significant synergies in co-locating manufacturing with research and development, and as manufacturing migrates overseas, R&D is destined to follow.

Young Chinese workers are willing to work twelve-hour days, plus weekends, without many of the benefits that Americans are used to, and at a fraction of what U.S. workers are paid—around $120 a month for blue collar production workers, and $2000 for highly skilled white- collar workers.[16] Highly skilled American workers are now competing in an international labor market, and this has led some people to ask, in what ways, if any, do American workers still have a competitive advantage? With the proliferation of the Internet and other high-tech communications, technology and capital are easily transferred and invested overseas to make cheap foreign laborers as productive as Americans. That has led to a lot more offshore outsourcing than economists ever anticipated.

"China presents both an incredible threat and an incredible opportunity," says Bart Hamilton. "If we're able to enter Chinese markets and have access to those markets, it would certainly increase the demand for American products. I also think that the more we can tap the skills of people all over the world, the better the products are likely to be, and that's better for consumers. But there are certainly threats, and to me, the biggest threat is the potential loss of highly skilled foreign labor. During the post-war era, the greatest thing that happened in the United States was that we were able to essentially import so much foreign talent and knowledge, to the extent that we became the world's knowledge factory. We probably have the greatest pool of talent in the history of the world in terms of generating innovation and entrepreneurship, and the immigration of Indian and Chinese scientists, engineers, and graduate students has been an incredible driver of growth for us.

"As places like China and India open up, however, I think more and more we will see people in those societies deciding not to come to the United States. There will still be innovation, but the returns from that innovation will be captured more by companies in those countries. Instead of having an Indian software engineer come to the U.S. and work for Microsoft, they're going to be more likely to stay in India and work for high-tech startups there. That may not be bad for the owners of capital, in that capital is able to move freely across countries, but where I think that can have some negative impact is in employment. We like innovation not only because it's a benefit for consumers, but also because it's a driver of employment growth, and I think that's a significant threat. If most talented people stay in their own countries rather than coming to the United States, there may be less of an employment gain for innovation than there has been in the past."

It would be vastly unjust to cast China in the role of a villain, stealing American business and American jobs. Having championed the superiority of capitalism over communism, we can hardly fault the Chinese now for embracing the profit motive and acting in their own self-interest, although their piracy of American intellectual property is a serious issue that needs to be addressed. Nor is China the only competitor we need to worry about.

Indians have proven themselves to be adept at doing white collar back-office jobs from overseas, and are using that experience to move into more creative work. India's economy has been growing at a rate of 6 percent annually, and it far outpaces China in exporting information technology and services. In fact, at its current growth rate, India will have a larger share of world domestic product than the European Union by 2050, and may well surpass both China and the United States a few decades after. Their entrepreneurs are re-inventing business models in the automobile, banking, cellular, and software industries, and their average return on capital is an incredible 16.7 percent.[17] With those kind of numbers, high-tech Indian service companies are going to be very attractive to American investors in the future.

Meanwhile, countries like Ireland, Germany, and New Zealand are carving out their own niches at the top of the income ladder. On a macro-economic level, the spread of capitalism certainly has the potential to grow the global economic pie, but on a micro-economic level, it is always a Darwinian struggle as to who will have the largest piece. Capitalism is by nature competitive, and America needs to rise to the global challenge and compete, for the goal of China and many other countries isn't merely to catch up with the United States but to surpass it. The American Dream is now being appropriated and morphed into the Chinese Dream and the Indian Dream.

Innovation and Economic Competitiveness

In the twenty-first century, the key to remaining competitive with China, India, and the rest of the world will be innovation, and while that is one of the things we do best, it is no longer a foregone conclusion that we will lead the world in this area. It is true that developing and formerly communist countries do not have the same systems for disseminating breakthroughs and turning them into commercial applications. They never developed the research networks, intellectual property rights, risk capital systems, and economic incentives necessary to sustain the momentum of innovation. Indeed, the main reason that countries like China violate intellectual property laws and focus so much on technology transfer is that they lack a system to generate innovation on their own. But they're working on it, and they're gaining fast.

"My sense is that the United States is still in the lead across most metrics, but that lead is narrowing, and in a couple of metrics other countries have pulled ahead," says David Attis. "If you look at the world at a single point in time today, the United States is still clearly in the lead, but many others are catching up, and might overtake us in some areas over the next decade or so."

Americans need to understand this and respond, because remaining the world leader in innovation is crucial to both maintaining our standard of living and retaining our current economic and geopolitical power. While the United States still has a tremendous advantage over the rest of the world in innovation, that advantage is in peril. We have been leading in the innovation race for so long that we have come to take that lead for granted, and our complacency is a dangerous mistake. The growing ranks of capitalist countries all around the world have come to see innovation as their ticket to a better future, and the gap between them and us is closing rapidly. In 1987, the number of U.S. patents granted to foreign citizens equaled the number of patents granted to American citizens for the first time, a result of more innovation and entrepreneurship across the globe. The world has joined the innovation race, and Greg Blonder, a venture capitalist and former Bell Labs scientist, predicts that in the future, "the United States can only count on making at most one in five inventions."[18]

Whether or not this is good news or bad news depends on your perspective. Clearly, other nations are becoming more innovative, which is good news overall, but that means there is more competitive pressure, which could be perceived as bad news for the United States.

Looking at what happened during the 1970s and 80s, it is clear that we lost ground as the overall number of patents granted to American citizens dropped. In the 1990s, however, we maintained parity while the total number of patents awarded to both foreign and domestic citizens jumped significantly. Does this mean that we as a country are responding to competitive pressure from foreign innovators? Possibly, and the 1990s were certainly an indication that we are capable of responding to such pressure and thriving in a global economy.

Patent rates, however, are only a small part of the story. The overwhelming majority of patents wind up having little economic value, so what really matters in the innovation race is our ability to build business models around and commercialize new technologies—in other words, entrepreneurship. Yet the United States is losing ground here as well, for globalization is not only bringing us into contact with new customers for our products and investors for our

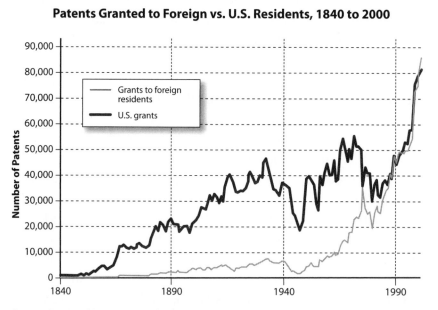

Patents Granted to Foreign vs. U.S. Residents, 1840 to 2000

Source: Reprinted by permission from Ken Harrington, the Skandalaris Center for Entrepreneurial Studies. Data from the U.S. Patent Office.

businesses, but a vast pool of hungry international entrepreneurs, especially in developing Asia. The United States ranks only eleventh in total entrepreneurial activity, a measure of the prevalence of working-age citizens engaged in starting up a business or managing one less than three-and-a-half years old.[19] Overall, it is part of a middling group of countries with average rates of entrepreneurship—a far cry from being the global leader.

The race is on in the global innovation and entrepreneurship game, and the lead the United States relies upon is in jeopardy. Some may argue that it is wrong to conceive of innovation as a race between nations, because economic progress is not a zero-sum game—the diffusion of innovation and entrepreneurship has benefits for all. Economic resources, however, are scarce, and those who control them reap the majority of the benefits. In the past, that meant accumulating the most land, labor, and capital; today, it means generating and commercializing the most innovations. While we should be glad to see more innovation and entrepreneurship in other parts of the world, we still need to remain the global leader if we want our standard of living to continue rising in the twenty-first century.

"We talked about that issue a lot at the Council on Competitiveness' National Innovation Initiative meetings," Attis told me. "Does the United States have to be number one? Or would we feel comfortable if we still had very high standards of living but other countries were simply catching up on us, if essentially we still had the same total amount of wealth, and our share of the pie was smaller because the pie is getting bigger? The consensus seemed to be that it's great that other countries are growing and building their capacity in science and engineering, but what we're seeing now is that research and innovation are increasingly essential to our ability to compete in global markets. The risk is if we lose our lead in innovation, we won't be able to sustain our standard of living, let alone continue to increase it."

Those who assume that Americans will have no problem remaining competitive and climbing the economic ladder do so because they believe American companies will always have a superior ability to

Total Entrepreneurial Activity by Global Region

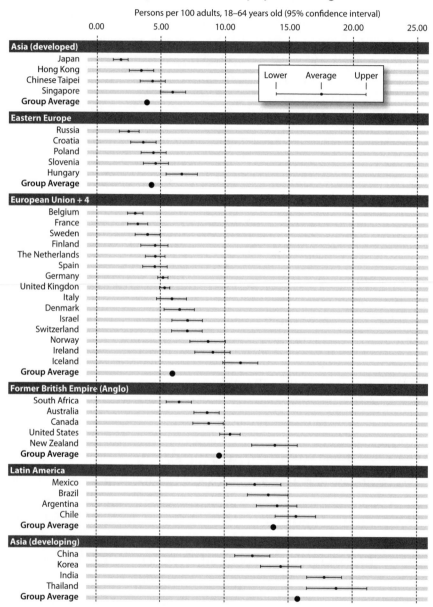

Persons per 100 adults, 18–64 years old (95% confidence interval)

Source: Global Entrepreneurship Monitor 2002 Executive Report. © 2002 Paul D. Reynolds, William D. Bygrave, Erkko Autio, Larry W. Cox, Michael Hay, and the Ewing Marion Kauffman Foundation.

innovate. But this is a dangerous illusion, and if we persist in believing it we are headed for serious trouble. Innovation is not our birthright, but a complex activity that is going to require a serious, sustained commitment of talent and resources. There is a widespread belief that America is going to continue to prosper by moving up the economic ladder into increasingly high-value-added services, that while the boring jobs are outsourced we Americans will do the fun, creative, high-paying work. While this may indeed be the only viable strategy available to us, the idea that Americans somehow have a lock on the top of the economic pyramid is ridiculous.

Americans have a habit of thinking that we can do high-value creative work better than anyone else, but there are brilliant, creative, hard-working Chinese, Indians, Russians, Indonesians, Malaysians, Singaporeans, Taiwanese, Koreans, Japanese, Irish, Brazilians, and many other people who can do this work just as well as we can—and who will do it for less. We have no more hold on the top of the economic ladder than we do on the lower or middle rungs. A lot of this highly paid creative work can, and will, go overseas. Meanwhile, low-paying service jobs will be taken by immigrants from Mexico and other countries hurt by low-cost Chinese manufacturing, immigrants who will work long and hard hours for wages Americans consider beneath them. On what is an increasingly level global playing field, the rest of the world will not sit idly by while America keeps the largest, tastiest slice of the pie for itself. Everyone wants the best, and they will go after it with everything they have.

It is time that Americans wake up and realize this fact. If business owners and managers believe their companies can survive merely by cutting costs and outsourcing, they won't be in business for long. If parents believe their children should have a good time in high school, with their primary focus on playing sports and going to dances rather than academic achievement, those children will not enjoy the same standard of living their parents did. And if the government of the United States believes that it can go blithely along without an industrial innovation policy, letting the invisible hand of the market single-handedly shape our economic destiny while we concentrate on the War on Terror, then this country will not remain an economic superpower for long. Free markets are good at allocating resources efficiently, but they are not infallible. There is one survival strategy in this global economy—innovate or die—and we're all going to be in the dogfight of our lives to innovate faster and better than everyone else.

As CEO of Microsoft, no one is more aware of this than Steve Ballmer. "I tell our employees that the most important thing to think about in terms of innovation is, are we first in the marketplace? I guess some companies have different strategies, those who say they're fast followers, but at Microsoft we don't want to be a fast follower. Our goal is to be first, and so we're going invest in innovation, to take those big bets. There may be some times when those bets don't pay off, when we're not first, but when that happens you can count on us to continue to push ourselves to innovate and improve upon that new offering. That's our philosophy—be first, but if you're not first, run extra, extra hard and make sure you're still in the game. Be tenacious.

> There is one survival strategy in this global economy— innovate or die.

"I think most companies give up on their innovation far too soon, before it ever has a chance to really pay off, and that's a mistake. You have to be willing to stick with it. As a company, you have to judge the breadth, depth, and value of your innovations. If your portfolio is not wide enough, if there is significant value being created in an area that you're not investing in, that's a problem. If you're not going deep enough and being tenacious enough to win, that's a problem. If you're not leading the industry and being first to market, that's a problem. You really have to ask yourself every day, are we working hard to have a portfolio of broad, deep, and valuable innovations? Are we getting the talent necessary so that our company can be dynamic and competitive? Are we succeeding in key new areas? These questions don't just apply to large, multinational corporations with big research and development departments. They also apply to small companies, non-profits, governments, and even individuals, because innovation can mean many different things. Your innovation may be in the efficiency with which you can deliver a service, help a customer manage a license, or leverage an asset. It may be on the efficiency side. It may be on the new ideas side. But all of us are in a position where we have to reach out, find appropriate partners, innovate in the fundamental work that we do, and then have excellence in execution for our target customers and listen very intently to what they say."[20]

Unfortunately, Ballmer doesn't sense this same level of focus on innovation from other American companies. "There's a dangerous complacency about innovation amongst people in the world these days, and that complacency threatens to leave companies behind in a world that will continue to change rapidly. What do I mean by innovation complacency? To put it simply, I think it's when corporations focus on short-term gains over long-term value, when they fail to exploit or even develop new technologies that could boost productivity, reduce order times, improve customer service, and open up new markets. That's a mentality I see everywhere these days. Sam Walton once said, 'You just can't keep doing what works one time, because everything around you is always changing. To succeed you have to stay out in front of change.' I think that's true for American companies, I think it's true for the American workforce, and most importantly I think it's true for America itself."[21]

Fortunately, there are a number of reasons to be optimistic about the state of innovation and entrepreneurship in the United States. The acceleration of innovation is creating a wealth of new opportunities, as the ever-expanding pool of knowledge and new technologies provides more possibilities for entrepreneurship. Globalization is giving American entrepreneurs the chance to access entirely new customers and markets, along with a growing number of foreign investors, and the diffusion of technology has made it faster, cheaper, and easier to communicate with these new customers and investors via the Internet and a number of other high-tech devices. In many ways, the Internet levels the playing field for small and large firms, creating an environment with low barriers to entry and easy access to information.

Young Americans are responding to these opportunities, as reflected in the huge increase in enrollment in entrepreneurship programs across the country. CEOs of established firms are also realizing that after decades of cost-cutting and maximizing efficiency, they are now going to need to emphasize growth and innovation in order to prosper in an ever more competitive global environment. In addition, state governments and economic development programs have become increasingly interested in fostering entrepreneurship as a means of creating jobs and economic growth, and technology clusters and innovation zones are being established across the country. Last but not least, the academic community is playing a greater role in the innovation process, and is taking more responsibility for technology transfer. All of these trends reflect our growing realization of just how important innovation and entrepreneurship is going to be in the twenty-first century. Yet there are significant challenges as well.

In the new millennium, entrepreneurial activity will be more global, although far from ubiquitous, and the process of innovation will become more competitive as additional countries opt to participate. While startup activity in the United States is relatively high, in terms of sheer numbers, India and China both have more entrepreneurs and new businesses than we do. The two countries combined have over 200 million entrepreneurs involved in over 140 million startups, while the United States has only 20 million entrepreneurs starting 11 million new businesses.[22] These figures do not automatically portend bad things for the United States, as more global businesses mean more trade and more overall wealth. What is clear, however, is that by the year 2050 the United States is very likely to have at least one, if not several, powerful economic rivals.

What I find most disturbing is not the fact that we have global competition, but that just when we need to rely on our entrepreneurs more than ever before, we are undercutting the very systems that support entrepreneurship. For example:

Distribution of Entrepreneurial Activity and Labor Force

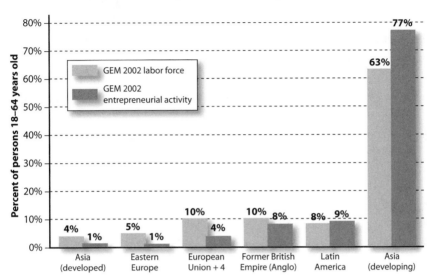

Source: Global Entrepreneurship Monitor 2002 Executive Report. © 2002 Paul D. Reynolds, William D. Bygrave, Erkko Autio, Larry W. Cox, Michael Hay, and the Ewing Marion Kauffman Foundation.

- **Federal research and development funding** has been cut in critical areas like information technology and nanotechnology

- **Entrepreneurial education,** while growing, still does not adequately prepare science and business students for the demands of entrepreneurship

- **Venture capital** funding has grown conservative and moved upstream, creating a funding gap for high-tech growth funding

- **Intellectual property** is not being adequately protected from foreign piracy and counterfeiting

- **Financial incentives** such as stock options that are used to motivate entrepreneurs and their employees are under fire due to intense scrutiny of corporate accounting

America's future can still be bright, but only if we address these problems and renew our commitment to innovation and entrepreneurship. The evidence suggests that global innovation will continue to accelerate rapidly in the future, which means that the United States can quickly regain our commanding lead in the innovation race if we make a focused effort. On the other hand, we can also fall rapidly behind if we fail to adapt the demands of a new, more global environment. Throughout our history, the United States has worked to develop systems that support innovation and entrepreneurship. The demands of the twenty-first century require that we update these systems and work to develop new ones as well, for in a world full of challenges, both foreseen and unforeseen, innovation will be the determining factor in who succeeds and who does not.

> America's challenge is to unleash its innovation capacity to drive productivity, standard of living, and leadership in global markets. At a time when macro-economic forces and financial constraints make innovation-driven growth a more urgent imperative than ever before, American business, government, workers, and universities face an unprecedented acceleration of global change, relentless pressure for short-term results, and fierce competition from countries that seek an innovation-driven future for themselves. For the past 25 years, we have optimized our organizations for efficiency and quality. Over the next quarter century, we must optimize our entire society for innovation.[23]
>
> —*Innovate America* report,
> Council on Competitiveness

In many ways, the United States is well positioned to take advantage of the benefits of globalization, but we cannot allow ourselves to become complacent. With a growing number of hungry new participants in the innovation race, there will be increased competition, and this, combined with advancements in technology and communication, will fuel the trends that are already accelerating the rate of change and innovation. In the future, those people, organizations, and governments that don't have a strategy to become a world leader in innovation will be displaced or at serious risk to become obsolete. Therefore, the message to individuals, companies, and countries is to examine their strategies for supporting innovation and entrepreneurship, for as the famous television chef Emeril says, we are going to need to "kick it up a notch."

3

THE CRUCIBLE OF INNOVATION— RESEARCH AND DEVELOPMENT

◇◇◇

Thomas Alva Edison was the most prolific inventor in American history, with an incredible 1093 patents to his name. He is most often remembered for inventing the incandescent light bulb, but Edison was much more than an inventor. He was an entrepreneur who had the scientific knowledge to invent what he needed to fulfill his vision. Whereas many inventors are happy just to invent for the sake of inventing, for Edison, the point was always to commercialize inventions and bring them to the world. To quote the man himself, "There is a wide difference between completing an invention and putting the manufactured article on the market."[1] The original invention was merely the first step in a larger process of creating the technological system, and then a series of businesses to manage that system. In commercializing the light bulb, for example, he not only had to invent the light bulb itself, but the entire electrical industry.

At the age of thirty-one, Edison established an "invention factory" at Menlo Park, New Jersey, from which he promised "a minor invention every ten days and a big thing every six months."[2] The invention factory was one of Edison's greatest inventions in and of itself, a precursor to the industrial research and development laboratory. We tend to picture Edison as a lone inventor—an image he deliberately cultivated—but the truth is that most of the patents in his name were the product of a team of researchers. He staffed his laboratory with a cadre of scientists and mechanics, and it was the exchange of ideas across multiple disciplines that created the seemingly endless stream of innovations that we have come to associate with Edison alone.

From the start, the Menlo Park lab was devoted not just to invention but to the commercialization of inventions, and a key part of this process was the sharing of insights from various seemingly unrelated projects. In addition to pursuing their own research, Edison and his employees served as freelance inventors for hire, and technical solutions developed for one client often found their way into other projects. It was an open process that would drive today's corporate research directors crazy, yet it was crucial to the Menlo Park lab's success. Rather than inventing in isolation, Edison acted as a knowledge broker, sharing and bringing together many different ideas from various people and disciplines.

Edison also created a unique environment that stimulated innovation and creativity. The schedule was brutal, for Edison and his employees would often work twenty-four hours straight and then crash for eighteen hours on the floor or a bench, never bothering to go home. Yet the lab was full of intelligent and talented people, and it was high on camaraderie. Working late into the night, the muckers, as Edison called them, would often stop for midnight meals of ham, pie, and beer, along with that all-important food for the creative soul—stimulating conversation. It was a culture more akin to a dot-com startup than today's typical research and development department, intense but informal, cooperative rather than functionalized, and it produced results. Menlo Park was so successful that within a few decades, the industrial research and development laboratory had become ubiquitous in America's top corporations. Innovation was seen as the best method of staying ahead of the competition, and the research laboratory had become the crucible where breakthrough ideas were born.[3]

I f you want to understand why America has led the world in innovation for over a century, there is no better place to start than an American research laboratory. There are many different kinds of innovation, and while some have nothing to do with science or technology, in most cases high-impact innovation is increasingly high-tech and built upon the foundations of scientific research. While breakthrough inventions like Henry Ford's first quadricycle and the Apple personal computer may have been created in a garage, the research into electricity and semiconductors that preceded these inventions was done in a laboratory. It is the birthplace of invention, and scientific research provides the fertile soil from which commercial applications can grow.

The research and development process that leads to a breakthrough invention like the personal computer has many steps and is far from linear, working both forwards from pure scientific exploration and backwards from a market need. The path that led to the development of the first microprocessor, for example, started with what is often called exploratory research in the area of solid-state physics, the kind of research we generally think of as being done by scientists at universities. Eventually, discoveries in this area led to a more focused research effort into semiconductors—what many would still consider basic research, but with a greater promise of eventual application. Indeed, later-stage applied research, primarily in industrial labs, did lead to the invention of a variety of patentable semiconductor devices such as transistors, diodes, solar cells, and of course, microprocessors. That, in turn, led to the development of commercial products such as Intel's 8080 and MOS Technology's 6502 microprocessors, which allowed Steve Jobs and Steve Wozniak to design and manufacture the first commercially successful personal computer.

For half a century, the United States has been recognized around the world as the leading center for this kind of scientific research and development. The rise of industrial and university research laboratories, and a massive increase in federal funding for research following World War II, placed the United States squarely at the forefront of scientific research—a position that has never seriously been challenged. That commitment to research and development has fueled the technological advances of the twentieth century and sparked an unprecedented rate of innovation. The discoveries in these labs have been crucial not just for established corporations, but also for entrepreneurs, who have developed breakthrough technologies on the foundations of this research that have created millions of new jobs. Indeed, middle class America owes much of its prosperity to the strength of American research and development, and will depend upon it even more so in the future.

The Evolution of American Research and Development Laboratories

In the first half of the twentieth century, industrial research and development labs were the primary crucible for commercial research and development in the United States. Thomas Edison's invention factory at Menlo Park had proven the value of research done explicitly for the purpose of developing new products, and by the start of the Great Depression, 115 of the largest 200 American companies had their own research labs.[4] In fact, one of the reasons the United States overtook Britain to become the world's leading manufacturing power was due to its superior applied research and development capabilities. In the late 1800s, British scientists had led the way in conducting breakthrough science and pure research, but American inventors and engineers had become consistently better at taking those breakthrough discoveries and applying them to develop marketable products.

During this period, neither the government nor universities played a major role in commercial research and development. The federal government had established a land-grant program designed to support science and technology development at state universities, and had funded a limited amount of agricultural research. As late as 1940, however, the federal government was only spending $614 million annually on research and development.[5] Universities spent even less, partially because they simply didn't have the financial resources to underwrite major research projects, but also because there was a strong feeling within the academic research community that true scientists should not debase themselves by getting involved in applications research for commercial purposes. The power of the profit motive was seen as a threat to the objective, independent nature of research, and scientists at universities generally had little involvement with the industrial research labs. Without significant support from the government or academia, American companies were on their own when it came to research and development.

That changed after World War II with the success of the Manhattan Project in developing the first nuclear bomb. This project marked the first time the federal government played a significant role in funding research and development, and from a military standpoint it had been a resounding success. In fact, President Franklin D. Roosevelt was so impressed with the results that in 1944 he commissioned a report to learn how the power of scientific research could be applied to peacetime problems. "New frontiers of the mind are before us," argued Roosevelt, "and if they are pioneered with the same vision, boldness, and drive with which we have waged this war, we can create a fuller and more fruitful employment, and a fuller and more fruitful life."[6]

> **Middle class America owes much of its prosperity to the strength of American research and development.**

Roosevelt put Vannevar Bush, the director of the Office of Scientific Research and Development, in charge of the report, entitled *Science: The Endless Frontier.* Bush came back with a bold suggestion—that the federal government should take a lead role in funding scientific research and development, particularly in the basic sciences. While Americans had long been recognized for their Yankee ingenuity, a certain knack for creating practical inventions, our success had always relied upon basic, theoretical research conducted by European scientists. Bush was adamant that this could no longer continue. If the United States wanted to retain its preeminent place in the world, it had to take the lead in funding research, particularly basic research.

A key policy decision that resulted from *Science: The Endless Frontier* was that government should fund research through universities as well as public and private labs, rather than conducting research itself. The massive amount of funding quickly transformed a select group of American universities into the premier research institutions in the world. Through sheer volume of investment, the United States became the leader in both basic and applied research in almost every discipline. Scientists and students from around the world came to work in American university laboratories, allowing us to benefit from a steady stream of top research talent that often went on to work in American industrial labs. The huge investment in basic research provided a continually expanding base of scientific knowledge from which to create commercial applications.

By 1955, the federal government had surpassed industry to become the largest provider of research funding in the United States, with an R&D budget of almost $18 billion.[7] Russia's launch of Sputnik in 1957 added fuel to the fire and created widespread fear that the United States was falling behind in technological innovation. As a result, federal research financing grew to over $53 billion by 1970.[8] As university, public, and private laboratories came to play a larger role in research, industrial research labs benefited tremendously from the rapidly expanding pool of general scientific knowledge, resulting in a golden age of American research and development in the decades following World War II that vaulted us into the lead in the innovation race.

For the remainder of the twentieth century, investment in scientific and technological research received widespread popular support in the United States, and federally funded research led to numerous breakthrough innovations such as the Internet, fiber optics, Doppler radar, computer aided design, and global positioning satellites. This funding also created a strong university research system that attracted the world's best science and engineering talent, and American industry continually increased its research and development spending over the last several decades. All of this investment has been a boon to

American entrepreneurs, creating a broad base of research to draw on in their quest to innovate.

At the start of the twenty-first century, however, cracks are starting to appear in the United States' research dominance. Federal funding for research and development as a percent of gross domestic product, which hit a peak of 2 percent in the mid-1960s, has slowly declined in real terms ever since, and is now less than 1 percent.[9] While corporate funding for research has picked up the slack and continues to escalate, a majority of senior executives report that they are unhappy with the return on their research investments.[10] The increasing pace of innovation is shortening product life cycles so that companies have less time to recoup their investments in new product development, and traditional industrial research labs are not generating the overwhelming competitive advantage that they used to provide. As a result, the United States is now in danger of losing its research lead.

When federal and corporate investment are combined, the United States still spends more on research and development than anyone else in the world—2.7 percent of our annual gross domestic product—but we've lost ground in comparison to other countries, especially those in Asia.[11] World-class laboratories are emerging in countries like India, Israel, Singapore, Taiwan, and China, whose government has doubled the percent of its GDP spent on research and development over the last decade.[12] Other countries are graduating an increasing number of scientists and engineers, publishing an ever greater number of scientific articles in prestigious journals, and leading the way in breakthrough research areas such as nanotechnology and stem cell research—and all while we have been sleeping.

The world is catching up to the United States, and while more spending on research is great for the global economy, it will be troubling if America fails to keep pace. If we fail to support federally funded research, build a strong science and engineering workforce, and improve the return on investment for research and development, in another few decades we will lose our lead in the innovation race.

With the ongoing loss of manufacturing, growth in the U.S. economy is now based almost exclusively upon knowledge and innovation—intellectual property is our largest export. If we are not at the leading edge of research and development, the center of gravity will shift overseas, and it will be much harder for American entrepreneurs to keep up with the global competition.

The Decline in Federal Funding for Research

Federal funding is what catapulted the United States to the forefront of scientific research in the 1950s and has kept it there to this day, allowing us to push the boundaries of scientific knowledge and experiment with new, unproven technologies. That investment has been an important source of U.S. competitive advantage in a wide range of disciplines, most recently the computer and telecommunications industries. While much of federal research spending goes to universities, it also benefits private industry directly—federal research grants comprise 26 percent of large firms' research and development budgets and 11 percent of small entrepreneurial firms' budgets.[13] Directly and indirectly, federal research funding is critical to innovation and entrepreneurship.

Unfortunately, a number of factors have chipped away at federal support for research over the last several decades, compromising our ability to compete in the future. One was the end of the cold war and the collapse of the Soviet Union, which left the United States without a serious military rival to spur continued investment in research. The massive federal deficit and mounting Social Security and Medicare liabilities produced pressure to cut federal spending across the board, and support for federally funded research, particularly basic research, took a back seat to other concerns. Fortunately, industrial research spending over the last twenty-five years has increased dramatically, producing a sharp spike in total R&D spending even while federal funding stagnated. While industry was spending more on research and development in general, however, most companies were pulling back from doing research and focusing more on development. With the decline in government funding, support for research started to falter during the 1990s.

This trend changed somewhat in 1998 when a Congressional initiative to double the National Institutes of Health budget was passed, significantly increasing the federal funding available for biomedical research over the next five years. The terrorist attack on September 11th and the war in Iraq initially restored some of the urgency to defense-related research and development that had been lost after the cold war. As a result, federal R&D funding soared to an estimated record total of $132 billion in 2005, a huge buildup that has resulted in a historically high base level of spending.[14]

Unfortunately, the federal deficit has become so large over the past five years that it is starting to negatively affect government support for research, as the cost of the war, domestic programs, and entitlement programs such as Social Security and Medicare are balanced against the need to control the deficit. As a result, federal research and

Defense Research and Development Spending, 1976–2006

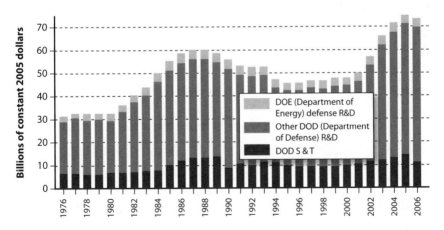

Source: American Association for the Advancement of Science, analyses of R&D in *AAAS Reports XIII-XXX*. FY 2006 figures are for the President's requested budget. DOD S & T figures are not strictly comparable for all years because of changing definitions. Revised February 2005, © 2005 American Association for the Advancement of Science.

Non-Defense Research and Development Spending, 1976–2006

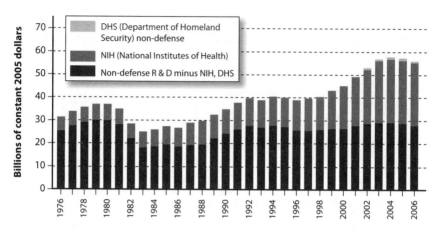

Source: American Association for the Advancement of Science, analyses of R&D in *AAAS Reports XIII-XXX*. FY 2006 figures are for the President's requested budget. R&D includes conduct of R&D and R&D facilities. Revised March 2005, © 2005 American Association for the Advancement of Science.

development investment, in real terms, is slated to decline for the first time since 1996. While the federal budget for development will increase 1.6 percent from 2005 to 2006, investment in basic and applied research will decline by 1.1 and 1.7 percent respectively.[15] The U.S. Office of Science and Technology Policy has attempted to gloss over these changes by pointing to the huge increases in investment during President George W. Bush's first term. The aggregate numbers, however, are misleading.

"It's true that the proposed cuts in 2006 will be coming off of historically high levels," says Kei Koizumi, the director of the R&D budget and policy program at the American Association for the Advancement of Science. "But on the defense side, almost the entire increase to get us to the record levels of investment has been for defense weapons development. That's fine in and of itself, but for the science and engineering community, what concerns us is that defense investments in basic and applied research have just barely returned to where they were in the late 1980s. It's taken almost two decades to restore the investment levels of the cold war. That's crucial to U.S. science and engineering because the Department of Defense invests a lot in computer sciences, engineering, physical sciences and mathematics research that's vital not only for national security, but also for our civilian economy."

When it comes to non-defense spending, Koizumi notes that the situation is similar. "Again, we are at a record level of investment, so the 2006 cuts would be coming off of record totals. But for the past few years, nearly all of the increases in non-defense research and development investment have come from the doubling of the National Institutes of Health (NIH) budget. As a result of the NIH campaign, biomedical research has done very well. For non-biomedical research, however, federal funding has been flat or just barely keeping pace with inflation for almost two decades now, which means that the cuts that are proposed for 2006 would really be cutting into historically flat investments. If you look beyond the big-level numbers to break out exactly where those federal research dollars have been going, the picture for many areas of research is not all that great, and so these proposed cuts represent very bad news."

While the doubling of the National Institutes of Health budget and the War on Terror have fueled significant increases in spending for biomedicine, homeland security, and defense weapons development, investment in other disciplines, particularly physical sciences, has stagnated. Increases in funding for space exploration and homeland security are being offset by funding cuts in other critical areas such as nanotechnology, information technology, and climate change. Non-defense R&D budgets for five of the largest research and development funding agencies—the National Institutes of Health, the Department of Energy, the National Science Foundation, the Department of Agriculture, and the Environmental Protection Agency—are projected to decrease in real terms through 2009.[16] We are withdrawing federal funding in critical areas of research just when we cannot afford to do so, hoping that we will be able to coast on the investments of the past.

"Biomedical research is doing much better because of the NIH doubling effort," explains Koizumi, "but with physical science and engineering it's been a kind of a double whammy. So much of physical science and engineering support comes from the military, and the Department of Defense has only reluctantly kept up its investments in basic and applied research these days. With the war in Iraq, the Pentagon is very much focused on the near term, what's happening this week, and not what it's going to need ten or twenty years from now. They're focused on this war, not the next war. Then on the non-defense side, agencies like the National Science Foundation, the Environmental Protection Agency, and the Department of Energy that fund physical sciences and engineering haven't benefited as much from these big increases in spending that this administration has been trumpeting, so it's been a struggle to sustain those investments."

> We are withdrawing federal funding in critical areas of research just when we cannot afford to do so, hoping that we will be able to coast on the investments of the past.

Having a balanced research portfolio is critical, because it shapes how companies and universities will direct their research efforts and thus has a significant impact on America's long-term economic competitiveness. Certain fields, such as information technology, nanotechnology, and biomedicine have strategic importance, both commercially and militarily. There are synergies between research, development, and manufacturing in these fields as well as significant economies of scale and scope, which is one of the reasons why China is pushing so hard to become a world leader in nanotechnology. Underinvestment in these research areas jeopardizes our ability to compete and create jobs in these industries.

On the other hand, overinvestment, particularly in defense weapons development, can have a negative impact on industry competitiveness as well. In the decades after World War II, the majority of federal research grants went toward non-defense projects and applications, because Franklin Roosevelt's intent in funding research had been to direct the power of science to solve peacetime problems. Yet over the years, federal research spending has slowly come to be dominated by military applications, particularly weapons development. In 1981, the first year of Ronald Reagan's presidency, federal defense research and development spending overtook non-defense R&D spending for the first time, and by the end of the Reagan era, military research accounted for three-fourths of government research spending.[17] The military has always argued that weapons research produces dual-use technologies that can be used for both defense and commercial applications, and there is some crossover—the Internet grew out of a project in the computer sciences that was spearheaded by the Department of Defense. Overly extensive spending on weapons development, however, diverts federal funding from basic and applied research in other important areas.

The negative impact that can have on American industry was evident during the 1980s when, with so much defense funding available, American corporations started devoting much of their development efforts to military applications, gutting their support for more basic research and commercial applications. The bidding process used by the military provided added security, for while bidding could be fierce, once the contract was won, profits were assured. There was no need for mass marketing or improvements in efficiency, the kinds of activities that keep a company competitive in a commercial environment, and the companies that engaged in military research often lost their leading technological and manufacturing edge. In fact, this was one of the primary reasons that American companies fell behind the Japanese in terms of innovation, quality, and productivity in the 1970s and 80s.

Part of the problem in trying to achieve a balanced research portfolio is that with federal research and development funding coming from a variety of different agencies, it is very hard to coordinate the government's overall investment efforts. In addition to determining the right balance between basic research, applied research, and development, there is also the question of splitting resources between various disciplines. Biomedical research, for example, is funded almost entirely through the National Institutes of Health, so policy makers understood that by doubling the NIH budget, they were boosting support for biomedical research. When it comes to the physical sciences, computer science, or engineering, however, support comes from a variety of different agencies, and without coordination it is very difficult to achieve an appropriate balance.

"There are a couple of possible strategies to deal with that problem," says Koizumi. "Maybe the easiest is to pick one agency, like the National Science Foundation, and try to double their budget, just like they did with the National Institutes of Health. Not necessarily because it would do the most good, but because it's a good focal point to energize investment in the non-medical sciences. Another is to try to work all of these agencies separately. Then you have to advocate not just for the NSF, but for the Department of Defense, the Department of Energy, and all the rest, which is the primary strategy of the science and engineering community now."

Aside from having an imbalanced research portfolio, the more basic problem is that Congress and the White House are caught in the classic trap of needing to balance investment in the future against the crises of today. The federal deficit has ballooned out of control thanks to Hurricane Katrina, the War on Terror, and the rising cost of health care and entitlement programs such as Medicare and Social Security, not to mention the growing trade deficit. It is a vicious cycle, one that does not bode well for future federal investment in research at a time when, on paper, we appear to be far in the lead. While there is broad, bi-partisan support for federally funded research in theory, in the current budgetary environment, basic and applied research is on the chopping block along with many other discretionary spending programs.

"Science is neither singled out nor immune from the budget pressures that effect most domestic programs," explains Koizumi. "The federal government already has an enormous budget deficit, and policy makers have chosen to focus on cutting domestic spending as the only way to reduce the federal budget deficit. The idea of getting out of this spending constraint by making cuts in entitlement programs or raising tax revenues is simply not on the table in Washington. As a result, it then follows that the only option is to make cuts in programs that support research and development such as the National Science Foundation, Environmental Protection Agency, or the Department of Energy, as well as programs that support education or transportation, labor training or veteran's care. Science is in the same boat as almost everyone else."

That may be true, but it is of little comfort as we look over our shoulder and see the competition bearing down on us while we've dropped anchor.

The University Research System

The effect of the federal government's research policy was driven home for me when I paid a visit to Dr. Randal Kaufman, a leading researcher and biological chemistry professor at the University of Michigan in Ann Arbor. As I walked through the central campus, I passed a number of science buildings, all of which looked as though they had been built many decades ago and hadn't been updated since. As I made my way north to the medical science research buildings where Dr. Kaufman's lab was located, however, I found that there was a lot of activity. There was a new biomedical science research facility under construction as well as renovations to several other buildings, and I noticed the recently completed life sciences institute on the edge of the medical campus. Clearly, this was where the federal research dollars were going.

One of the United States' most significant competitive advantages in the global innovation race is its university system, which performs 60 percent of all the basic research done in this country. The federal government invested heavily in research and education following World War II, and many of our native-born scientists and engineers were products of the National Defense Education Act of 1958, which provided student loans and graduate fellowships to advanced science and engineering students in response to the Soviet Union's launch of Sputnik. American universities have contributed greatly to the innovative process, both by conducting basic research and by training the scientists that go on to do applied research in industrial labs and startup companies. At universities, federal research grants provide a triple bang for the buck, because not only do they support research, they also attract students to science and engineering and support their graduate educations as they work with their professors on research projects.

One of the United States' most significant competitive advantages in the global innovation race is its university system.

One of the people all of this investment attracted was Randal Kaufman. "I always liked medicine in terms of health care and biology, ever since I was very little," he explained when I asked him why he decided to go into medical research. "I always enjoyed the courses. It was fun to try and answer questions, to understand things that you don't understand. I went to college and got a degree in molecular biology at the University of Colorado. Originally I had planned to go on to medical school, but I decided not to because I couldn't stand the sight of blood, so I went into research instead," he laughed.

It was as a doctoral candidate in pharmacology at Stanford University that his career path came into focus. "In graduate school is when things really clicked, because that's really when your experiments start to work. All of a sudden you're not just reading about science, you're doing science, and that makes a huge difference."

Kaufman went on to do his post-doctoral studies at the Massachusetts Institute of Technology and, after a decade long stint as director of molecular and cellular genetics at a company he co-founded, he eventually accepted a position at the University of Michigan. He now leads research into the fundamental processes that control signaling proteins, which help stressed cells to make new proteins—exactly the kind of biomedical research that has been helped by the increase in the National Institutes of Health's budget. Even in this seemingly booming area of research, however, Kaufman sees cause for concern.

"They're building new buildings, and there is a tremendous amount of growth going on in life sciences, but that doesn't mean the grants are there. It goes through cycles. Right now we're going into a bad cycle, because the federal government basically is not funding any new grants this year. There are jobs, but only for those at the top of the crop."

The depth of this problem is apparent from the acceptance rate for research proposals. The National Science Foundation (NSF), for example, projects that only one out of every five research proposals made to the NSF will be funded in 2006, and that in some areas such as computer science, the acceptance rate could be as low as 10 percent.[18] While they have attempted to compensate by tweaking the size of grants and shifting money out of education programs to shore up their research efforts, there simply are not many attractive options. Even the National Institutes of Health, which benefited from the recently completed campaign to double its budget, estimates that fewer than one out of four of their grant applications will be funded in 2006.

Kaufman is fortunate because half of his work is funded through the Howard Hughes Medical Institute (HHMI), the largest private non-profit organization in the world. Its mission is to support the progress of science, in part by funding cutting-edge research at universities across the country. As an HHMI investigator, Kaufman knows that he will receive funding for the duration of his five-year grant, and that renewal of the grant depends on his results and the foundation's endowment rather than federal budgetary pressures. His colleagues at the University of Michigan who are funded primarily through the

National Institutes of Health and other federal agencies are far less secure, as university faculty members are evaluated in large part on their ability to obtain grant funding. This lack of security and the increasing competition for grants has the effect of making research proposals more conservative, as researchers are less likely to push the boundaries in new areas and more likely to make proposals with a high probability of research success.

"Pressure for productivity is up, so in some ways university labs are being run more like businesses," explains Kaufman's lab manager, Robert Clark. "Over the past forty years, the universities have taken bigger and bigger cuts out of grants to cover overhead expenses. Now they take nearly a third of the grant's total cost, so you have to do more with less. At the same time, productivity is one of the ways funding agencies like the National Institutes of Health decide whether to renew grants, and it's also a primary factor in how the university evaluates faculty. The problem is, even with published scientific work, only a tiny part of all the research that's done, something like less than 2 percent, leads to a product or medical technique. When civilians outside of the research community look at that figure they ask, 'Why can't it be higher?' and the pressure for results pushes research towards more near-term, applied research. That's one of the reasons behind the shift towards medical research—it has a definite end product. Even if it isn't immediate, it has promise."

Whether or not there has been an actual shift from basic towards more applied research is a matter of some debate. The line between the two is often blurred, but in the proposed 2006 budget, both basic and applied research are being cut while development spending is increased, and it is clear that the research process is being increasingly driven by market needs rather than moving forward from pure exploration. While this approach may seem like a good idea in theory, it may also have major drawbacks.

"To a certain extent directed research is helpful, but it can be shortsighted in the long run," says Clark. "For example, the basic research that started molecular biology, restriction enzymes, wouldn't be able to get funded today. The original research was about bacteria protecting themselves. If you look at it from the perspective of wanting to achieve a commercially useful result, well, who cares about bacteria protecting themselves? How is that useful? The motive in looking at it was just curiosity. The researchers weren't looking to make a product or file a patent, they just wanted to find out something new that was interesting and publish it. But then after the initial research was published, the light began to dawn on people that these restriction enzymes would be a useful tool in manipulating DNA structures, and that opened up a whole new world of opportunities. The research wasn't enough by itself, but there were a number of pieces that various people were working on independently simply out of interest, and then someone saw the potential applications and did more directed research to fill in the missing pieces. You couldn't get that kind of curiosity-driven research funded today, and that narrows the research field. Universities hire and evaluate you based on your ability to get grants, and if you're researching something that doesn't have an apparent return, you aren't going to get hired or funded."

"Government funding is very anti-risk, they want to see results," Dr. Kaufman agrees. "Howard Hughes Medical Institute places more emphasis on risk taking and claims to tolerate failure, although in practice those who fail don't get their grants renewed. But at least with HHMI you can get cutting-edge research funded, whereas federally funded research is more conservative.

The difference is that Howard Hughes Medical Institute, while still focused on results, takes a long-term view of scientific progress, and as a private foundation it can afford to do so. "HHMI has a real lofty goal—to better mankind through science," notes Jeffrey Tefft, HHMI's Assistant Manager at the University of Michigan Medical Center. "Many places would not fund the research that we do, because they want those immediate results, whereas HHMI focuses on the long run and what is best for mankind. Often times we are doing research that a drug pharmaceutical company, for example, wouldn't be able to fund because they can't look twenty years down the road and hope something hits. As a for-profit corporation, they've got to have some viable product in mind shortly down the line. So while the level of funding we provide is a drop in the bucket compared to the National Institutes of Health or industry, I think we're a needed component. Even though we don't have the final product or aren't working directly with patients, we are still that needed step that might not even be there if HHMI wasn't around."

As federal research becomes more applied, organizations like Howard Hughes Medical Institute are playing an increasingly important role in sustaining basic, exploratory research. As large as it is, however, HHMI can't fill the gap being left by the federal government, a gap that is undermining the very foundation of America's entrepreneurial ecosystem. The investments in basic research that we made back in the 1950s are driving our industries today, but if we stop making them, it will soon be too late to repair the damage. Our continued prosperity hinges upon revitalizing our commitment to funding basic and applied research.

America's Science and Engineering Workforce

The availability of federal funding affects not only the type of research being done, but the willingness of domestic students to pursue science and engineering as a career. Unfortunately, a quarter of our science and engineering workforce is now over fifty years old and approaching retirement, and we aren't graduating enough new PhDs to replace them. The United States ranks seventeenth internationally in the proportion of the college-age population that is studying science and engineering, and even if interest increased, only 15 percent of American high school seniors have the educational prerequisites necessary to pursue degrees in these fields.[19] For those who do study science and engineering in college, the future employment situation in academic sciences seems bleak.

"While there is a lot of growth right now, and there's space and buildings to put people in, the resources for grant funding are going down, even in biomedicine," explains Kaufman. "On one hand, what that does is weed out the people who are not competitive. Researchers that had four grants will be cut back and will only have three grants, the people with three grants will be cut back to two grants, and people that have one grant, they'll lose their jobs. So it's a way to select for the most productive people, survival of the fittest, but then the number of PhDs doing academic research goes down. There are fewer positions, fewer people coming up going into that area of research or into science in general. Then when money does become available, we don't have enough qualified domestic students and PhDs who can compete for the funds and set up labs, so we have to go overseas."

The United States has come to rely on foreign science and engineering talent to supply its research and development brainpower.

This is one of the reasons the United States has come to rely on foreign science and engineering talent to supply its research and development brainpower. American universities are the envy of the world, and for decades the best and brightest minds from across the world have gravitated to them—about half of the students pursing graduate degrees in engineering and computer science at American universities are foreign nationals.[20] In the past, many of them stayed and worked in the United States after their education was complete, which has been something of a double-edged sword for the American science and engineering community. On the one hand, these highly educated foreign scientists and engineers have added much to the U.S. economy through their talent, hard work, and innovation. On the other, their presence has suppressed wages for American science and engineering jobs, and has driven domestic students towards other, better-paying careers.

Since September 11th, however, it has become much more difficult for top foreign talent to study and work in this country. More stringent immigration rules have reduced the number of foreign students and researchers who are being allowed to come to the United States, and the visa rejection rate, particularly for the highly skilled, has almost doubled. As a result, talented foreigners are looking to study elsewhere—graduate applications from foreign students dropped 32 percent in 2004.[21] This trend means that the United States needs to increase the number of qualified domestic candidates and the funding necessary to attract and employ them, or risk losing its preeminent position in the world research community.

With federal funding for research declining, however, it is even harder to encourage American students to pursue science and engineering careers. Cuts in grant funding mean fewer research positions for graduate students, post-doctoral students, and professors. This is a particular problem for students who are attracted to research areas that were not being well funded in the first place. Science is not personally rewarding unless you're excited by the research area, so if you're not interested in cutting-edge molecular biology, homeland security, or weapons development, you're not likely to pursue a career in science at all. When grant funding is cut, students in the physical sciences see that there are no jobs available for them, so they decide to major in something other than science.

"It all depends on having the resources available," says Kaufman. "You don't want to go into a field, spend ten years in school, and come out and not be able to get a job. When students look around and see professors struggling to get grants, they think, "Do I really want to do this? Or do I want to go into business or law?' Good people get turned off by not having the resources available. There are a lot of post-docs who can't get jobs."

Albert Teich, director of science and policy programs for the American Association for the Advancement of Science, agrees and sees this as an issue that goes far beyond the cuts in federal funding. "We need to pay attention to the issue of the pipeline for scientists in this country. In recent years, we have found it increasingly difficult to get as many students as we would like to go into scientific, engineering, and mathematically-based careers, because they're intellectually rigorous and perhaps not as financially rewarding as some other fields.

Business and law have drawn a larger share of students in recent years because people see them as opportunities to make good money, and they don't necessarily require as many years of education or—in some cases at least—make the same kind of demands on your life as scientific careers do. So we need to try to do what we can to draw people into scientific careers, because we need the brightest people in these fields. Otherwise, we won't be competitive in the long run. I don't think that's an issue right at the moment, but it could be an issue twenty years from now, or maybe even less."

Teich's concerns are echoed by much of the science and engineering community, as foreign countries continue to ramp up their technology workforces while the United States struggles to channel students into those fields. The United States now produces only 100,000 engineers per year, while China will soon be graduating 350,000 annually.[22] Universities in India, Russia, Israel, Singapore, Taiwan, and South Korea are gearing up and producing more scientists and engineers as well. While the United States has been a magnet for the world's top science talent in the past, in the future these countries are going to redouble their efforts to stop the brain drain and channel that resource into their own research and development activities. All of the countries who have joined the innovation race are working aggressively to retain their top talent, and as more people choose to study and work in places other than the United States, the supply that we've enjoyed of foreign science and engineering students and workers may be drying up as they find more attractive opportunities in their home countries.

The growth of science and engineering talent in other countries is not necessarily bad for the United States, as Teich is quick to point out. "This is not a zero-sum game. If others gain, we do not necessarily lose. In fact, we benefit from the knowledge generated by people in other countries. We read their research papers, just like they read ours, and they guide us in further research and sometimes in applications. In the past, many countries like Japan, Taiwan, and South Korea have taken advantage of the knowledge that we've generated to develop new products and processes to become more competitive in technology in the international marketplace. We can do the same kind of thing with the knowledge that they've generated. I think it's an indication that other countries are beginning to pull their own weight in the scientific enterprise as well as in the technological and high-tech trade areas."

The danger, however, is that if the United States fails to fund research adequately and provide attractive career options for domestic science and engineering students, then research and development will follow U.S. manufacturing overseas to Asia. While China and India are cranking out thousands of new science and engineering graduates, they aren't utilizing all of them yet, and so American companies are taking advantage of that comparatively cheap talent by establishing more research laboratories abroad. Leading companies like Microsoft, General Electric, and IBM, for example, now have important research and development labs in places like China, Israel, Switzerland, Japan, and India.[23] Over the long run, if the United States cannot support a domestic science and engineering workforce, research and development will move overseas, which will seriously impact the U.S. job market and American competitiveness.

Industrial Research and Development

One bright spot for American research and development is that while federal support for research in key areas has stagnated, industrial research and development spending has increased dramatically, rising from $30 billion in 1980 to $181 billion in 2001.[24] Unfortunately, the return on investment for industrial research has declined. Market-leading companies used to invest a significant amount of money in creating self-sufficient, vertically integrated programs that did everything from basic research to fabrications development. Henry Ford led the way in this area when raw materials shortages during World War I forced him to take control over his supply chain. At his River Rouge plant in Michigan, he integrated production, assembly, and transportation in order to gain complete control over the production process. He purchased coal mines, acquired timberland, built a saw mill, and even purchased a glassworks to deliver the necessary raw materials. He also bought a railroad company and a fleet of freighters to transport both the raw materials and the finished product.

In a vertically integrated environment, superior research labs gave companies like Ford, Bell, DuPont, General Electric, and Hewlett-Packard a distinct advantage in their respective industries, and leading companies were willing to invest a great deal in research and development in the hopes of winning a patent monopoly. When successful, this created a self-perpetuating cycle where research and development spending led to breakthrough products, which increased sales and profits, and thus made more money available for research and development. The cycle fueled growth and, as the company got bigger, led to significant economies of scale.

Industrial research and development labs created strong barriers to entry in many industries, for research and development required significant investment up front that often took years to generate a return. As industries consolidated and the market leaders' research laboratories became more sophisticated, they became deterrents to smaller competitors who knew that if they wanted to survive, they would have to keep up with the big companies' research output. This encouraged vertical integration and created a business landscape dominated by big companies that were relatively autonomous and required extensive internal research and development in order to compete.

Industrial research labs worked hard to maintain secrecy and control over their research output, but when companies reneged on the promise of lifetime employment in the 1980s, workers found themselves changing companies far more often. When they switched jobs, their knowledge went with them. Gradually, the control of information that corporations had relied upon to maintain secrecy began to break down. The increasing number of college graduates also changed the game by helping suppliers to become more sophisticated and reliable. This allowed big companies to outsource more of their work, but it also required greater trust and exchange of information, which changed the business environment. The proliferation of the Internet in the 1990s made information even more accessible, and research breakthroughs, which had once been tightly controlled, spread rapidly among competing firms. As intellectual and human capital has kept leaking out of their companies, return on research investment has fallen, and it has become harder to support the extensive internal research and development departments that served large companies so well in the past.

The demise of vertical integration is easy to see in today's outsourcing trend, a 180-degree change in American corporate philosophy that encourages extreme focus on core competencies while contracting out all other activities. Consider T-Mobile USA, the fourth-largest wireless carrier in the United States with 20 million customers and 25,000 employees. When customers decide they want to buy a cellular telephone, they're really buying two things—the handset and the wireless service. In most cases, people decide on the wireless carrier first by evaluating the different calling plans. Then they select the handset, but they do so assuming that they'll be able to get the kind they want, with the latest features, from whichever carrier they pick. If one carrier offered a breakthrough product like a Blackberry and the others didn't follow suit, that carrier would have a huge competitive advantage. Thus, T-Mobile depends on having cutting-edge products to attract and retain customers.

"I think it's critically important to have innovative products," says T-Mobile co-founder and former executive vice president Alan Bender. "The problem is that over time, the wireless world is becoming more commodity-oriented. You can walk into any major urban market and have your choice of wireless carriers and handsets, and in some cases you can go into a Costco or Circuit City or Good Guys and have a choice of all four or five national carriers under one roof. So why choose T-Mobile over Sprint or Verizon or Cingular? The features of the handset or the wireless device that you're buying are a key differentiator, so it's very important in a world where your product is being commoditized that you have innovative technology features."

Fifty years ago a company like T-Mobile probably would have wanted to control internally all of the research and development that went into creating wireless handsets, in the hopes of developing a unique product that would take years for their competitors to copy. The idea of outsourcing product development to a company that might be working on a competitor's product at the other end of the shop would have been unthinkable. But information and technology are diffused so rapidly now that any new handset could be reverse engineered quite rapidly. Under these circumstances, it makes more sense to let another company do the handset design and manufacturing, while the carriers concentrate on providing the wireless service and building out their networks for better coverage. As a result, T-Mobile does not do its own research and development. It lets the wireless handset manufacturers like Motorola, Nokia, and Samsung handle research and development, although they work closely with these companies to shape the product.

"It's a very open, collaborative process, because each of us needs the other," Bender explains. "If we couldn't deliver a physical handset, Blackberry, or similar device, obviously we wouldn't be able to add customers, and if they developed handsets that we couldn't move through the distribution channels and which didn't meet our customers' needs, they wouldn't be in business. So we work together. Basically, we have the read on the consumer needs, so we will sit down with a company like Research in Motion, which manufactures the Blackberry, and we'll say, 'Listen, what our 20 million customers need is this, and do you think you could configure a bigger screen, easier keypad, more functionality, and these other features?' Then they go back to their plant and actually create the prototypes, deliver them to us, and we test them and send them back in an iterative process. So it's a cooperative effort, but it's not as if we are doing the actual research and development ourselves. We don't have the capital for that."

This approach to research and development isn't unusual, as in today's world, product development, production, and distribution are often done by different companies. "Product development is a whole different mindset, frankly," says Bender. "You have to raise capital and generate different prototypes that may or may not meet a consumer need. We are one step further removed in the supply chain. We are the distribution channel to the consumer need, and we help dictate what the product looks like, but we don't have the capital to develop it ourselves, and T-Mobile is not alone in that. Cingular, Verizon, Sprint, and Nextel don't have R&D departments either.

"Obviously, there are innovators who have accomplished both under one roof successfully. Microsoft comes to mind. But for every Microsoft, which has done a great job, there are thousands of others who try to be both the developer of the product and the distributor who haven't succeeded. You need a lot of capital, a lot of patience, and a lot of trust that the market isn't going to move away from you if you're going to do research and development, because it's high risk. You have to put all of your eggs in one basket to a certain extent, and that's a big gamble. If you hit the development of the product that you need for your customer, that's terrific. But the world changes so rapidly, and consumer and business demands change so quickly, that what the customer needs on day one may be a lot different once you reach day one thousand when you polish off the product and bring it to market. If you guessed wrong, you're nowhere. You're not just halfway across the river, you're swimming in another river entirely, and nobody is buying what you're selling.

"It is not necessarily a mistake to be in the research and development field, but it is a bigger gamble, a bigger risk. For me personally, if I was to start another business, I wouldn't start a development company. I would start a company that has its face directed towards the customer need and work with the entity that has the R&D budget to withstand ebbs and flows, to be able to switch quickly. When you're dealing with a Samsung or a Nokia or a Motorola, for the most part, they're on their toes. They've got the big infrastructure, and they're capable of switching funding internally, quickly, to go with the flow."

The problem for the United States and American labor in this scenario is that once research and development is taken outside of the company that interfaces with the customer, there is no limit in a global economy to how far it can be outsourced, particularly if the manufacturing function has already been moved overseas. There are synergies between research, development, and manufacturing, so once manufacturing moves offshore, research and development often follow as well. The assumption has been that research and development will continue to stay in the United States, but why? Multinational wireless carriers like T-Mobile need to have a presence in the United States, because they're the ones that interact with the customer. But there is no particular reason the handset manufacturers that do the research and development need to be in the United States, as the success of Nokia and Samsung demonstrates. Scientists and engineers don't generally interact directly with the customer, so there's no reason for them to be located in any particular place other than the one that is most cost efficient. There are five national wireless carriers in the United States, but only one U.S.-based handset manufacturer, Motorola, that is truly competitive. And in order to remain competitive, Motorola has had to offshore some of its research and development. It is a simple economic imperative.

> Once research and development is taken outside of the company that interfaces with the customer, there is no limit in a global economy to how far it can be outsourced.

T-Mobile, with 20 million customers in the United States and another 75 million worldwide, has a tremendous amount of buying power. They are a global company, and thus it matters little where they get their handsets from. They will make their buying decisions based on product quality, price, and efficiency. Motorola has to do whatever it must in order to compete effectively with Nokia, Samsung, and the other global handset manufacturers, or it will go out of business. Competing effectively increasingly means setting up research and development centers overseas in places like China, India, and Israel, not just because you can utilize five top-quality scientists and engineers for the price of one back home in the United States, but because they are equally if not better trained and educated, hardworking, and just as innovative and creative.

Until recently, research and development has been considered a strategic activity by most American businesses, and thus something to be kept in house. After decades of cost-cutting, however, not to mention radical improvements in the technological capabilities of overseas suppliers, corporate managers are now considering outsourcing basic research and development—70 percent of the design work for PDAs and 65 percent of the design work for notebook computers is now offshored or outsourced.[25] The financial benefits can be significant, as outsourcing highly skilled design work can generate even greater savings in labor costs than outsourcing manufacturing and back office work. Yet it is a dangerous game to play, because if too much research and development is relocated to offshore suppliers, those suppliers can easily become direct competitors, and American companies will then be left with no sustainable competitive advantage.

I asked Bender what he thought about the trend towards outsourcing research and development, and he replied, "You have to ask me what hat I'm wearing when you ask me that question. As a businessman, you go where the talent is. You go where the deliverable comes to you most effectively, with the highest quality, at the best price, and the most efficiently. If that's a Chinese firm or an Indian firm, rather than an American firm, so be it. Historically, our largest handset purchases have clearly been overseas, and we're not alone in that, it's true of all the carriers. Nokia is the dominant handset manufacturer in the world, and is based in Finland. Samsung is growing in market share faster than any other manufacturer, and they're based in South Korea. American companies need to figure out ways to come to a company like T-Mobile or Verizon and say, 'Hey, we can deliver that product with better quality, at a lower price, and a quicker deliverable.' That's a winning argument. But you can't expect a business to buy an American-developed product that might be inferior in quality or more expensive or slower to market, just because it's American. We owe it to our shareholders to be as good as we can be.

"If I switch hats and view it from the perspective of an American citizen, then I think we need to do a better job of recognizing the global economy. Remember, T-Mobile, or VoiceStream as it was called then, was created here in Washington. Now it is part of a larger, global company, and where is it headquartered today? Bonn, Germany. The reason Deutsche Telekom came to the United States and bought VoiceStream is because they wanted to fill out a significant void in their worldwide map. Our biggest infusion of capital before we became T-Mobile was from Hong Kong, and if we hadn't sold to a German company, it's likely we would have sold to a French, British, Chinese, or Japanese company. We are now the walking definition of a global company, and it's unreasonable to think that today's businesses are somehow framed by geographic borders. As a country we need to recognize that. Is it bad for our economy that great technologies are coming out of China, India, and elsewhere? No. Ultimately I think it forces us to be better, sharper, more innovative, and more efficient than ever before, and that's how you grow. But I think there are challenges, and I think we have to alter the way we do things to meet those challenges. We are no longer the shining city at the top of the hill when it comes to product development."

The Future of American Research and Development

The only way that research and development will stay in the United States, and create jobs here, is if we do it better and more cost effectively than anyone else in the world. At a time when the federal government is cutting back on research spending, and corporate executives are questioning the wisdom of doing research in house, this requires doing more with less. One approach to maximizing our return on investment is to focus more on multidisciplinary research. Many of today's breakthrough innovations occur at the intersection of different disciplines, like biochemistry and computer science, and thus multidisciplinary research is critical. Fostering greater interaction between scientists from various disciplines, however, can be quite a challenge and requires a change in approach.

"Universities are traditionally organized into academic departments around specific disciplines, and those departments are the primary means of exercising quality control and distributing rewards," explains Albert Teich. "Scientists publish in their fields, for an audience of peers in their fields, who are the best judges of how good it is. That's how researchers get recognition, which is the basic currency of scientific careers. As a result, universities are set up so that the reward structures operate through the departments. The departments are the units that award tenure, raises, and promotions for faculty members. If we want to foster more interdisciplinary research, we need to modify that. We need to keep the good parts of that basic structure in place, but we need to broaden it in a way that allows people to get recognition for their contributions in multidisciplinary research as well. Once faculty members see that they're getting rewards for collaborating with people in other departments, as well as simply doing the traditional kinds of things they've done in the past in the confines of their own departments, that will be a major step towards facilitating and making multidisciplinary research more attractive to people in the universities."

Two institutions that are already working to encourage more multidisciplinary research are the University of Michigan, with its life sciences initiative, and Howard Hughes Medical Institute, with its new Janelia Farms facility outside of Washington DC. "The whole principle behind a life science institute is that you bring people from completely different disciplines together to tackle the same problem," explains Jeffrey Tefft. "The chemists, for example, might have something very different to say about a problem than the physicists, and by talking, they may gain new insights and spark new ideas. In an old-style laboratory, the head researcher would generally have the same type of people working for them, and so they would really be looking at problems only from one viewpoint. In a life science institute, however, the more openness you have, and the fewer walls there are between labs, the more you can get everybody involved. At the University of Michigan, they encourage people in life sciences to sit in each other's labs, and just having scientists who would not normally have much of a chance to interact with each other working in close physical proximity can sometimes pay huge dividends."

With the Janelia Farms facility, Howard Hughes Medical Institute is taking the approach one step further by constructing a state-of-the-art facility dedicated entirely to research. "Under the old system, the National Institutes of Health or Howard Hughes Medical Institute would give money to an investigator in a lab that might have been there for fifty years and where the infrastructure is worn out," says Tefft. "By starting with a whole new state-of-the-art facility with all of the latest equipment, like Janelia Farms, that allows the investigators to just concentrate on their science. You don't have to be shipping new equipment to these locations or spending money repairing old equipment, because everything is brand new and set up in the most advantageous way. In an old lab you might have to go down the hall or down the floor to get to a specific machine or computer, but in a life sciences building everything should be within easy walking distance. There will be a big lab with little rooms off of it—a meeting room, a tissue culture room, a microscope room—and the entire building is just for research. In a university lab you have teaching going on at the same time, and things are just haphazardly put together. Whereas a life sciences institute, if it is done right, is set up with research in mind. But to do it right you need a lot of startup money."

To some extent this explains why grant funding is going down while the government is pouring money into new biomedical research buildings. It is an investment in the future. Without sufficient support for grant funding across all disciplines, however, these new facilities will be of little use. We need a well-balanced, stable federal research portfolio that recognizes the strategic importance of certain industries and fosters a strong domestic science and engineering workforce. The United States research and development system is still the envy of the world, with investment levels that far exceed that of any other country—but the world is fast catching up. To compete, the United States is going to need to pay much more attention to our research and development policy.

"The big question is, where will the next innovations take place, and which nations will be best poised to take advantage of innovative knowledge?" says Kei Koizumi. "Historically, where innovation has taken place and where the benefits have accrued have been primarily in the same location. Research has been conducted and the results have been commercialized in close proximity. If that continues to hold true, then a lot of our technological lead will continue to depend on a strong U.S. research enterprise. Even if it doesn't hold true and research results are discovered and commercialized in different places, in order to take advantage of those research results we're going to need a scientifically literate, technologically adept workforce, including entrepreneurs."

What will matter in the coming decades is who controls the world's major research and development networks, for in all likelihood that will determine where the new products, jobs, and companies are going to be created. There are those who argue that federal investment in basic research is wasted in a global economy because there is no way to ensure the benefits accrue to the United States. Yet someone has to do basic research and development, and where it is done is a strategic issue. Research and development that is done in the United States tends to create jobs in the United States, at least for a while. Innovators do not like to manage the evolution of their idea from afar. They prefer to be deeply involved, and they create businesses and jobs around them in the process of bringing their vision to the world. Eventually, as the companies mature, jobs may be lost to automation, consolidation, and outsourcing, but if innovation itself moves offshore, those supporting jobs will never be created here in the first place. The United States has a vested interest in continuing to support research and development at a level that will attract the world's best talent and ensure our ability to lead the world in innovation. If the United States wants to maintain its economic competitiveness and create high-paying jobs, we are going to have to devote more funding, more time, and more talent to our domestic research efforts in the future.

4

THE INCUBATOR OF INNOVATION—
ENTREPRENEURSHIP EDUCATION

<><><><><><><><><><><><><><><><><><><><><><><><><><><><><>

A friend of mine sent me the following joke about Lawrence Ellison giving a commencement speech to a class of Yale business students. It's a hoax— several versions of this joke are floating around on the Internet with various people giving the speech—but it's a hoax with a point. It goes something like this:

"Graduates of Yale University, I apologize if you have endured this type of prologue before, but I want you to do something for me. Please, take a good look around you. Look at the classmate on your left. Look at the classmate on your right. Now, consider this: Five years from now, ten years from now, even thirty years from now, odds are the person on your left is going to be a loser. The person on your right, meanwhile, will also be a loser. And you, in the middle? What can you expect? Loser. Loserhood. Loser Cum Laude. In fact, as I look out before me today, I don't see a thousand hopes for a bright tomorrow. I don't see a thousand future leaders in a thousand industries. I see a thousand losers.

"You're upset. That's understandable. After all, how can I, Lawrence Ellison, college dropout, have the audacity to spout such heresy to the graduating class of one of the nation's most prestigious institutions? I'll tell you why. Because I, Lawrence Ellison, fifth richest man in America, am a college dropout, and you are not. Because Bill Gates, the richest man on the planet—for now, anyway—is a college dropout, and you are not. Because Paul Allen, the third richest man in America, dropped out of college, and you did not. And for good measure, because Michael Dell, number four on the list and moving up fast, is a college dropout, and you, yet again, are not.

"Hmm . . . you're very upset. That's understandable. So let me stroke your egos for a moment by pointing out, quite sincerely, that your diplomas were not attained in vain. Most of you, I imagine, have spent four to five years here, and in many ways what you've learned and endured will serve you well in the years ahead. You've established good work habits. You've established a network of people that will help you down the road. And you've established what will be lifelong relationships with the word 'therapy.' All of that is good. For in truth, you will need that network. You will need those strong work habits. You will need that therapy.

"You will need them because you didn't drop out, and so you will never be among the richest people in the world. Oh sure, you may, perhaps, work your way up to No. 10 or No. 11, like Steve Ballmer. But then, I don't have to tell you who he really works for, do I? And for the record, he dropped out of grad school. Bit of a late bloomer.

"Finally, I realize that many of you, and hopefully by now most of you, are wondering, 'Is there anything I can do? Is there any hope for me at all?' Actually, no. It's too late. You've absorbed too much, think you know too much. You're not nineteen anymore. You have a built-in cap, and I'm not referring to the mortar boards on your heads.

"Hmm . . . you're really very upset. That's understandable. So perhaps this would be a good time to bring up the silver lining. Not for you, Class of 2005. You are a write-off, so I'll let you slink off to your pathetic $40,000-a-year jobs, where your checks will be signed by former classmates who dropped out two years ago. Instead, I want to give hope to any underclassmen here

today. I say to you, and I can't stress this enough: Leave. Pack your things and your ideas and don't come back. Drop out. Start up."

A nation that supports research and development provides a strong foundation for innovation—but that is not enough. The nature of the scientist is to discover and invent, and the nature of the engineer is to refine and develop applications, but for both the joy of their work tends to be in the intellectual challenge. It requires an entirely different skill set, and in many cases a different type of person, to commercialize an invention and bring it to the world. It takes someone who can marshal resources and bring together people with diverse talents in order to create a business model around a new technology. It also requires someone who is flexible and can adapt quickly to changes while transforming an invention into a marketable product. In short, it takes an entrepreneur.

A commonly held belief is that entrepreneurs are born and not made, that entrepreneurship is not something that can be taught. Those who are meant to be entrepreneurs gravitate towards it naturally and often believe they have no need of a formal, entrepreneurial education. It is certainly true that to succeed as an entrepreneur you must have a talent for it, and talents are innate and cannot be taught. Talent alone, however, is not enough. Meryl Streep is an incredibly talented actress, but would she have two Oscars if she had never taken an acting class, if she had never studied her craft? A talent for entrepreneurship, as with any talent, must be trained and nurtured, and entrepreneurial aptitude must be supported by knowledge of strategy, marketing, finance, management, and other "soft" skills like leadership and negotiation. To be successful, entrepreneurs need to know a little about a lot of different things.

Part of the reason Ellison, Gates, and Dell dropped out of college is that they each saw a market opportunity, and if they had waited until they had finished their degrees, they might have missed those opportunities. Beyond that, however, I also suspect that they left school because they felt the system was stifling their innovative impulses. I imagine they felt, to paraphrase a line from the movie *A Beautiful Mind,* that classes were dulling their mind and destroying their potential for authentic creativity. Someone once said that if Henry Ford had gone to business school, we might still be riding around in horse-drawn carriages. While universities certainly provide a more creative atmosphere than high schools, the bureaucracy and systematic approach, at least in business schools, still tends to stifle innovation.

> Knowledge is power, and as the world becomes more technologically sophisticated, college education has become increasingly important.

The fact that several highly successful entrepreneurs have dropped out of college does not mean that a college education is unnecessary for entrepreneurs, however. Henry Ford, Andrew Carnegie, and John D. Rockefeller may not have had a business degree, but they did make an effort to attend their local colleges and expand their expertise by taking business courses. Knowledge is power, and as the world becomes more technologically sophisticated, college education has become increasingly important. Most millionaires are entrepreneurs, and while many only have a high school degree or at most some college, they nevertheless disagree overwhelmingly with the statement that "college education is of little use in the real world."[1]

The problem is not that a college education is useless for entrepreneurs, but rather that it often fails to meet their needs. When Bill Gates and his peers were going to college in the 1970s, only a handful of universities had programs in entrepreneurship. If you wanted to become an entrepreneur, the most logical approach was probably to double major in business and a technical discipline like science or engineering. But traditional science programs teach students nothing about entrepreneurship, and business programs are designed to teach students how to run and maintain established businesses, not how to innovate and create new ones. While certain basic business skills like accounting are broadly applicable, in many ways what potential entrepreneurs are taught in traditional business programs is all wrong. Business requires innovation to grow, and there is a constant need to explore the edges for new opportunities.

Unfortunately, business schools, almost out of necessity, are condemned to teach history. In many ways, they are similar to our modern day audit firms who must accurately report the past, for the tenure system preserves old teaching methods and traditions, and can lock out new ways of doing things. This is not the right way to foster innovation. It only serves to perpetuate conventional thinking, by both students and faculty, in an environment where critical thinking should be taught and challenged. Given this backward-looking focus on the part of most business schools, no wonder many people with a talent for entrepreneurship have a tendency to drop out.

Now, slowly, colleges and universities are starting to realize the value a distinct entrepreneurial curriculum can offer. What exactly are the benefits of formal entrepreneurship education? First and foremost, businesses founded by people with four or more years of college education have far lower failure rates than average.[2] While this correlation may be due to other factors—for example, it is probably easier for those with a college degree to obtain investment capital—it is reasonable to assume that educational experience itself is a significant contributor to entrepreneurial success. In particular, students have found that entrepreneurship programs are extremely helpful in three areas: 1) learning the mechanics of writing a business plan and obtaining funding; 2) developing essential finance, negotiation, and marketing skills; and 3) instilling confidence and motivating people to pursue their ideas.[3] A good entrepreneurship program can provide aspiring entrepreneurs with focus, teach them what pitfalls to avoid, and greatly improve their chance of success.

Entrepreneurship programs are also useful in teaching potential entrepreneurs about the realities of starting a business, and can guide them in developing more realistic expectations. For many people, being an entrepreneur is all about money and success. A study of middle and high school students found that three out of four boys and one out of three girls expected to be millionaires by the time they are forty years old.[4] Thus, all of the publicity surrounding young millionaire entrepreneurs in Silicon Valley during the late 1990s is one of the reasons there is increased interest in entrepreneurship today. Yet succeeding in business is a relative concept, and those who pursue entrepreneurship for fame and fortune usually burn out. Entrepreneurship requires vision, passion, and determination, and entrepreneurship programs help make it clear to students whether they have the necessary drive and motivation to succeed.

Last but not least, entrepreneurship programs help to introduce potential entrepreneurs to other people with a wide variety of talents, experiences, and interests. Most entrepreneurs have a broad view of the world. They expose themselves to many cultural and societal issues, and through this process they identify trends and opportunities. One of the key contributions a university can make to an entrepreneur's future is to place him or her in an environment with people of varied interests and then, through education and exposure, mold their appreciation for people with different talents than their own. This appreciation, when combined with broad-based business skills, enables future entrepreneurs to ask good questions and make wise decisions.

The Growth of Entrepreneurship Programs

In the early 1980s, Dr. Randal Kaufman, a biomedical scientist who at the time was a post-doc at the Massachusetts Institute of Technology's Center for Cancer Research, was approached by a friend to join a fledgling biotechnology company called the Genetics Institute. He was offered a position as director of molecular and cellular genetics and became one of the founders of the company. "We started this company with six founding scientists, and the original idea was that it was going to be like Bell Labs, except for biotechnology," explains Kaufman. "Two professors at Harvard had raised about $5 million dollars in venture capital, which back in those days was quite a bit, and our investors were looking for a long-term investment with a return of 100 to 1. The company was set up as a research boutique, and for the first five years, we were very successful scientifically cloning genes and making proteins."

For scientists, this was research heaven. They had access to a significant amount of capital and were able to do cutting-edge, exploratory research. Over the long term, however, it became evident that operating as a research boutique wasn't going to create the type of return their investors wanted. "After about five years, we realized the only way we were going to create value was by having a product," says Kaufman. "We brought in a CEO, and soon the resources were focused on development, manufacturing, marketing, and clinical studies. It seemed the research department became more of an appendage to the company rather than the focus." The goals of the founders, who wanted to continue their cutting-edge research, and the CEO, who wanted to create a marketable product and sell the company, were at odds. "Since our CEO was very familiar with how to make money by manufacturing and marketing, that was the focus of what he wanted to do, while the other scientists and I just wanted to concentrate on the research," recalls Kaufman.

The clash of objectives between the founders of the Genetics Institute, their investors, and the CEO who was brought in to manage the company was typical of what happens in many startups. For the founders, who were scientists, the research and its potential to help solve medical problems was the focus of the company. Yet scientists and engineers who become entrepreneurs generally know little about running a business—Kaufman and his colleagues didn't even have a business plan when they received the initial investment. They had a general idea that they wanted to function as a research boutique, but no specifics about the business model or how they were going to generate a profit. At first, the investors wanted to break even each year, so the company developed pharmaceutical compounds for outside clients and either licensed or sold them the technology, rather than investing in producing and marketing a product themselves. They had done the research and development work, but didn't have any of their own products to show for it.

Eventually, the founders and investors decided that business model wasn't going to produce the return on investment they wanted, so the focus of the company changed and they brought in an experienced CEO to take charge of producing and marketing a product. But the CEO had experience running established businesses, not startups, and was interested in generating high-yield profitability as soon as possible. Thus, when presented with a choice of two potential products, he chose the one with the larger potential market share. The founders, on the other hand, wanted to produce a drug for the treatment of hemophilia which, although it had more limited market potential, they considered to be more of a sure bet. A strategic decision was made to produce the potentially bigger product, but unfortunately, the company became involved in a patent dispute over the product and lost. Having spent $200 million on development costs with nothing to show for it, Kaufman and some of the other founders left. With the original idea and several important research members gone, the company could not move forward, and so the remaining assets were sold to American Home Products.

Dr. Kaufman's story is a perfect example of what can happen to a technology company with high growth potential when it lacks an experienced entrepreneur. The founders, while brilliant scientists, did not have experience running a biotechnology startup, and neither did the CEO who was brought in to manage the company. The scientist founders and the CEO saw the company's mission and objectives from completely different viewpoints, and without an entrepreneur to bridge the connection, to know when to invest and when to be patient, when to push for a product and what product to push, the result was almost inevitable. Each of the key players involved had made a tremendous investment in their education, but at the time entrepreneurship education just wasn't available.

Over the past three decades, however, there has been a steady increase in the demand for entrepreneurship education. In 1970, there were just sixteen courses in entrepreneurship being offered nationwide; now over fifteen hundred colleges and universities offer entrepreneurship courses or programs.[5] The increase in interest has come from a variety of sources: the government wants to promote entrepreneurship to create growth and new jobs; students are exploring entrepreneurship because they like the idea of being their own boss and the potential of earning a greater income; and finally, businesses want to develop managers and employees with entrepreneurial skills in order to gain an advantage over their competitors.[6] As a result, all of the top twenty business schools in *BusinessWeek*'s 2004 rankings had comprehensive entrepreneurship programs that were among the top fifty nationally according to *Entrepreneur* magazine.[7]

Over the past three decades there has been a steady increase in the demand for entrepreneurship education.

By and large, however, the interest in developing entrepreneurship programs has not come from within the top business schools themselves, which in many cases resisted the foundation of such programs and accepted them only grudgingly. Of the top fifty business schools, ten offer only an emphasis in entrepreneurship rather than a full concentration or major. Of the forty schools that do offer complete programs, twenty-seven have a distinct name— such as the Heizer Entrepreneurship Center (Northwestern), the Eugene M. Lang Center for Entrepreneurship (Columbia), and the Michael P. Polsky Center for Entrepreneurship (University of Chicago)—generally indicating that someone outside the university was the catalyst for the program. These programs exist because wealthy individuals donated the money and fought the political battles necessary to create them. The name serves not only to recognize the person who donated the money, but also to separate the entrepreneurship program from the regular business school so that it is seen as a distinct entity.

Why the resistance to entrepreneurship programs among business schools? There are several reasons. First, business school deans are evaluated based on their ability to generate revenue, and the incubators and seed funds necessary for a successful program are often viewed as a drain on the financial and human capital of the department. In reality, it is possible for entrepreneurship programs to pay for themselves—the one at Washington University in St. Louis was financially self-supporting within three years. Nevertheless, the perception that entrepreneurship programs are a drain on revenue persists, and is a key reason why individuals have had to donate money to start entrepreneurship programs.

Second, the failure rate for entrepreneurs is high, and students who pursue entrepreneurship rather than taking a job with a big company can lower a school's placement rate and average income for graduates, which are key factors in business school rankings and recruitment. Also, many successful entrepreneurs are not the best students. In fact, only a small percentage of successful entrepreneurs graduated from a top business school, a fact business school deans are well aware of. As they have not yet seen a meaningful reversal of this trend, they find it difficult to justify making the required investment for the program to succeed.

Both of these objections point to a deeper, root cause of resistance. Starting an entrepreneurship program is in itself an entrepreneurial venture, as it requires startup money and new approaches to teaching such as experiential learning. Business schools, however, are run not by entrepreneurs but by academics. They function within a larger university bureaucracy, are dedicated to training professional managers, and are deeply versed in the theories of how to maintain an established, successful entity. They are also concerned about improving the quality of the overall program, cutting costs, attracting and retaining talented students and faculty, and making incremental improvements in the programs and services provided by the school. Establishing an entirely new and unique program is often seen as risky. It's a job more naturally suited to an entrepreneur than the typical business school dean, which explains why so many entrepreneurship programs have been founded by wealthy alumni.

In the past, a business school could get away without offering a comprehensive entrepreneurship program. But now, so many students are interested in entrepreneurship, and so many top business schools offer comprehensive programs, that the lack of an entrepreneurship program is increasingly becoming a key deciding factor against the schools that are still holding out. To be taken seriously as a top business school, a university will have to have an entrepreneurship program or risk sliding backwards in the rankings. Entrepreneurship programs are no longer an unknown quantity but are a proven business model that has been shown to be self-supporting and even profitable—not to mention highly popular with students and successful in creating entrepreneurs. Many of the administrators who were once opposed to establishing entrepreneurship programs at their schools are now avid supporters, and the holdouts are finding themselves playing catch-up.

The Building Blocks of Entrepreneurship Education

One of the more successful entrepreneurship programs in the country is the Stanford Technology Ventures Program (STVP) which, interestingly, is run out of the school of engineering rather than the business school. "Our philosophy is that it's not good enough for scientists and engineers to come out of school with pure technical training," explains Tina Seelig, executive director of the STVP. "They really need to have an understanding of the business environment in which they're going to work and develop the entrepreneurial skills to be successful. There's a huge demand among science and engineering students to get this type of education, especially at Stanford where we're right next to Silicon Valley and students are very entrepreneurial.

"At the STVP, we do three different things—teaching, research, and outreach. We have twenty-five quarters of courses, most of which are offered through the Department of Management Science and Engineering, and many of our entrepreneurship courses fill the requirements for students who are getting a degree in that department. Other students major in electrical engineering, computer science, medicine, biology, or other scientific fields, and they take our courses for enrichment. There's no major, no minor, no special certificate, but students can take as many of our courses as they want. In addition to teaching, we also have a very strong research group including fifteen PhD students, and then as part of our outreach program we share what we're doing with faculty members around the world."

The fact that the entrepreneurship program at Stanford is run through the Engineering School gives it a unique opportunity to focus on high technology ventures. "The interesting thing is that in some universities, the business school faculty have the responsibility for teaching entrepreneurship to the whole university. At Stanford they don't, and because we do this through the Engineering School, we have a very technology-based focus. The cases we use often are high-tech cases, and the speakers we bring in generally have high-tech backgrounds as well. Our focus is really on high-growth, high-impact, high-technology entrepreneurship."

Whether run through the business school, engineering school, or some other part of the university, successful entrepreneurship programs tend to have a number of elements that are distinctly different from the traditional approach to college education. It is not enough to teach the same core business curriculum—accounting, finance, marketing, operations, and strategy—from an entrepreneurial perspective, although this is an important step in the right direction. Starting a business is a demanding, creative activity, one where you need to jump in and make mistakes in order to learn. Thus entrepreneurship education, almost by its very nature, demands a less theoretical, more interactive approach that focuses less on memorization and testing, and more on exploration and critical thinking. The best entrepreneurship programs use an approach that blends traditional educational methods with experiential learning, guidance from successful entrepreneurs, exposure outside of the business school, and the development of practical experience through incubators and internships.

Experiential Learning

Successful entrepreneurship programs combine practical, experiential learning with the traditional lecture format. Students absorb a great deal more of what they learn from doing than what they learn from books or lectures, and while classroom activities are harder to structure, when done well they're far more effective. Tangible subjects such as the mechanics of writing a business plan and financial concepts can be addressed through lectures, but many other critical skills—such as developing and analyzing ideas, conducting market research for emerging markets and products, and presenting an idea to investors—can only be learned through practice and experience. Theories build analytic smarts, but practice and experience creates street smarts.

"At STVP, our courses have a huge range of formats," says Seelig. "We do have a large lecture seminar series that is open to everyone, which is called our Entrepreneurial Thought Leader Lecture Series, but our other courses range from small seminars to workshops to interactive work-study programs—the entire range. I teach a course in creativity and innovation which is very much a workshop-type course with lots of lab experiences, field trips, and extensive teamwork. In fact, I would guess almost every one of our courses has some type of team project associated with it."

A good entrepreneurship program provides a safe environment in which to develop street smarts and where students can learn from some of their early, inevitable failures. This establishes a safety net for failure, and promotes the idea that it is acceptable and normal. The problem with most business schools is they teach students to respond only to the information being taught, memorize the "correct" answer, and then repeat it back later on a test. This flies in the face of reality and encourages narrow thinking. Learning there are many right answers in the business world should be a priority, and experiential activities help students to realize this. The answers in an experiential learning environment aren't prefabricated, so students learn to think, remain flexible, consider the alternatives, act decisively, and then adjust to new facts. Individual businesses don't fit a mold, especially entrepreneurial businesses, so why should business schools require students to find a single correct answer?

The traditional lecture-and-test approach to education assumes the human brain is like a funnel, and that a teacher can pour in information day after day and the knowledge will simply collect in the repository of young minds. But it is well established in educational literature that we only retain 10 percent of what we read and 15 percent of what we hear in a lecture. Mid-terms and finals are of little use, for after the exam most of what students cram into their short-term memory is lost. So why do we continue to teach this way? It has been shown time and time again that the human brain only retains information which is applied, and applied repeatedly. The lecture-and-test approach encourages short-term memorization of facts rather than mastery of basic principles.

> **A good entrepreneurship program provides a safe environment in which to develop street smarts and where students can learn from some of their early, inevitable failures.**

In addition to providing street smarts, one of the most valuable aspects of experiential learning, for business students in particular, is that it provides an opportunity for them to integrate everything they've learned. "It allows students to actually see how finance and marketing fit together, how strategy and operations fit together," says Dr. Barton Hamilton, a professor of entrepreneurship at the Olin School of Business at Washington University. "A big problem in business schools is that professors don't usually make those kinds of cross-disciplinary connections in their classes. All of those specialized skills like accounting, finance, marketing, economics, and strategy are taught separately. Experiential learning is important because it gives students an opportunity to finally integrate all of these different pieces, and that's the kind of experience people need whether they're going to be an entrepreneur, or a manger working in a mature corporation."

Experiential learning also allows students to learn about themselves. Typically, at the beginning of an entry-level entrepreneurship class, the percent of students who think they are potentially founder-entrepreneurs can be quite high. By the time the class is over, however, many realize that their role is not necessarily to be the founder, but to be a contributor or collaborator. Others learn they're not an idea person, and they need an idea person. Learning about themselves, relative to what their motivations are and what their skills are, allows them to fit themselves into the role and career path that's most appropriate. While a lot of people are going to need to work in an innovative entrepreneurial environment, not everybody is going to be a founder-entrepreneur in the traditional sense, and it's important for students to learn what their role should really be. Experiential learning, properly structured, allows people to learn this in a process of self-discovery.

While traditional business programs often use some experiential learning, the vast majority of the time in college classrooms is still spent on lectures and analysis of business cases. This can be a great disappointment to students. In one survey, about 40 percent of students reported that they were bored by their classes, and a majority said they came to college hoping to learn through discussion only to be faced with endless lectures.[8] When done well, entrepreneurship education is a "pracademic"—it combines the practical and the academic. While entrepreneurship education should not be completely lecture-free, it does require a curriculum full of experiential learning to be successful, and traditional business education would benefit from a greater emphasis on learning-by-doing as well.

Interaction with Successful Entrepreneurs

One of the big political obstacles that can develop when an outside entrepreneur attempts to establish an entrepreneurship program at a university involves the decision as to who is most qualified to teach entrepreneurship. The university generally wants to use academics who have a PhD and published research, for that is how expertise is judged in the academic world. Many entrepreneurs, on the other hand, argue that the only people who are truly qualified to teach entrepreneurship are those who have successfully started a business. This debate over which type of expertise is most appropriate is one that has raged since business schools first began, and each side has a point. Practitioners lack the well-researched theoretical knowledge that professors bring to the table, while professors often lack real-world experience.

While business schools readily bring in industry practitioners as guest speakers, they are often very resistant to use adjunct faculty from industry to teach full courses. Since entrepreneurship is a relatively new academic field with very few doctoral programs, however, there is a shortage of qualified academics. The recent growth in entrepreneurship programs across the country has exacerbated the problem and practically forced business school deans to hire practicing entrepreneurs as clinical faculty members. This is a welcome addition for entrepreneurship students, as one of the key success factors in fostering greater entrepreneurship is exposure to successful entrepreneurs.

"At STVP, about half of our faculty members are regular faculty, and half are adjuncts," says Seelig. "That's critical, because in an area like entrepreneurship you need to have those scholarly teachers who are looking at problems from the academic perspective, but it's just as important to have entrepreneurs with practical experience." When I asked Seelig if they ever had trouble getting adjunct professors, she replied with an emphatic, "No! We practically have to fight them off. In fact, we have people volunteering to do this on a daily basis. Lots of retired executives, venture capitalists, and other people in the entrepreneurial community want to give back, and they really enjoy teaching."

Established entrepreneurs, for their part, generally love the chance to get into the classroom and pass on their knowledge to the next generation. They tend to serve on corporate advisory boards at universities, and often welcome the opportunity to get more involved by teaching. But the transition can be difficult. While most entrepreneurs champion proactive learning-by-doing and tend to argue for a more vocational approach to education, once in the classroom they sometimes fall back on lecturing. When this happens, the ambivalence displayed by students who are tired of listening to yet another lecture can throw adjunct faculty for a loop, for as entrepreneurs they are accustomed to commanding the attention of their employees and associates. Clinical professors are also criticized for basing too much of their classroom lectures on personal experience, telling "war stories" rather than teaching methods and principles.

"Using former entrepreneurs to teach entrepreneurship is very important, but it's actually much more difficult to do than you might think," says Hamilton. "The problem with many former entrepreneurs is they don't have any perspective on what they've done, and to be honest, probably 75 percent of being a successful entrepreneur is luck. When entrepreneurs teach, there's a real temptation for them to focus on what they did that made them successful, and to think what they did will work every time. That's not useful, because every startup is somewhat unique, and so you really have to search for entrepreneurs who have some perspective on what they've done. Often, experienced venture capitalists and angel investors are very good teachers and mentors, because they've seen a lot of different ideas, and they've seen a lot of failures. I think you probably learn more from failures than from successes, and people who have seen the failures and seen what's gone wrong are incredibly valuable mentors."

Most students find the opportunity to learn from practicing entrepreneurs and venture capitalists is priceless.

Most students find the opportunity to learn from practicing entrepreneurs and venture capitalists is priceless, and adjunct faculty members provide students with contacts, which are invaluable later in their careers. One of the keys to fostering greater entrepreneurship is finding a way to bring the experience and capital of established entrepreneurs together with the energy and technical knowledge of young, aspiring entrepreneurs. Adjunct faculty provide an important link between these two groups, and thus they are a vital part of a successful entrepreneurship program. The strengths and weaknesses of traditional and adjunct faculty members tend to balance each other, and often the best approach is to integrate the use of both professors and entrepreneurs as teachers, in teams when possible, so that students have exposure to both viewpoints.

Exposure Outside of the Business School

Another key opportunity that makes entrepreneurship programs extremely valuable is the cross-pollination of ideas between students in various disciplines. Thus, the best entrepreneurship programs offer joint classes through the science, medical, and engineering schools, as well as the business school and other areas. Due to their limited range of experience, business students who are isolated within the business community tend to develop service industry ideas that require few job skills and have low barriers to entry. Access to other academic communities broadens entrepreneurship students' perspectives and helps to generate better business ideas. Similarly, the students from other disciplines such as science and engineering benefit from the business students' knowledge, and some great business ventures can emerge from the mix of ideas and expertise.

"Business students have very good management, marketing, and financial expertise, but the kinds of ideas they have for new businesses are often not that good," says Hamilton. "The flip side is that the people from engineering and the sciences often have great ideas, but they have no clue how to exploit those ideas. That's why it's so valuable to bring those two groups of people together—take biotech, for example. Unless the business student has an undergraduate degree in biology, has worked in biotech, or has a partner with those skills, they don't really have deep enough knowledge of biotech to find a really good idea to work on. They know how to market products, but they don't understand what they're marketing. That's where it's invaluable to bring together people with different skills, and a university is a kind of neutral environment where you can do that relatively easily. It's like a really big incubator, and it's rare to find incubators where you can mix really smart people who are medical doctors with really smart people who are getting MBAs. The cost of doing that in a university setting is much lower than anywhere else, and people seem to feel more comfortable collaborating in a university setting than they would out in the real world."

University leadership tends to like the idea of cross-functional classes, at least in theory, but the idea can be complicated to implement. Academic departments tend to be territorial, and an equitable way of sharing the revenue from joint classes has to be developed and agreed upon, along with ways around various other bureaucratic hurdles. Students sometimes have to be very persistent in order to cut through the red tape necessary to take a cross-functional course, trudging across campus from building to building in order to waive prerequisites and secure the necessary paperwork and signatures. Often it's even worse for students outside of the business school who want to minor in or take a second major in entrepreneurship, for there is an attitude that entrepreneurship is strictly a business discipline that should be open only to business students.

"While the business school here at Stanford is fabulous, it does not open its doors to engineers, and only in very rare cases are there open slots in their classes," explains Seelig. "Also, there isn't an undergraduate business program at Stanford, just the graduate one, which is part of the reason why the STVP was formed in the Engineering School. We absolutely encourage our students to mix with students from other disciplines—we have many students from arts and sciences, the medical school, and the business school who come and take our classes. In fact, we work very closely with a student group on campus called BASES, the Business Association of Stanford Engineering Students, which has four to five thousand members who are students from all across campus. We are always thinking about broadening our audience beyond just the engineering school."

Business schools have worked hard over the past century to establish themselves as professional schools that, like law and medicine, are distinct from the rest of the university community. This makes little sense, as a majority of liberal arts majors will eventually wind up in the private sector, in which case a minor in business or entrepreneurship might be extremely helpful to their careers. Moreover, it works against the cross-pollination between different disciplines that has become so crucial to innovation in the university setting, and which is now an important alternative to large companies in discovering and developing new technologies. Business schools, especially ones who run entrepreneurship programs, need to reassess their approach and move towards greater integration with the university rather than greater exclusivity.

Practical Experience

One of the biggest problems with business education, particularly at the undergraduate level, is that it lacks the kind of practical training clerkships and residencies provide in professions such as law and medicine. Medical students do rotations and a residency, law students clerk for judges, yet most undergraduate business students only get job training if they seek out internships of their own accord. A lack of applied experience is a critical problem for both business and liberal arts students, and is one of the main reasons many find themselves underemployed after graduation. A head full of theory is a waste if graduates don't have the experience or contacts to get their feet in the doors of companies. This is also a significant shortcoming for entrepreneurs, because people who are considering starting their own business report one of the key factors holding them back is the feeling that they don't have the skill set to succeed. An effective entrepreneurship program should not only provide students with this skill set, it should also give them practical experience using their skills so they develop confidence in their abilities.

One approach to practical training for entrepreneurs is to provide a forum for students to experiment and develop ideas to the point where a mature business plan can be presented to investors, for the best way to learn how to be an entrepreneur is to actually start a business. The problem, however, is that this requires a steady stream of seed funding to develop prototypes and get business ideas off the ground, enabling them to fly long enough for students to obtain additional funding. Most business schools are often unwilling to take a chunk out of their budget to fund risky student ventures, although it should be noted that student ventures aren't always that risky. An entrepreneurship program is an ideal place for investors to find solid business plans, because the students and their ideas are watched, nurtured, and evaluated over the entire length of the program. As investment funds are generally limited, only the best ideas are funded, and they tend to have a high success rate. Venture capitalists are often interested in the business plans that emerge from business schools because the ideas have been so carefully mentored and reviewed.

> An effective entrepreneurship program should provide students with practical experience using their skills so they develop confidence in their abilities.

On the other hand, there are potential legal and ethical complications. It is generally considered to be a conflict of interest for a faculty member to serve as a board member or invest in a student venture. Less clear is the issue of whether it's ethical for schools to fund student ventures when those same students are paying the university tuition, and business schools certainly have no desire to become legally liable for the student ventures they fund. Thus, they prefer to have a donor create an endowment to provide seed funding and keep it separate from the business school, as this bypasses many of the legal and ethical issues. Yet students often need just a few thousand dollars to get an idea to the stage where it can be shown to angel investors, and sometimes networking contacts are the most valuable resource a university can provide.[9]

In addition to business incubators, consulting courses and internships are also crucial to developing entrepreneurial experience, and the more the better, for they serve the same function as rotations for medical students. The more young entrepreneurs try different things, the better feel they have for their own particular strengths and weaknesses, which allows them to make more informed career choices. At the Stanford Technology Ventures Program, their approach to practical training has been to establish the Mayfield Fellows Program, an intense, nine-month program open to a dozen students every year.

"We hand pick twelve top science and engineering students through an interview process early in the year, and it's almost like getting into a PhD program, it's so competitive," says Seelig, who is co-director of the program. "The students start out in the spring quarter and get what amounts to a mini-MBA. They do two business cases a week, and the focus is on strategy, finance, organizational behavior, and leadership. They also spend the spring semester looking for summer internships. We help them with that, but it's their responsibility. Then during the summer they work at these startup companies, and they all host open houses for the other students in the program. When they return to school in the fall, they each do a case presentation on some key aspect of what happened at their company during the summer. It's like a work-study program on steroids, because the students get exposure to all twelve companies and essentially have twelve internships, so it's a very intense program."

For students at universities without an entrepreneurial internship program like the one at Stanford, finding internships with smaller, entrepreneurial companies can be particularly problematic. While these companies need cheap labor, they have little time for training and no established mechanism for utilizing temporary student help. Meanwhile, college students often prefer to take summer jobs where they can make some money rather than taking an unpaid internship for credit. This is a mistake, because practical experience or exposure is a critical element to the education of entrepreneurs, and it is imperative that internships be available to entrepreneurs in training. Just ask Steve Ballmer, the CEO of Microsoft. "I certainly think that many schools are encouraging young people to think like entrepreneurs, but I know from my own experience that theoretical knowledge doesn't always translate into real world skills. So it's critical to balance getting a great formal education with experience in the business world via internships."

Who is better able to provide these internships than a major institution of higher education with its alumni and business contacts? Universities and four-year colleges have always resisted providing vocational training, but practical experience is crucial in making the leap from college to the business world, and entrepreneurial companies should not have to shoulder the complete burden of job training. Business schools need to take a much greater interest in establishing effective internships, both for entrepreneurship and traditional business students.

Creating a Successful Entrepreneurship Program

How can all of these elements be brought together to create a successful entrepreneurship program? I helped establish the Skandalaris Center for Entrepreneurial Studies at Washington University in St. Louis because I believe entrepreneurship education is incredibly important to the future of our country, and that research universities have a crucial role to play in innovation. The Skandalaris Center grew out of the Olin Business School's Center for Experiential Learning, which was founded in 1991 to promote hands-on learning in entrepreneurship as well as other areas. The program has grown rapidly since then, and was ranked amongst the first-tier entrepreneurship programs in the country in the 2003 *Entrepreneur* magazine poll.[10]

The Ewing Marian Kauffman Foundation selected Washington University as one of eight schools to receive funding to create new models for entrepreneurial learning in 2003. The result was the Skandalaris Center for Entrepreneurship, which has grown into a multidisciplinary program that targets learning and research in corporate innovation, application and commercialization of early-stage science, social entrepreneurship, and student-started ventures. Beyond training students to lead entrepreneurial businesses in the future, the center also fosters networking, supplies resources for ideas to mature, and provides a forum in which these ideas can partner with venture capital. As an early resource along the idea-to-business path, the center acts as a funnel through which an idea starts on its way to becoming a business, and has helped form numerous partnerships across Washington University and the broader St. Louis community.

The Entrepreneurship Curriculum

The entrepreneurship curriculum at Washington University requires students to both study entrepreneurship and experience it directly. Both the undergraduate and graduate degree programs have an entrepreneurship track, which consists of both foundation and elective courses customized for students pursuing that degree. The program's curriculum is designed to teach students the fundamentals of starting a new business and provide them with ample opportunity to participate in the process in a real-world setting.

The Startup Game is the first foundation course for all entrepreneurship students. It focuses on the earliest stages of the venture process including idea creation and evaluation, company formation, team recruitment, and fundraising. Students come to the Startup Game with an idea for a new business, which they then attempt to sell to their fellow classmates. Each is allotted a set amount of dollars, which they can use to fund the most promising of the other students' ideas. Those who attract the most money form mock companies and compete with the other winning entrepreneurs to hire their classmates. The companies then work on developing their business ideas, and at the end of the semester they make a presentation to a group of student bankers.

"One of the most memorable ideas that emerged from the Startup Game came from a student who had already been accepted to medical school, and who just wanted to learn something about entrepreneurship," remembers Dr. Hamilton, who used to teach the course. "Sitting in the class, he was thinking what a pain it was to apply for medical school, in particular preparing for the interviews. While there are lots of services that do test preparation, once you do well on the exams, it's really important to follow up by doing well in the interview with the admissions people. This student was taking the Startup Game course, and he was thinking about all of the work that went into preparing for these interviews. You have to read up on all of these different aspects of medicine and public policy, and he realized that there were a whole bunch of other people out there who were in the same boat as he was. So he put together a team of students who knew marketing and finance and so forth, and developed this business idea of a medical school interview preparation service. Unfortunately, he went to medical school and had no time to develop the idea further. But it was a really nice idea, one of the best ideas to come out of that class."

I believe the Startup Game is critical in the development of the entrepreneurial thought process. Students are asked to compete for funds without a full business plan, and those students with the best idea, the most charismatic personality, or who are simply the most persistent ultimately win. They see on a first-hand basis that an idea is just that and nothing more, while a business is the process of developing that idea into a product for sale.

The second foundation course in the Skandalaris Center curriculum is known as the Hatchery. The best teams from the Startup Game go on to develop their ideas in the Hatchery, while other students submit resumes to work on business ideas developed by entrepreneurs from outside the university. As part of the Hatchery, students learn how to write a business plan, develop a business model, and make investor and customer presentations during the course, and they are supported by both a mentor and a faculty member. Some recent projects have included commercializing biotech innovations developed by Washington University scientists, helping to found a company that develops platform technology related to stem cells, and a social entrepreneurship venture to create a sustainable revenue stream for Glacier National Park. The Hatchery is where the real entrepreneurs begin to show, as they are good at creating momentum for a project. Others join their team, and through their combined energy attempt to create a business plan that can be presented to investors. With the help of a team of seasoned professionals, the students' plans and assumptions are constantly under review. Upon giving the final presentation, these students have a better understanding of their product and the steps required to get it to market.

"It's really good experience for students to work on developing a real business plan and putting together all of the pieces of a business," says Hamilton. "Usually, the people in the hatchery are MBA students in their late twenties. While they generally haven't had enough experience to come up with a really good business idea of their own, it's great practice for what to do when the right idea actually comes along. A good example of this was one of our first Hatchery graduates, Andrew Rubin. He wrote a business plan for a company called Ice King, and he actually got some funding and opened a shaved ice stand at a mall here in St. Louis. It closed within a year, but the important thing for Andrew was the experience of writing the business plan and opening the store. He subsequently started a network security company five years ago and it seems poised to be a big success."

Another aspect of the Hatchery is the seed capital fund, an investment fund managed by mentored student investment teams. The fund originally targeted investments in student-initiated ventures, and the investment board was composed entirely of outside members who approved or rejected investment recommendations. They would look for startup companies that involved current students or alumni, and would co-invest with other angel investors or venture capitalists. Since then, the seed capital fund has morphed into a fund operated by the students themselves, giving them real-world experience as investors in performing due diligence and making investment decisions. This is an unusual demand to place on the typical student, but is critical to the understanding of the entrepreneurial process.

In addition to the Startup Game and the Hatchery, there are over forty cross-disciplinary courses combining entrepreneurship with other subjects offered throughout the university. One of the most interesting aspects of the curriculum is that undergraduate students in any discipline can receive a second major in entrepreneurship; in other words, an art history major could also major in entrepreneurship without needing to get a second degree from the business school. All students have to do is complete the two foundation courses and a combination of six other required and elective courses. This has been an appealing option, because many students are discovering that entrepreneurial behavior and change management skills are highly desirable in many environments and situations, not just starting businesses. As a result, some of the entrepreneurship coursework at Washington University is now broadening into areas such as addressing how to apply entrepreneurial activity and innovation to social welfare programs, where the goal is simply trying to make them sustainable rather than trying to make a profit. Entrepreneurship classes lend themselves well to the whole issue of creativity and breakthroughs, and it is desirable for people to have those skills no matter what their job is. A lot of what the Skandalaris Center has tried to do, particularly cross-functionally, is to teach those skills to a wide audience of students.

Entrepreneurship Training

Entrepreneurship courses are only part of what is offered by the Skandalaris Center for Entrepreneurship. Students also have the opportunity to develop practical experience through practicums, internships, and business plan competitions that connect students with the local entrepreneurship community. The entrepreneurship practicum offered through the Skandalaris Center is a consulting course that allows students to receive academic credit by completing defined projects for outside organizations. It is a form of service learning, integrating community service with practical experience, which is particularly helpful in developing interpersonal and operational skills.

As part of the practicum, companies propose projects, student teams are matched with client companies, and detailed work plans are developed and agreed upon. In one project for Boeing, students helped to form spin-off ventures created around intellectual property that Boeing had developed. Company managers direct the student teams, who are assigned a faculty adviser with expertise in the area of their project. The students who participate in this program are asked to work on the validity of the idea, the marketing plan, budgets, job-costing schedules, and product conceptualization. Many ideas come from the local community, but others are generated by large corporations, and faculty advisors have found the quality of output and the energy staff and students devote to these projects is outstanding.

> Entrepreneurship classes lend themselves well to the whole issue of creativity and breakthroughs, and it is desirable for people to have those skills no matter what their job is.

The Entrepreneurial Internship Initiative is another experiential program which allows students to apply what they have learned in the entrepreneurship program's foundation courses in an internship setting. The students serve as management team members in early-stage ventures or recently-formed venture capital or private equity firms, and the participating companies offer students the opportunity to take a significant role in an entrepreneurial environment. Interns perform a variety of tasks such as financial, market, and competitive analyses, as well as pitching in to help in all areas of the new business. This ensures valuable student experiences with young companies that could not otherwise afford student support, and in many cases, the companies offer the students full-time positions or extended internships.

Andrea Meacham, an MBA student who participated in the internship initiative in 2004, found the experience to be incredibly valuable. "My internship showed me how an entire organization can be entrepreneurial, and how important it is to have innovative leadership. It was eye-opening to see how I could apply marketing, finance, and strategy skills I learned at Olin to social entrepreneurship projects that are making a real difference in the community. I gained valuable experience in business and strategic planning, real estate, community development, retail marketing, and not-for-profit management and operations."

Perhaps the ultimate entrepreneurship training experience at Washington University is the Olin Cup, an annual business plan competition designed to promote cross-campus and community collaboration. "The Olin Cup has been an incredible catalyst for entrepreneurial activities on the part of our students and the St. Louis community," says Bart Hamilton. "In particular, it has been a great opportunity for undergraduate students and also our executive MBA students, who traditionally hadn't really participated as much in the Hatchery and the entrepreneurship program. It used to be that the best idea from the Hatchery would win the Olin Cup, but now we've expanded the competition university-wide and created a lot of programs and support to help people develop their business plans outside of the strict confines of a class environment. It's interesting how a lot of our undergraduate and executive students, as well as students from outside the business school, have really gotten much more involved as a result. If you're a forty-year-old manager and you're working full time, you can't really come to class twice a week, but if there's somebody once a month explaining how to do the financials or a marketing plan, that opens the opportunity to a lot more people."

As part of the competition, teams of Olin students, alumni, and people from the greater St. Louis region develop business plans and make presentations to potential investors. The competition offers an opportunity for rigorous review and constructive feedback, exposing students to key resources and increasing the likelihood of funding. Competing teams gain exposure to a large number of potential investors, and the winners of the competition receive investment funds to help start their businesses. Over the years the program has grown, providing wonderful exposure for students and creating several successful business ventures. The Olin Cup is but one aspect of what has become a highly successful approach to practical entrepreneurship training.

The Center for Research in Innovation and Entrepreneurship

In addition to teaching students about entrepreneurship and providing them with practical training, the Skandalaris Center also seeks to promote interdisciplinary research within the university community. A new Center for Research in Innovation and Entrepreneurship has been established in the Law School to support research related to technology transfer, corporate entrepreneurship, female and minority entrepreneurship, entrepreneurial learning, and the impact of entrepreneurship on economic development. Each project is eligible to receive up to $40,000 a year, and all university faculty members have been invited to submit proposals. In addition, the Skandalaris Center has also developed incentive programs for university deans and faculty that encourage them to develop innovative new courses, research projects, and other activities.

"The Center for Research has been really important for us on the academic side of entrepreneurship," says Hamilton. "Programs like the Olin Cup, the Hatchery, and the Internship Initiative have emphasized the practical and teaching aspects of entrepreneurship, but in a university, you also need to have academic research on entrepreneurship. We understand so little about why people become entrepreneurs, what the key determinants of success are, and how corporate entrepreneurial programs should be designed. The Center has really facilitated research into those important questions, and not just in the Olin Business School. There are so many different facets to entrepreneurship that from a research perspective you really need to attack it from a number of different directions. The Center is now funding entrepreneurial research grants to faculty in law, business, art, science, engineering, social work, and medicine, so what it's really done is foster research into entrepreneurship in a variety of disciplines, from a variety of perspectives. That's been a very positive thing, because at most universities the people in the law school rarely talk to the people in the business school, and the people in social work *never* talk to people in the business school, so what the research center has done is really enhance that communication. It's encouraged research across disciplinary boundaries, and hopefully we'll learn a lot more that will help us to foster entrepreneurship much more effectively."

Another goal of the Skandalaris Center is to promote the local entrepreneurial economy by increasing the level of interest in, and understanding of, the commercialization process by researchers and faculty. In conjunction with the Washington University Technology Transfer Office, the Skandalaris Center works to connect innovative scientists and researchers within the university to experienced entrepreneurs, business incubators, and sources of funding in order to help commercialize their discoveries. The interdisciplinary approach has clearly produced results, as the School of Engineering alone has produced eighteen startup companies over the past eight years, and the university currently owns over 150 federally funded inventions, half of which are being licensed to private companies. Newly expanded science and biomedical engineering laboratories are expected to spur even more cross-disciplinary learning and innovation in the future.

The Center for Research is an important step in legitimatizing entrepreneurship as an academic discipline, which is vitally important. Entrepreneurship is critical to the growth and prosperity of American business, and also to the ability of individual Americans to maintain their standard of living. Business schools must address the need for entrepreneurship education, and recognize they have an institutional responsibility not just to train professional managers, but also to train entrepreneurs. Students in all universities ought to have access to entrepreneurship education without having to go to alternative sources. The schools that do not have entrepreneurship programs need to develop them, and the responsibility for doing so should not have to rest on outside entrepreneurs. It is time for the deans and directors at these schools to shoulder the responsibility for championing the cause of entrepreneurship education themselves.

One of the great things about entrepreneurship education is that it has value not just for people who want to start a business, but for those managing established business as well. The analytical and leadership skills that entrepreneurship education develops are desirable in many career paths. "Entrepreneurship education is a way for students to put together everything they've learned in business school and apply it," says Hamilton. "A big problem a lot of people have with management education today is that you learn specialized things like finance, marketing, and operations, but there's no practical integration of those disciplines. Entrepreneurship programs are valuable for business schools because they are a way to integrate these specialized skills in a real-world environment. So even if you're never planning on being an entrepreneur, it's still valuable to have entrepreneurship as a key piece of the curriculum, because it will make you a better manager and leader."

Not everyone will start their own business and become an entrepreneur, but if Americans want to retain their high-paying jobs, they are going to have to find a way to add value, to solve problems, to create new products. In an innovation economy, entrepreneurship is a critical skill, and it deserves a central place in the American educational curriculum. There are many students who have the desire to start a business, but they often lack the knowledge of how to go about it. Entrepreneurship education bridges that gap and can help turn young people into successful entrepreneurs.

5

THE LIFEBLOOD OF INNOVATION— VENTURE CAPITAL

◇◇

One of my favorite stories about being a successful entrepreneur involves the introduction of a highly successful business person at a banquet in his honor. The person giving the introduction discussed the millionaire entrepreneur's large holdings, both corporate and real estate, his community contributions, and his sizeable foundation. He was an American success story. "Your support is overwhelming," said the honoree. "Many of you are aware of my accomplishments, and not one of them would have been possible without your help, for I came to this community with the clothes on my back and a paper bag containing my worldly belongings." At the close of the speech, a young admirer asked, "What was in the bag?"

"My two million dollar inheritance," he replied.

Underlying this story is a deeply held but erroneous assumption that most wealthy people inherit their fortunes. In fact, nothing could be further from the truth, for 80 percent of American millionaires are self-made. Nonetheless, it is true that it takes money to make money, and since the majority of entrepreneurs don't inherit their wealth, they have had to access capital from other sources. Indeed, it is America's ability to come up with innovative approaches to financing, particularly venture capital, which has maintained our lead in the innovation race for so long.

Venture capital, which has financed many innovations, is an innovation in and of itself, one that we owe to Georges Doriot. He founded the world's first publicly owned venture capital investment company, the American Research and Development Corporation, in 1947, which launched a whole new way of funding entrepreneurial ventures. Before then, it was left to wealthy families like the Vanderbilts and the Rockefellers to fund the sort of high-risk ventures—like Eastern and Pan American airlines—that no bank or investment company would dare touch. A professor at Harvard Business School for over forty years, Doriot created a business model that provided not only capital, but also management advice, which proved to be integral to the venture capital system's success.

Doriot's vision was never about making a quick profit. A war veteran, he saw venture capital investment as a patriotic duty, for he feared that American innovation would lose its leading edge if left to the traditional banking and investment community. He and his associates saw themselves as partner-managers who were in for the long haul, and they had the patience to wait years for results. "Your sophisticated 'long term' stockholders make five points and sell out," said Doriot derisively. "But we have our hearts in our companies. We are really doctors of childhood diseases here. When bankers or brokers tell me I should sell an ailing company, I ask them, 'Would you sell a child running a temperature of 104?'"[1]

Doriot's focus was on developing technology, and the companies he helped to finance and manage commercialized high voltage accelerators, liquid fuel rockets, ultrasonic generators, cancer therapy, hydraulic pumps, various pharmaceuticals, ceramics, and optical scanning—for an average return of 15 percent. Even more important, he established an entirely new financial business model that, half a century later, almost single-handedly financed the New Economy. As a professor, he told his students, "Always remember that someone, somewhere, is making a product that will make your product obsolete." Doriot, for his part, was always on the leading edge.[2]

Capital is the lifeblood of an innovative economy, and obtaining startup funding is generally one of the biggest hurdles that emerging entrepreneurs have to overcome. Banks and other lending institutions are often reluctant to loan money for startup financing, and while the government has a number of loan guarantee programs available, the application process is complex and arduous. For high-tech entrepreneurs in particular, raising the seed financing necessary to develop prototypes and prove the business concept can be daunting, and generally requires some form of equity financing. While venture capital became relatively easy to obtain in the 1990s, now that the dot-com craze has subsided it is generally awarded only to entrepreneurs with a proven track record and an established business with high growth potential. Although there are "angel" investors who are willing to provide early stage seed and startup capital for high-tech ventures, gaining access to the angel investor network is difficult if you don't have the right connections.

As hard as raising startup capital can be, however, it is much easier to do in the United States than anywhere else in the world. While countries like Chile, Uganda and Venezuela have higher rates of entrepreneurship, they do not have a high-performance financial system. Their citizens do not have the same access to startup capital in the form of credit cards and home equity that most middle class Americans do. Moreover, developing nations lack the vast network of private investors, venture capital partnerships, investment banking firms, and small business investment corporations necessary to finance the expansion of high-growth businesses. In fact, one can argue that the United States' ability to produce highly accessible capital underlies our economic success and distinguishes us from non-Western nations.

The relative ease with which American entrepreneurs can obtain capital for investment has been crucial to our economic development and prosperity, and throughout our history the variety and complexity of financing options has grown. While the government, banks, and other lending institutions provide important sources of debt financing for small businesses, it is equity financing that fosters the type of entrepreneurship that creates significant jobs and economic growth. No other country comes close to having a venture capital network of the same magnitude as the United States, which is a primary reason why we are currently the world's leading economy.

Venture capital is particularly critical for high-tech startup firms. To start a more traditional small business like a restaurant or a hardware store, an entrepreneur would generally mortgage their home and borrow money from friends and family in order to raise seed capital. Once off the ground, they would apply to a bank for a loan, often with the assistance of a loan guarantee from the U.S. Small Business Administration, and they would expect to finance their monthly interest payments from sales revenue. If they wanted to expand, they would use their proven track record at the bank to obtain larger loans, and if the business grew large enough they might eventually sell stock in the company.

The relative ease with which American entrepreneurs can obtain capital for investment has been crucial to our economic development and prosperity.

High-tech startups, by contrast, often go through a long period of research and development where they aren't generating any revenue. Venture capital is well suited to the needs of these startups, because it provides a lump-sum payment up front without the need for collateral and monthly payments. While first-time entrepreneurs in high-tech sectors generally use credit cards, home equity, and loans from family to get started, the nature of their startups soon drives them to look for equity financing, and experienced entrepreneurs go to those sources right from the start. They generally turn either to angel investors, who are accredited investors with a net worth of at least $1 million, or to venture capital funds that specialize in providing early stage seed and startup financing.

The returns to the American economy from this investment in high-impact entrepreneurship are enormous. Venture capitalists invested over $338 billion in more than 21,600 American companies between 1970 and 2003, and those companies generated 10 million new jobs and over $1.7 trillion in sales revenue in 2003 alone.[3] A study conducted by the consulting firm Global Insight showed that companies backed by venture capital experienced greater job and revenue growth than private firms during the economic downturn from 2000 to 2003, and invested significantly more in research and development as well. These findings aren't really surprising, as venture capital firms select their investments with growth potential in mind. Nevertheless, it seems clear that venture capital investment has an important role in helping promising companies to achieve their potential. Without it, the United States won't be able to create all of the new jobs necessary to replace the ones we're losing.

The American Venture Capital System

The concept of equity financing first took root during the sixteenth and seventeenth centuries when charter companies were developed in Northern Europe to establish colonies and trading empires. Previously, the idea of dividing ownership of a company into small pieces and selling those pieces to investors was not widely accepted, as investors didn't want to share liability for a company they were not directly involved in running. Colonization, however, was so risky that for the first time, the idea of limited liability was introduced to protect investors. This made it much easier for entrepreneurs to raise capital.

The acceptance of limited liability joint-stock corporations soon gave rise to stock markets such as the famous Exchange Alley in London, where people started to trade shares on the open market. While this idea dated back to the thirteenth century, it was only with the rise of chartered companies that it took firm root. Unfortunately, speculation eventually created the largest financial bubble in history—the South Sea Bubble—which, when it burst, created tremendous backlash and public suspicion towards joint stock companies and the concept of limited liability.[4] As a result, governments made it difficult to create joint-stock corporations, and also reserved the right to revoke and rewrite company charters at will. Slowly, however, the concept of limited liability was accepted. Entrepreneurial capital began to flow, and the first corporate stock was traded on Wall Street in 1798.

As the American industrial revolution gained momentum during the 1800s, joint-stock corporations started to be used extensively to finance canals and railroads. These projects required even more capital than trading voyages and colonization, and without limited liability and the ability to sell stock to raise capital, it is doubtful that major railroads could have been built. "The limited liability corporation is the greatest single discovery of modern times," noted nineteenth century economist Nicholas Murray Butler. "Even steam and electricity would be reduced to comparative impotence without it."[5] By the time the transcontinental railroad was completed in 1869, the power of equity financing had been unleashed and was at the disposal of entrepreneurs across the country. This, combined with widespread property rights and a centralized national banking system, created unprecedented access to capital that fueled the massive growth of the American economy over the next century.

The next leap forward came with the development of the modern venture capital industry, which got its start after World War II. Many promising technologies had been developed during the war that were waiting to be commercialized, but by that time Wall Street had become a mechanism for trading established stocks rather than financing new businesses. In response to this problem, Georges Doriot and a group of wealthy bankers and industrialists in Boston formed the country's first institutional venture capital fund, the American Research and Development Corporation, in 1947. Meanwhile, Congress created the Small Business Administration, which issued and guaranteed loans to small businesses, as well as the Small Business Investment Company program, which allowed commercial banks to form SBICs and leverage their capital by borrowing from the government at below-market interest rates.

The true financial breakthrough, however, came with the invention of venture capital limited partnerships. This new type of venture capital fund allowed the general partners who managed the fund to raise money from outside limited partners, which included not only wealthy independent investors but banks, corporations, and eventually pension funds and other institutions. This greatly increased the pool of venture capital available, and over time it became clear that venture capital investments could produce unprecedented returns which, according to one early estimate, were five times that of corporate stocks and bonds. Indeed, some early venture capital-backed firms like Digital Equipment Corporation provided a return on investment of over 100 percent!

Over time, the lowering of the capital gains tax and loosening of restrictions governing pension funds made venture capital investments even more attractive. By the 1990s, risk capital was pouring into these limited partnerships. The annual amount invested in venture capital funds soared from $2.8 billion in 1990 to $106 billion at the height of the Internet bubble in 2000, arguably an unsustainable and even imprudent level of high-risk investment.[6] Then the bubble burst, and the subsequent falloff in venture capital funding appears to have bottomed out in 2003 and stabilized at a healthy level of around $20 to $23 billion annually. Venture capital investment was up $2 billion in 2004, the first increase in the three years after the bust, and fund performance is continuing to improve. All in all, the American venture capital system seems to have regained its equilibrium in the wake of the dot-com bust.

The Venture Capital Funding Gap

While the American venture capital industry is strong and healthy, it is nonetheless very different from the way it was a few decades ago. The exuberant investment levels from 1998 to 2001 made venture capital available to an unprecedented number of entrepreneurs at a very early stage in the process. They often had little experience and not much of a business plan, but this was an anomaly in a

Annual Venture Capital Invested in U.S. Ventures, in Billions

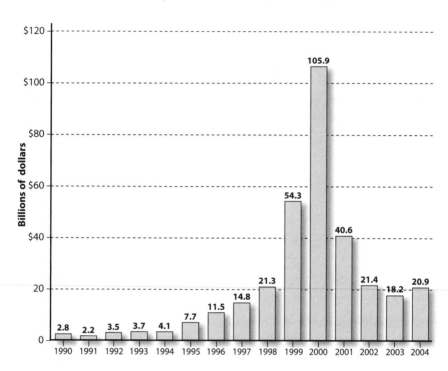

Source: Data from the MoneyTree™ Survey by PricewaterhouseCoopers, Thomson Venture Economics, and the National Venture Capital Association, March 28, 2005, http://www.nvca.org/ffax.html (accessed September 1, 2005).

much longer-term trend towards funding larger deals at later stages. Entrepreneurs generally raise venture capital through several rounds of financing tied to development milestones, increasing the valuation of the company with each round. Venture capital funds rarely provide early-stage seed and startup capital. Instead, they normally come into play once a company has a working prototype and initial orders from at least one customer. A typical first-round investment might be for $5 to $7 million, followed by a second round of $15 to $25 million and subsequent initial public offering. Venture capitalists often specialize in funding particular stages of a company's development, but in general, they tend to invest in companies that have the potential to generate at least $100 million in revenue within ten years.

This is a big change from when Robert Kuk, a long-time venture capitalist based in St. Louis, got started over twenty-five years ago. Kuk founded his first venture capital limited partnership in 1981 with three other partners, raising a fund of $20 million. Before the 1980s, venture capital was generally early-stage, high-risk capital. Funds averaged in the $4 to $5 million range and were raised mostly from wealthy individuals, with the fund managers generally making investments of $500,000 to $1.5 million. By the time Kuk started his fund, however, the size of the funds and their investment strategies were already changing. Federal regulations were relaxed to allow pension funds to invest in riskier assets, and by 2005 the average deal size was $7.3 million.

"When we raised the money for our first venture capital fund in 1981, our limited partners were mostly institutional investors. We did not have many individual limited partners," Kuk explains. "It was mostly pension funds and other institutional investors, so in general, we did not like to get involved in very early stage rounds of venture funding. We were a later-stage investor looking for growth situations. It was a more conservative investment strategy with less downside risk, but with significant upside potential in terms of return on your investment."

The growth of institutional investors in venture capital funds also pushed investment towards later-stage deals, simply because of the amount of money available. Venture capital funds have grown significantly in size over the years, so a $20 million fund would now be considered very, very small. When the managing partners have a bigger pool of money, it's easier to invest it in larger chunks than to enter into a number of smaller deals. The time horizon for generating a return on investment is also a critical issue.

"Time horizon is very important to venture capitalists," says Kuk. "They want to get into and out of a deal in three to ten years, depending on their investment strategy, and that is driven by the stage of the deal. If you go into a very early stage deal, generally you're looking at a longer investment cycle, and if you're looking at later-stage deals you should be looking at a shorter investment cycle. We always liked later-stage growth situations because they gave us an opportunity to cash out in three to five years as opposed to seven to ten years. I would guess that's probably the strategy with an increasing number of venture capital firms, having lived through the last few years of the dot-com bust."

Indeed, that's exactly what's been happening in the American venture capital community as of late. The economic growth America experienced during the 1990s was due, in great part, to a venture capital system that was efficiently funding promising new companies all the way from the startup phase to leveraged buy-outs. The bursting of the dot-com bubble changed all of that, however, and we now have the makings of a potential problem. In search of more stable returns, venture capitalists are investing less in early stage ventures, preferring to channel their money to investments requiring at least $5 million.[7] This has opened up a funding gap for early stage risk capital. While entrepreneurs can generally scrape together some initial capital, beyond that the potential to raise capital for early and mid-stage ventures is somewhat limited. The dearth of venture capital funding at the $500,000 to $5 million level could weaken our ability to nurture promising high-tech businesses into the kind of companies that create significant economic growth, profits, and jobs.

> The dearth of venture capital funding at the $500,000 to $5 million level could weaken our ability to nurture promising high-tech businesses.

Tom Anderson, director of the technology center at Automation Alley in Detroit, finds this to be one of the most significant challenges facing entrepreneurs today. "The gap between what friends, family and the entrepreneur himself can provide, and where venture capitalists are funding these days, is a significant problem. Venture capital has moved upstream, for a couple of reasons. First, the funds have gotten larger, so they're looking for larger opportunities because you can only manage so many investments at one time. Second, the limited partners have gotten a little more risk averse. The early stage venture capital firm that was funding technology coming directly from universities five years ago is now looking at companies that have started to generate a little bit of revenue, and the venture firms that were looking at early stage revenue companies are now looking at companies that are closer to breaking even. So the gap between what you can fund yourself and what can be professionally funded with growth capital is widening."

According to the annual MoneyTreeSurvey™ conducted by PricewaterhouseCoopers, Thomson Venture Economics and the National Venture Capital Association, funding for later-stage ventures increased almost 50 percent in 2004, reflecting a preference for later-stage deals. In total, 71 percent of all completed deals and 81 percent of all venture capital dollars went to expansion or later-stage investments.[8] This venture capital funding gap is a growing concern for high-tech entrepreneurs, and the question is, how does America increase the amount of venture capital funding being channeled to startups with high growth potential?

Angel Investors and Investor Networks

Equity financing is critical to fostering entrepreneurship, and the biggest challenge in financing the entrepreneurial economy is not providing access to credit for small businesses, but rather providing access to patient risk capital for high-growth ventures. The strength of the American venture capital system, particularly in Silicon Valley, is that it is a loose network where the active venture capital partners share information, are actively involved in businesses they fund, and are patient investors. The drawback to venture capital limited partnerships, while they have certainly provided a much greater pool of venture capital, is that they are less patient and more averse to risk. The fund managers must please their passive, limited partners, who in general have grown more cautious about investing in small high-tech companies. Their institutional investor clients are not focused on the long-term health of the American economy. They are more interested in achieving steady returns on their investment, and their patience for high volatility is somewhat limited.

While some venture capital funds focus on smaller, early stage investments, over the years it has increasingly fallen to individual "angel" investors to provide seed and startup funding. This is exactly what happened to Maxine Clark, the founder of Build-a-Bear Workshop, when she attempted to raise venture capital in 1996. At the time, venture capital was available in record amounts, but it was flowing primarily to Internet-based business opportunities. No one was interested in financing bricks-and-mortar stores where kids could make their own stuffed animals. Clark was forty-eight years old, had been president of Payless Shoe Source, and had twenty-four years of experience in retail. She'd created a well thought-out business plan and had invested her own money to open the first store. On paper, she should have been a venture capitalist's dream, but she found that raising outside capital wasn't so easy.

"Prior to starting Build-a-Bear Workshop, I'd only worked for large corporations, and I'd never had to worry about raising money at all," explains Clark. "In fact, I'd had no intention of using venture capital when I started the company, because I had my own money to invest. But I would talk to people and they would say, 'Why would you use your own money? You can go out and get venture capital.' So I started doing some research, talked to people, and got a few introductions. Unfortunately, at that time people were so hot on the Internet that they didn't want to talk to anyone about a bricks-and-mortar concept. Everyone thought that was going to go away, that malls were going to burn down or something. It was an interesting philosophy, that once women discovered shopping on the Internet they would never shop in malls again.

"Venture capital firms at that time were doing seed money, but they were just looking at Internet companies. Hundreds of millions of dollars were being given to startups, or to ideas that hadn't yet even been formulated. People were offering me jobs to run Internet businesses they had in their portfolios, they just weren't as willing to listen to my business idea. They couldn't understand why anyone would want to make their own stuffed animal. There's a misnomer that venture capital people are visionaries, but that's not necessarily true. They only take calculated risks, and if there are a lot of risks being thrown at them, they're kind of like lemmings. They all fly together. The venture capitalists who had traditionally developed retail businesses were devoting their attention to the Internet, and while some of the other more sophisticated companies that I talked to were interested, they didn't do seed money.

"I found it to be very discouraging, because so many people were talking negatively about bricks-and-mortar retail. So I decided I would just put my own money in, start the business, and worry about raising more when I wanted to expand and people could see the store as a reality. Then in July of 1997, a local business writer saw a sign at the mall that the first Build-a-Bear Workshop store would be opening soon, and she interviewed me and ran a story in the local business journal. It came out on a Friday, and that Friday afternoon I got a call from a local entrepreneur who owned a relatively large business. He said, 'You don't know who I am, but I read this article and I'd like to know more about your business. Could you meet with me on Monday?' So I met with him and he asked how much money I needed. I told him between $4 and $5 million for the next three to five stores, depending on how well they did and if that's the size we wanted to stay with, and he said, "Would next Thursday be soon enough?" He was truly an angel investor, and he continued to invest in future rounds of capital we raised for Build-a-Bear Workshop. He's still an investor today, continues to be part of our board, and is a good friend." Six months after the first store opened, it was so successful that traditional venture capitalists were lining up to invest, and by 2004 Build-a-Bear Workshop had become a public company with revenues of $302 million and a market capitalization of $464 million.

Clark's story is typical in that an angel investor, rather than a venture capital fund, provided her first source of outside financing, although he provided an unusually large amount of funding for a single investor. Unlike the fund managers from limited partnerships, angels invest on their own behalf, tend to be actively involved in the ventures they fund, and are not beholden to passive institutional investors. They also tend to be more patient with their investments and, as many are successful entrepreneurs, they have a personal interest in mentoring the next generation. For angel investors, such investments aren't just about making money, they're also about giving back to the community. Most invest locally or regionally, whereas institutional investors will put their money wherever they expect the highest return, whether that is in a company down the street or in Beijing.

The problem with relying on angel investors to fund early stage ventures is that for many, an investment of more than a few million dollars is beyond their individual means. The typical angel investor has an annual income of $90,000, a net worth of $750,000, and invests an average of $37,000 per venture.[9] As part of a formal angel investor network, however, they have the ability to fund much larger deals. Angels invested $22.5 billion in over 48,000 ventures in 2004, as opposed to venture capital funds, which invested $20.9 billion in 2876 deals.[10] By working together, angel investors have the ability to fill the funding gap and make the overall venture capital pipeline much more balanced and efficient. The question is how to encourage the growth of these networks.

One approach is to use tax credits. The Council on Competitiveness, for example, recommends creating a 25 percent tax credit for early stage investments of at least $50,000 made through qualified angel funds.[11] While tax credits are always welcome to investors, venture capitalist Robert Kuk isn't sure that reluctance to invest in small deals is the real problem. "If there's a good quality deal, it will get funded," he declares. "It might be by angel investors, it might be by venture capital firms, but there are a host of possibilities for finding venture funds. I think the driver is the quality of the deal. For an outstanding investment situation, there is money at the $1 to $5 million range the same as for $5 to $20 million. I wouldn't have any problem looking at $1 to $5 million deals if they present themselves, have great people, a great marketing concept, and a great product or service."

> Angel investors have the ability to fill the funding gap and make the overall venture capital pipeline much more balanced and efficient.

Tom Anderson, however, finds in his work at the Automation Alley Technology Center that local investor risk tolerance is also a factor. "In Michigan, the angel investment community is starting to fill the funding gap, but only very slowly. This is partly because a lot of the high net-worth individuals in the community haven't seen their portfolios rebound from the dot-com bubble the way they had hoped. It's also partly because for Michigan, and likely some other areas with large established businesses, many of the potential angel investors made the bulk of their money in pretty mature businesses. Maybe they ran a division for General Motors or Ford, or they operated a tier one supplier. The level of risk they assumed and became comfortable with was very different from that facing a startup business. While Michigan's early heritage was strongly entrepreneurial, the double-edged sword of successful business growth is that the executives of these very large companies have a preference for more stable investment opportunities."

Angel investor organizations are important because by pooling investment resources, they give new investors the opportunity to learn from more experienced investors, so they can avoid the major pitfalls and stumbling blocks associated with venture capital investing. In a group, there also tends to be better matching of entrepreneurs and investors, and performing due diligence is much more efficient than doing it individually. Angel investor networks have a lot of potential benefits for both investors and entrepreneurs, and they are crucial to supporting a robust innovation economy. There are now over two hundred angel investor organizations in the country, and as the word gets out about the funding gap, hopefully independent angel investors will band together and form even more.

Funding Women and Minority Entrepreneurs

Another major challenge America faces in fostering high-tech entrepreneurship is that it currently under-funds women and minority entrepreneurs. Women and minorities have made great strides over the past century, and the National Women's Business Council reports that most of the cultural, legal and structural barriers to accessing capital have been eliminated. Yet in practice, some access issues still exist, and the venture capital industry needs to take a serious look at how to channel funding to women and minorities more successfully.

Motivation for minority groups is certainly not the problem— African Americans are 50 percent more likely to start a business than their fellow white Americans, while Latinos are 20 percent more likely.[12] Meanwhile, the number of women-owned businesses is growing two-and-a-half times faster than the national average, and they are generating jobs at three times the national average.[13] Yet there are still significant inequalities when it comes to funding, particularly venture capital funding. Minorities receive only 2 percent of venture capital, while women receive about 4 percent.[14]

Is this discrimination? While the percentages are low, most venture capitalists say the problem is not that they won't fund women or minorities, but that women and minorities don't come to them for funding. "I would have no trouble investing in a business started by a woman or a minority," says Robert Kuk emphatically. "If there's an investment opportunity I like, I'm going to go for it. It doesn't matter to me who started the company. In fact, I don't know anyone in our industry who has decided not to invest in a business because it's run by a woman or a minority. I have never in all my years in venture capital heard anyone say that. The problem is that over the years I wasn't approached by many women or minorities looking for venture capital."

For venture capitalists, the key deciding factor is the quality of the deal—they're generally looking to fund ventures with high growth potential that have a proprietary technology. Investment decisions are made based on assessment of risk, which is determined by a variety of factors ranging from the entrepreneur's education, age, and managerial experience, as well as the size of the venture and the location of the business. Thus, the reasons women and minorities don't receive funding are far more complex than simple discrimination.

Amy Millman, president of Springboard Enterprises, is intimately familiar with these complexities. Springboard is a non-profit organization whose mission is to accelerate women's access to the equity markets, and as its president, Millman has seen first hand the challenges that women and minority entrepreneurs face. "It's like trying to walk into a casting director's office in Hollywood and saying, 'Hi, I'm here, cast me.' The chance of you getting an audition are slim and none, and that's exactly the way the venture capital industry is. It's a very small industry, there are probably only one thousand funds in this country. So when you look at that as an entrepreneur you think, 'How am I going to get in the door?' If you're a biochemist, how are you going to know anybody in the investment world? It's not your world, that's not what you went to school for, that's not where you built your career. You may be able to tell people about the intricacies of cell structure, but you don't really know how to raise capital. So why is it easier for men to raise capital than for women or minorities? Well, it's not that it's easier, it's hard for everyone. It's just that there are fewer women and minorities starting businesses that are attractive to investors. It takes time to build a career and a reputation in these fields, and a natural connector had not emerged for women and minorities until about five years ago."

One of the factors which often works against women and minorities is their choice of industry and business sector. About 70 percent of women and minority entrepreneurs start either service or retail businesses, and with the exception of high-tech services, these sectors are less attractive to venture capitalists than the computer, biotech, and communications sectors. The low participation of women and minorities in high growth potential sectors is a major reason why they don't receive more equity capital.

"What you have to understand is that venture capital is appropriate for only a very small percentage of all of the businesses in America. It is not and should not be for everybody," explains Millman. "Some people are very successful at growing companies using venture capital, because they understand what the impact on their business will be. On the other hand, some people go after venture capital when they shouldn't and they waste a lot of time. They hear about people raising all of this money and they think it's going to be easy, but it's the hardest, most expensive money you'll ever get. Venture capitalists are known for taking risks, but they're really a conservative group of people who are looking for a certain type of business and a certain type of management that will ensure a big return on their investment. You may be able to grow a successful service business that's worth hundreds of millions of dollars, but it's unlikely that you can achieve such growth in the short amount of time that investors expect to see a return."

Another factor working against women and minorities is that while they are slowly gaining access to seed and startup funding, they are less likely to receive later-stage capital for expansion and leveraged buy-outs. The reasons for this are unclear, although one possible explanation is that women and minorities are more likely to start a business due to a lack of satisfactory career opportunities and the desire to be their own boss. As a result, they are content to keep their businesses small and manageable, and are less willing to give up control. Thus, the fact that venture capitalists have started to concentrate on funding larger deals has worked against smaller businesses owned by women and minorities.

"I think a lot of the businesses that women start are typically smaller," says Maxine Clark. "Often they start out of their home, because one of the reasons they're starting businesses is to be able to have a family. So they really don't register in the venture capital wavelength, they're too small. Some of them eventually get there, and then the problem is often that they don't want to share. They're afraid someone is going to take the company away from them, or take advantage of them after they've worked so hard to create the business."

The control issue is crucial to both women and minorities. "A lot of business owners don't want to give up control," agrees Millman. "That's the basic issue driving whether you seek investment capital or not. For women and minorities, it used to be that those sources of investment and credit weren't available to you, regardless of whether you wanted it or not. Now they're available, and you have to ask yourself whether you want it. Say you have a company with growth potential that might be attractive to a venture capitalist, but you don't want to give up control, which will happen if you bring in investors. Taking on investors often necessitates giving up a significant amount of your equity in that company and in many cases majority control. It's like a marriage, and some entrepreneurs don't want that."

> The lack of equity capital going to women and minority entrepreneurs is due in large part to their lack of familiarity with the venture capital world.

Perhaps most importantly, the lack of equity capital going to women and minority entrepreneurs is due in large part to their lack of familiarity with the venture capital world. Funding is obtained through a web of networks and personal connections, forged through elite universities and corporations, by people who speak the language of business and finance. Fewer women and minorities are part of this world in the first place, so as entrepreneurs they come to the venture capital system as outsiders without the benefit of contacts they can leverage. Those already in the system generally have more business experience, connections, and assets, and thus they tend to propose more sophisticated business models that appeal to investors and have a better chance of success.

"It's very analogous to the whole supplier diversity issue," says Millman. "Forty years ago, when people realized that African Americans were not getting any supplier contracts because they were basically being discriminated against, the government decided it was time to create a program that would help open up the doors for this group. But it took twenty-five years for the programs to take hold and yield benefits for minority businesses. Similarly, it's really only been within the last thirty years that women have been pursing professional careers in any appreciable numbers. How many women scientists were there thirty years ago? How many women in technology? When you think about it, we're really talking about a very short time period. So how do you get into the networks if you're new at the game and there aren't many women on the investor side? It's very hard. I remember in the early 1990s, women would call me and tell me that banks wouldn't give them a loan unless their husband co-signed it. That was 1993, and that's not so very long ago. In the six years from 1998 until 2004, three hundred women-led businesses received venture capital, which is the same number that received venture capital in the thirty years leading up to 1998. We've come a long way, but making substantial progress in accessing venture capital may take a little longer."

A closely related issue is the lack of women and minority venture capitalists. Less than 10 percent of venture capitalists are women, and they've been leaving the industry twice as fast as men since the dot-com crash. African American and Latino venture capitalists are even rarer. "I think that's a big problem," declares Millman. "If you're sitting across a table and looking at a person, and that person looks nothing like you, has nothing in common with you, and you can't relate to them, are you going to want to invest with them? People invest in people that they feel comfortable and are familiar with, people that they have a connection with. If I'm an engineer, most likely I'm going to invest in other engineers. If I worked at Pfizer and you worked at Pfizer, most likely that's going to be appealing to me. If I went to Harvard and you went to Harvard, that's going to open doors. There are all kinds of ways that people make those connections, but without them, women and minorities simply have limited access to the informal angel and venture networks essential to raising business capital.

"Many times white men have a better opportunity to access equity capital simply because there are more investors in their personal networks. There aren't a whole lot of women and minorities in the investment world, so it's less likely that potential women and minority entrepreneurs will know investors. That's changing, but it's an evolutionary process, and it's been painfully slow to change. Women in particular were encouraged to go into the soft sciences or areas that were considered more acceptable for women, and not into finance or technology or engineering. Those are the areas that get venture capital, and if you don't have contacts in those fields, you're unlikely to get funding."

Fostering Access to Venture Capital

As more women and minorities pursue careers in finance, science, and engineering, their networks are growing and they are more likely to access risk capital. But the process is slow, and if America wants to foster greater innovation and entrepreneurship, we cannot afford to wait while we ignore this wealth of untapped potential. So how do we address this inequity? Should the venture capital industry adopt some form of affirmative action for women and minority entrepreneurs? For many years, the U.S. Small Business Administration has attempted to level the playing field for women and minorities in terms of accessing credit by offering specialized prequalification loan programs for seed and early stage capital. Businesses that are at least 51 percent owned by women or minorities, employ less than one hundred people, and have annual sales less than $5 million generally qualify for the special assistance, which offers loan packaging support and a pre-qualification form letter than can be used to help secure loans.

In many ways these programs have been helpful in opening up access to credit and debt financing for women and minority small business owners, but the SBA's approach does have some problems. For example, one of the areas where women- and minority-owned businesses distinctly lag behind their white male counterparts is in securing federal government contracts, so the government has made a point in recent years of using more minority- and female-owned suppliers. Unfortunately, the contracts they are awarded are often for products and services with razor-thin profit margins that existing suppliers have shied away from. In many cases, they are being awarded the table scraps the big dogs don't want.

In addition, the incentives and support offered to women and minority entrepreneurs also come with rules and conditions that become problematic down the road. In order to qualify as a minority-owned business, a minority entrepreneur must own 51 percent of the company, control the board, be the largest shareholder, and often employ a minority CEO. While the intent is to ensure that the business is really minority-owned, in effect these rules limit a minority entrepreneur's ability to raise capital from non-minority investors, hire the best-qualified executives, and take the company public. There are also succession rules that prevent minority owners from passing their business on to a child resulting from an ethnically mixed marriage who isn't considered to be a minority. These restrictions are a mistake.

One of the unique aspects of the venture capital and angel investor network approach is that it pairs promising entrepreneurial talent with seasoned managers and investors. Insisting on using minority investors and CEOs for minority businesses interferes with this crucial mentoring process. While the rule makes sense in theory, in practice it segregates women and minority entrepreneurs from the capital and expertise of non-minority investors, CEOs, and board members, keeping them out of the informal investment network rather than helping them gain greater access to it.

Trying to promote greater entrepreneurship among women and minorities by giving them a special status is ultimately ineffective, and does them no favors if it creates restrictions or lowers the bar to success. This allows businesses to be created that ultimately will not maximize their potential. What is needed is to create greater access, by bringing women and minorities into the venture capital network and letting them compete for capital on their own merit, which they are fully capable of doing. The key is not to give them a special status, but rather to equip them with the knowledge and the connections necessary to succeed in the venture capital world.

"The basic thing to understand is that women and minorities really haven't been in the professional world long enough to create a familiarity with, and an understanding of, the process," says Millman. "They haven't had time to own and grow significant size businesses that would be interesting to investors, and investors haven't had a lot of familiarity working with women and minority entrepreneurs. For example, in Washington DC, a lot of the area's investors came out of government. They worked for agencies like the Department of Defense, the Central Intelligence Agency, and the National Institutes of Health. A few decades ago, there weren't many women or minorities running programs at any of those agencies, and the relationships that were formed influence the type of investments those former officials are likely to make now that they are investors. The investors are mostly white men, and their colleagues were mostly white men. It is clear that the workforce is changing and that many talented women and minorities are taking the helm of federal departments and agencies. However, it will take some time before we see a change in investor behavior. It's just human nature."

Convincing women and minorities to take a risk and start their own businesses in some cases can be just as difficult. "A lot of women don't leave the laboratories or academic postings because, in many cases, they're the first woman in their family who has had a professional career," explains Millman. "Why would you take that big risk? A lot of African American women tell me that. They say, 'I'm the first one to graduate from college and now I've got this great career with an expense account, and you're asking me to leave it all and go start a business? Are you kidding me? My daughter can do that.' The women we work with at Springboard are in their thirties and forties, and have spent ten or twenty years going to school, building their professional careers and developing a marketable expertise. They are very attractive to corporate recruiters, so by choosing entrepreneurship, they're making a bold move."

In making this bold move, one of the key success factors for entrepreneurs is developing the business acumen and confidence that comes from knowing they have the skill set to succeed. Rather than providing a protected environment for women and minority entrepreneurs, we should provide them with the educational opportunities they need in order to compete and succeed in the global marketplace. Also, we need to educate the investment community as to the success of women- and minority-owned businesses in order to overcome any biases against these groups. Capitalizing women and minority entrepreneurs makes good business sense, and as investors come to realize this, capital will flow to women and minority-owned businesses naturally. To do this, we need to generate greater access. The venture capital industry in general, and the angel investor network in particular, is all about connections. Like a 1920s speakeasy, you need to know at least one person who has the password and can get you in the door.

What is needed is a forum to bring investors and promising women and minority entrepreneurs together, an approach that has in fact been tried with great success by Springboard Enterprises, which holds periodic venture capital forums for women-led companies. Women running emerging growth businesses apply to be part of the forum, and around twenty to twenty-five applicants are selected and coached on how best to present their business opportunity to investors. The forum eventually culminates in a showcase for investors, and great emphasis is placed on networking and fostering relationships. The program has been extremely successful, as the women who presented their companies at the fourteen Springboard Forums held since 2000 have raised over $3 billion dollars in venture, angel, and corporate investments for their businesses.

"We started our program because we wanted to increase investment in women-led firms by introducing investors to women entrepreneurs," says Millman. "When we started Springboard, venture capitalists would tell us they don't really care about the entrepreneur's race or gender, they just evaluate whether the company fits their investment profile and is a good deal. But they admitted they rarely saw business plans or had meetings with companies that were founded or led by women, and so they assumed there weren't many women running companies that would fit their investment criteria. We decided to fill the deal pipeline with women-led ventures and developed a means to foster relationships for these women with investors."

> **What is needed is a forum to bring investors and promising women and minority entrepreneurs together.**

Springboard Enterprises is an important organization which recognizes that many of the barriers women and minorities face in getting capital are due to a lack of communication and access. Information, coaching, and networking are critical to breaking down these barriers, as entrepreneurs need to learn what sources of funding are available and how to effectively communicate with potential investors. By doing so, we can develop the networks necessary to capitalize a much greater percentage of women and minority entrepreneurs.

The Threat of Investment Capital Migration

While we search for ways to make venture capital available to a broader range of entrepreneurs, we also need to be concerned with how that capital is invested. In the past, venture capital that was invested in American businesses tended to produce jobs and wealth in the United States. As globalization progresses, however, that is changing. A key element of the globalization agenda over the past several decades has been the liberalization of financial and capital markets. This involved the removal of national restrictions on the free flows of capital so investors could easily move their money into and out of various countries. Through the International Monetary Fund, the United States has encouraged foreign governments to eliminate restrictions on investing abroad, allow their currencies to float so their value is determined by the market, and promote financial transparency so investors can more easily determine the health of the economy. The argument is that these measures promote stability and attract more direct foreign investment in developing nations, and the United States has largely succeeded in pushing this agenda. As a result, investors have increasingly put their money into foreign ventures, particularly in emerging countries.

What is good for the investor class, however, isn't necessarily good for American entrepreneurs. Increasing investment overseas leads to capital migration, which leaves less venture capital available to support new American ventures. While direct foreign investment by American multinationals is generally long-term, much of the push for liberalization of capital markets is motivated by the desire of private investors to speculate rather than invest for the long term in productive assets, and speculation is generally counterproductive. At best, it enriches those who are already wealthy without doing anything to create jobs or meaningful economic growth. At worst, it induces financial panics, like the Asian banking crisis in 1987, that can cripple economies and destroy massive amounts of wealth.

After World War II, the primary method of directing international capital flows was through foreign aid, but since the liberalization of capital markets in the 1970s, the most important methods have become foreign direct investment by multinationals and private portfolio investment through capital markets. For several decades, the United States has been both the biggest provider and recipient of direct foreign investment by multinational corporations, and following the passage of the North American Free Trade Agreement, our share of world direct investment grew rapidly. At its peak in 1999, the United States provided $224.9 billion of direct foreign investment, and we received almost as much. Since the bursting of the dot-com bubble, however, our share of world direct investment has plummeted. The United States still provides the most direct foreign investment, yet we received only $39.9 billion in 2003, the smallest inflow in over a decade.[15] We are now only the third largest recipient of direct foreign investment, having fallen behind both India and China. Going forward, it is by no means assured that the United States will continue to be the preferred place to invest, especially if China and India continue to grow and provide more lucrative deals.

> Since the bursting of the dot-com bubble, the world has invested less in the United States and more in emerging markets.

Since the bursting of the dot-com bubble, the world has invested less in the United States and more in emerging markets, and over time this may make it harder for American entrepreneurs and entrepreneurial firms to obtain capital. This trend has been reflected in private portfolio investment as well, which has emerged as an important conduit for capital flows to developing countries. There was a huge increase in net foreign portfolio investment in developing countries in the early 1990s, particularly in Asia where it grew from $1 billion in the late 1980s to $25 billion in 1993.[16] Much of this was the result of the growth of institutional investors, as their diversification strategies led them to invest in emerging markets. As the U.S. stock market boomed in the late 1990s, however, a tremendous amount of portfolio investment poured into the United States. Since the crash, the trend has reversed once again, and portfolio investors are now investing more heavily in emerging markets. Total foreign portfolio investment by American investors reached $72.3 billion in 2003, while net equity capital inflows to U.S. companies declined for the third consecutive year to $62.2 billion.[17]

Private investors are the primary source of entrepreneurial capital in the United States, and if we are going to rely on them to fund high-growth ventures, we need a tax policy that encourages private investors to invest here in the United States. The key to maintaining a strong and innovative economy is for investors to continue investing domestically in order to develop the leading-edge technologies, companies, and industries of the future. While keeping capital gains and corporate tax rates low is a start, this does not necessarily help to direct the flow of investment capital to ventures that specifically benefit America and create American jobs. An angel investor may use his capital gains to buy a yacht rather than invest in a startup. A corporation may use its tax break to build a new plant in China rather than investing in research and development. Overseas competition for investment dollars is increasing, and if markets overseas are perceived to be more lucrative than markets in the United States, capital will flow overseas.

As of yet, this is not a significant problem, because venture capitalists and angel investors have a tendency to invest close to home. Angel investors in particular like to fund businesses within a day's drive of their home base, as they like to be actively involved, and many of the smaller and mid-sized venture capital funds share this philosophy as well. As Robert Kuk notes, however, "There's nothing more mobile than a venture capitalist's dollar. If you're convinced there's a good deal, even though you may like to invest in your backyard, you will get on a plane and fly to meetings half way across the country to do that deal. So the mobility of the venture capital dollar is a fact of life. Everyone likes to have deals within fifty miles of their office, and there's a lot to be said for doing that, but every once in a while you swing the bat at something that's not in your back yard."

The big venture capital funds in Silicon Valley and New York City, however, are doing much more than occasionally swinging their bats at opportunities in emerging markets. According to a study by *USA*

Today, venture capitalists on the coasts are increasingly investing in micro-multinationals—young, growing firms that employ offshore employees and have global business strategies. The newspaper's study of 106 software firms that received venture capital after 1999 found that 40 percent employed engineers, marketers, analysts, and other white collar employees in India and other foreign countries.[18] These jobs aren't counted as offshored because they were never in the United States in the first place, and because most of the firms are still privately owned. Yet the impact is the same, for there are fewer jobs being created to offset the ones lost to automation, consolidation, and offshoring.

Interestingly, it's the venture capitalists, rather than the entrepreneurs, who appear to be driving this trend, insisting on a global strategy as a condition for funding. A survey by Deloitte & Touche and the National Venture Capital Association found that 20 percent of U.S. venture capitalists expect to increase their global investments over the next five years.[19] Although for now they plan to sustain their investments in the United States, there is no guarantee this will continue. Capital moves towards opportunity, so if America wants to ensure that capital flows towards domestic entrepreneurial ventures, we need to provide the appropriate incentives.

> Capital moves towards opportunity, so if America wants to ensure that capital flows towards domestic entrepreneurial ventures, we need to provide the appropriate incentives.

One way to do this is through tax credits, but we need to use highly targeted credits that encourage desired outcomes, such as job creation and investment in research and development. Otherwise, tax credits simply erode the overall tax base, which is needed to support public education, worker retraining, and basic research.

Our first priority should be to give tax credits to investors who, either as angels or limited venture capital partners, invest in small entrepreneurial companies in the United States. We need to make it financially more attractive to invest here than overseas, effectively creating a higher capital gains tax rate for foreign investment as opposed to domestic investment. This will help discourage capital flight. Particular attention needs to be given to closing the venture capital funding gap by rewarding investors for funding early stage and expansion stage ventures with capital needs in the range of $500,000 to $5 million.

Secondly, we need to offer personal and corporate tax credits that reward entrepreneurs and business owners for reinvesting capital into their business rather than taking it out as profit or income. While some argue that by buying a boat, sports car, or other luxury goods the wealthy are stimulating demand, which creates jobs, it doesn't necessarily create jobs here in America, as an increasing number of products are being manufactured overseas. The use of capital that is most beneficial to America as a whole is to invest it in small, high-tech businesses that are creating jobs here in the United States, and tax credits granted specifically for creating jobs would help to align the interests of entrepreneurs and employees.

Third, we need to eliminate any tax loopholes and credits that unintentionally provide an incentive to American companies to outsource jobs overseas, such as the tax deferment companies receive on foreign income. Instead, there should be a deferment for income that is generated overseas only if it is repatriated and invested back in the United States. On the flip side, we need to tax all profits earned in the United States by foreign investors and corporations before allowing them to expatriate earnings back to their home countries. If people invest and make money in the United States, some of the earnings should flow back into the American economy rather than being taken completely out of the country. Of course, in response, foreign nations may increase their tax on profits earned by U.S. companies operating in their countries. In adjusting the tax code, we have to be careful not to create a tax structure that makes it more difficult for American companies to compete internationally, as this would hurt

U.S. manufacturing. The key is to use tax credits to develop human capital, encourage research and development, and maintain our ability to create leading-edge technologies.

The use of tax incentives can be tricky. Politicians have a habit of using tax credits and other exemptions as a way of rewarding their constituencies, or as backdoor subsidies to prop up failing local industries. Used this way, tax credits amount to little more than corporate welfare. Nevertheless, it is the best tool we have to help direct the flow of investment capital, and if incentives are structured properly, capital will flow to the best opportunities as with any other efficient market.

The American venture capital system is strong and is likely to remain so for quite some time, as it generates two-thirds of all the venture capital in the world.[20] To retain our status as an economic superpower, however, American capital has to be invested in American businesses in a way that creates jobs domestically rather than overseas. Venture capital can dry up quickly in a bear market—the amount of available venture capital dropped sharply after the Internet bubble burst, and as a result Silicon Valley is competing more and more with tech clusters in places like Bangalore, Tel Aviv, and Seoul for American venture capital. While investing internationally is good for the global economy, there is a temptation for investors to seek out big returns in emerging markets while neglecting to invest in growing businesses at home. In the big picture, retaining a sufficient amount of venture capital in the United States is critical to fostering an innovative, entrepreneurial economy at home.

6

THE CATALYST OF INNOVATION—
INTELLECTUAL PROPERTY RIGHTS

◇◇

Eli Whitney is best remembered as the inventor of the cotton gin, but while his invention changed the fortunes of many Southern planters, it did little to enrich Whitney himself. After graduating from Yale in 1793, Whitney traveled south to make his living as a tutor. At the time, Southern plantation owners were struggling to make a profit—the tobacco they had relied upon was wearing out the soil, the indigo market had collapsed, and no other crop had proven as profitable without Britain as an export market. While cotton had potential, the short-staple variety that grew in the South had seeds that were sticky and difficult to separate from the cotton fibers. While a field hand could pick fifty pounds of cotton in one day, it took twenty-five days to separate the seeds from that much cotton.

Whitney heard repeatedly about this problem as he traveled south, and it was generally agreed that if a machine could be invented to process short-staple cotton, it would revive the Southern economy and make the inventor extraordinarily wealthy. At the urging of his friends, Whitney mulled over the problem and soon drafted a plan for a machine that would solve it. His fellow Yale alumnus Phineas Miller financed the building of a prototype and, abandoning his plans to become a tutor, Whitney turned his whole attention to the project.

Within ten days, Whitney built a cotton gin that was simple and ingenious. He made a hand-cranked drum cylinder studded with hook-shaped wires that rotated past a wire sieve containing the cotton. The hooks caught the cotton fibers and pulled them through the sieve, while leaving the seeds behind. A rotating brush then swept the cotton fibers off of the hooks. With this new machine, a single laborer could process as much cotton in a day as ten people working by hand; a water-powered or horse-driven model could equal the work of fifty men. Whitney and Miller resolved to go into business together manufacturing cotton gins and applied for a patent on the invention.

Unfortunately for Whitney, his invention was so mechanically simple, and the need for it was so great, that it was being pirated before he could even obtain the patent. News of the machine had spread like wildfire, and Whitney's workshop was broken into and raided. Soon cotton was being planted in huge quantities throughout the South, and Whitney couldn't manufacture gins fast enough to meet demand. The design was so straightforward that the farmers simply built their own, without a single penny being paid in royalties.

Whitney turned to the courts to enforce his patent rights, but a loophole in the wording of the patent law, and the fact that most of the courts were in Cotton Country, led juries to rule in the planters' favor. The cost of the legal battles drove Whitney and Miller deeply into debt, and desperate for cash, they agreed to license the patent to various state governments. South Carolina offered $50,000, of which it paid only $20,000. North Carolina levied a tax of 6 percent on every gin in the state for a period of five years and gave Whitney and Miller the proceeds, amounting to a total of $30,000. Tennessee followed suit with another $10,000. In total, their licensing royalties amounted to around $90,000, which barely covered their expenses and the cost of litigation. To add insult to injury, the states then repudiated their agreements in 1803 and demanded the money back. By that time, Southern planters were making nearly $10 million in profit annually from cotton; Whitney, for all of his trouble, was penniless. Only when he gave up

*on the cotton gin and started manufacturing rifles with interchangeable
parts did he finally make his fortune.*

If you want to have an innovative economy, you have to have
incentives for people to innovate, and some of the most effective
incentives are intellectual property rights. Innovation requires
considerable investment of both time and money in research and
development, and if a competitor can simply copy one's invention,
it is hard to recoup your investment and earn a profit. This insight is
what led to the development of intellectual property rights such as
patents, copyrights, and trademarks. By granting the inventor some
form of exclusivity, at least for a limited time period, intellectual
property rights block the ability of competitors to gain a free ride
from others' development efforts. This encourages more people to
innovate, providing a catalyst for entrepreneurship.

Unfortunately, granting intellectual property rights has its
drawbacks as well, especially in the case of patents. They create
limited monopolies, which can be harmful to consumers, and patents
that are too broad lead to unfair competitive advantages. They also
encourage secrecy amongst scientists and inventors, making them
reluctant to share research before winning a patent. This slows the
dissemination of knowledge and sometimes works against the public
good. There's also the temptation to use intellectual property rights
to collect rents in the form of licensing fees, rather than using them
productively to create new products, jobs, and economic growth.

In a knowledge economy, intellectual property rights are incredibly
valuable and important, more so now than ever before. In a world
where knowledge is power, owning the rights to a particular piece
of knowledge can be extremely profitable, and the United States has
fought hard to protect its intellectual property rights in the face of
piracy from nations that have never had or respected such protections.
At the same time, changes in the patent law at home and the increasing
complexity of inventions has led to a rash of extremely broad patents

and predatory litigation. There is a worldwide intellectual property gold rush going on with people claiming exclusive rights to everything from witty sayings to mice, and companies must negotiate a rapidly growing number of license agreements in order to bring new products to market.

Currently, much of the world's knowledge is being carved up and assigned ownership just as if it were real, physical property. Within a few decades, there may be only a few repositories of knowledge left in the public domain. Already, more than 85 percent of the price of a product such as a semiconductor goes to pay for design and engineering services, patents, and copyrights.[1] The remainder has to cover everything from the cost of raw materials and traditional labor to distribution and marketing, leaving very little for profit. The problem of how to enforce our intellectual property rights abroad, while preserving the repository of public knowledge at home, deserves our utmost attention. If we allow the world to steal our ideas there will be less of an incentive to innovate, and that would be disastrous for the American economy.

The Development of Patents and Intellectual Property Rights

One of the critical developments that allowed entrepreneurship to flourish in the United States was the establishment of patent and copyright law. The foundation for entrepreneurship stems from the individual's right to retain a meaningful portion of the wealth they create, and the history of invention tracks closely the development of the rule of law and governance that led to individual freedoms such as patent protection.

"The development of the rule of law was extremely important to fostering innovation and entrepreneurship," says Dr. Charles McManis, a world-recognized legal scholar and intellectual property law professor at Washington University in St. Louis. "If you didn't have a rule of law to put some restraints on what a non-innovator can do with an innovator's invention, piracy would result. For example, you need a rule of law to honor contracts so that an innovator can hire employees and contractually oblige them not to share trade secrets or use inventions for their own interest. That's just one example of how the rule of law has been enormously important."

The development of the rule of law and intellectual property rights has been a long and slow evolution. In medieval times, patent rights, such as they existed, were awarded by the sovereign. The grant of exclusive rights monopolies were often used as a substitute for taxes, which were always difficult to collect, and many European rulers used this system. Monopolies were granted in various industries, such as mining and textiles, to favored members of the aristocracy or merchant class. In some cases, the granting of these monopolies was linked to the development of a particular innovation. In general, however, patent law as we know it today did not exist, and most individuals had little reason to innovate as there was no potential to gain personal profit from an invention.

> The foundation for entrepreneurship stems from the individual's right to retain a meaningful portion of the wealth they create.

The first known law that granted exclusive ownership rights specifically to inventors was enacted in Venice in 1474. After a long war with the Turks, Venice lost most of its trading empire in the Eastern Mediterranean.[2] The city was forced to turn to manufacturing to revitalize its economy, and as trade continued to weaken, it adopted laws prohibiting emigration of skilled artisans and the export of critical materials. As the strength of the European monarchies slowly started to subside, the rule of law and individual ownership rights gradually began to take root.

A significant breakthrough occurred in 1624 when the English Parliament passed the Statute of Monopolies. The statute allowed monopolies only in industries that were new to the country and the direct result of a new innovation, and even then only for a limited period of fourteen years. While the main purpose of this law was to restrict the power of the sovereign to grant exclusive rights monopolies, it also served to protect the rights of inventors. In general, the purpose of the English law was to encourage the development of new inventions for the benefit of society as a whole. The French system, developed later, placed more of an emphasis on the right of the individual inventor to profit from their invention. In both cases, however, it was clearly an improvement over the sovereign-controlled exclusive rights system.

As the rule of law was refined to protect individuals' rights and democracy began to take root, innovation increased dramatically. Many significant inventions were developed throughout the 1600s including the microscope, telescope, blast furnace, mercury thermometer, and precursors to the power loom and the bicycle. There was a major shift in motivation for the individual, and the entrepreneurial innovation engine began to sputter, then to chug, and then to run. By the end of the seventeenth century, developments in the rule of law in Europe had finally progressed to the point where they had enabled a connection between inventions and the availability of capital.

By the time the United States of America was founded, intellectual property rights were firmly established in the Western world. From the beginning, the U.S. government recognized the importance of entrepreneurship and innovation to the economic development of the country, and established laws to help support it. The United States Patent Act was passed in 1790, and was one of the earliest American laws relating specifically to innovation and the right of ownership. The drafting of this law is attributed largely to then Secretary of State Thomas Jefferson, who defined what was patentable as being "any new and useful art, machine, manufacture or composition of matter."[3] Congress also passed the Copyright Act in 1790 as well, giving authors, scientists, and artists the exclusive right to publish their work for a period of fourteen years, which over time has been extended to the life of the author plus seventy-five years. Interestingly, Jefferson was initially opposed to these measures because he disliked the idea of even limited monopolies, but he was eventually won over by the argument that it was the best way to encourage innovation and disseminate ideas. Even so, he never sought to patent any of his own inventions, considering them to be for the good of the public.

Thanks to the establishment of patents and intellectual property rights, the pace of innovation accelerated steadily throughout the first half of the 1800s, and then skyrocketed after the Civil War. The total number of patents registered in the United States went from just 36,000 before 1860 to 640,000 in the four decades after,[4] as the ability to patent and profit from one's invention made innovation and entrepreneurship much more attractive. The evolution of intellectual property rights explains why entrepreneurship in America took firm root at the end of the eighteenth century and blossomed throughout the nineteenth century. The result was to instigate over two hundred years of massive economic growth.

As this graph shows, the pace of both patent applications and grants has accelerated significantly over the last twenty years. Why has this occurred? While there are many reasons, two changes in particular

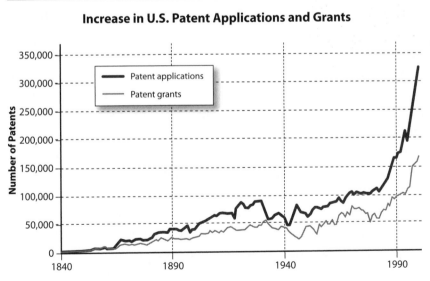

Increase in U.S. Patent Applications and Grants

Source: Reprinted by permission from Ken Harrington, the Skandalaris Center for Entrepreneurial Studies. Data from the U.S. Patent Office.

have happened over the last thirty years to spur the acceleration of patent grants in the United States.

One is the creation of the U.S. Court of Appeals for the Federal Circuit in 1982, a semi-specialized court that has subject matter jurisdiction over patent and trademark cases. It reviews the decisions of the more generalist federal district trial courts, and also provides guidance through published opinions. This has resulted in more consistent and predictable rulings, and a higher level of certainty about what rulings might be anticipated. Since the establishment of these appellate courts, patent law has been redefined to include business process patents, which allow individuals and businesses to receive patents for processes or methods that are unique and new. This was a significant change in the law, one that recognized a broad new type of knowledge and invention in a world that is becoming more driven by software and business process improvements. The courts have also ruled that it is legal to patent biological life forms such as genetically altered plants and animals, and these changes led to a sharp increase in the number of patent applications and grants.

The second significant change was the passage of the Bayh-Dole University and Small Business Patent Act in 1980. The purpose of the act was to strengthen the connection between academia and industry by granting universities the right to retain control of intellectual property resulting from federally funded research. It supported the negotiation of exclusive licenses between universities and private enterprise regarding such rights, in the hopes that this would result in increased technology transfer between university laboratories and industry, ultimately resulting in greater commercialization.

Before the passage of the Bayh-Dole Act, university scientists would often spend years refining and improving new discoveries because there was very little incentive to commercialize them. Over the past three decades, however, commercialization of university research has increased significantly, as the passage of the act spurred more patent filings and attention to intellectual property by universities and government research entities. The Bayh-Dole Act also began an evolution of relationships and dialog that better connected researchers, entrepreneurs, and mature companies in a chain of relationships that accelerated commercialization. As a result of this act and the creation of the specialized district courts, more than 300,000 patent applications are now being filed in the United States annually, three times as many as in the 1970s. These changes are a prime example of the systemic improvement that takes place in a culture that benefits from, and has the infrastructure to support, intellectual property rights.

The Growing Piracy Threat

While the American intellectual property system has been continually evolving, it is not keeping up with the tremendous challenges posed by globalization and the digital age. Theft of American intellectual property is rampant—in the first half of 2004 there was a 60 percent increase in arrests in the United States for intellectual property rights crimes.[5] Piracy and counterfeiting have increased markedly over the last five years, and protection of intellectual property rights in foreign countries varies greatly, posing many difficulties for American entrepreneurs who do business overseas.

America's biggest export is intellectual capital in the form of royalties and licensing fees; at our peak in 1999 we exported $37 billion worth of intellectual property.[6] The theft of this intellectual property, including patented industrial products as well as copyrighted material and even trademarks, is a significant threat. For example, the copyright industries—which include motion pictures, music, books, and software—generate 6 percent of our gross domestic product, 4 percent of American jobs, and over $89 billion in exports and foreign sales.[7] Yet the International Intellectual Property Alliance estimates that in 2004, the United States lost $12.5 billion in trade due to copyright piracy, with piracy rates for DVDs and business software over 90 percent in countries like China and Ukraine.[8] After adding in piracy of patented products like pharmaceuticals, the Alliance estimates that piracy accounts for 7 percent of global trade and is costing American businesses between $200 and $250 billion a year in lost revenue.[9]

"Piracy is a big problem," agrees professor Charles McManis, "although I should qualify that statement by noting that a lot of American intellectual property owners will give you outrageous figures for how much they're 'losing' on intellectual property piracy. The figures assume that for every pirated copy, they could sell a legitimate copy. But the reality is that the reason so much pirating is going on is because in a lot of developing countries they can't afford to pay the price for a legitimate copy. The actual amount of loss is very speculative, because it turns on how many legitimate copies would in fact be purchased if there was no piracy going on. Companies are trying to argue that without piracy, their revenues would be X amount higher. How do you prove that? It's very difficult, and unfortunately the federal government too often takes at face value private industry's cost estimates for what the price tag for piracy is. It assumes that poor people in developing countries would cheerfully pay $12 for a CD if they couldn't get it illegitimately for fifty cents, and that's just not going to happen every time. When it comes to software, on the other hand, that's a more plausible argument. People who are wealthy enough to own a computer are wealthy enough to at least pay something for software. There are definitely some legitimate concerns, but still, you've got to question how realistic the cost estimates of piracy are when we don't really know who could afford to pay what."

Piracy amounts to 7 percent of global trade and is costing American businesses between $200 and $250 billion a year in lost revenue.

Piracy isn't just a cost issue, however. It is also a safety issue, because world piracy goes far beyond downloading music, sharing software, or buying bootlegged DVDs. Foreign pirates also counterfeit American products and not only sell them abroad, but export lower priced products directly back to the United States. In 2003, the U.S. Department of Homeland Security confiscated $90 million worth of pirated goods from countries like China, Russia, Brazil, India, and Pakistan. The goods being counterfeited include products that potentially pose a danger to consumer safety such as pharmaceuticals (the World Health Organization estimates that 10 percent of medicines sold worldwide are fake).[10] As Tom Davis, the Chairman of the U.S. House Committee on Government Reform, noted in a hearing during September 2004:

> If the markets for U.S. goods derived from intellectual property are to be sustained and expanded, our products must be adequately protected in every market where they are found. Otherwise, jobs will be lost, not only the jobs of executives or movie stars or recording artists, but also technicians, carpenters, factory workers, and retailers. Moreover, consumer safety will also be in jeopardy if knock-off goods such as airplane, ship, auto parts, or consumer products get into the mainstream of commerce and fail to perform as expected. Incentives to stimulate and encourage innovation will also be diminished, as capital necessary to foster this creativity will be lost to illegitimate interests . . . Our copyright, patent, and trademark laws protect intellectual property domestically, but foreign intellectual property laws are often either totally lacking or woefully inadequate to protect legitimate U.S. intellectual property interests.[11]

As the technical production capacity of developing nations has increased, so has piracy, for when combined with cheap labor, high technology lowers the cost of producing counterfeit goods. Thanks to the Internet and increasingly sophisticated digital imaging technology, counterfeiters can reverse engineer products and recreate the brand logos, packaging, and even catalogs of American retailers, making their products virtually indistinguishable from the real products, or tweaking them just enough to avoid infringement lawsuits. The problem is particularly bad in China, which is now responsible for two-thirds of global piracy. Some of the larger Chinese electronics companies actually have internal groups dedicated to reverse engineering global market-leading products, and many of the smaller firms that American companies outsource their manufacturing to have no qualms about producing knock-offs as well.

The manufacture of golf clubs is a case in point. Almost all of the major American golf club manufacturers now outsource most of their manufacturing to China, but with the cost savings has come an increased risk of piracy. In less than a week, a top-selling golf club can be reverse engineered by a Chinese tooling company, and it can be mass produced and sold back in the United States within two months. Photographs are digitally sent to tooling factories in China, which have computer programs that convert them into three-dimensional images used to create master clubs. They are then mass produced by Chinese laborers who work twelve-hour days, seven days a week, and do not have benefits like paid vacation days or workers' compensation. Many of the clubs are flown into Canada and then trucked into the United States, or are shipped to an intermediate country that is not known for piracy. Eventually, they are sold in America, either as counterfeits or under private labels, for 25 percent or more off the regular price.

Even Chinese firms who as contractors perform tooling and manufacturing of legitimate clubs are often a source of piracy due to theft. A master club created by a Chinese tooling company can go for $10,000 on the black market, and thus the benefits of piracy for the average Chinese worker, who makes less than $100 a month, far outweigh the risks.[12] As a result, piracy rates in China are truly staggering. An estimated 90 percent of business software in China is pirated, and the country leads the world in producing and exporting counterfeit software. Yet China has failed to outlaw the unauthorized used of software in business and government organizations. Piracy of movies is as high as 95 percent, and while raids and seizures are on the rise, the fines are so low that pirates simply dismiss them as a cost of doing business. Piracy rates of music and entertainment software are similarly out of control at 85 and 90 percent respectively, and the Chinese government is doing little in response.[13] It has utterly failed to comply with the commitment it made in 2004 to the Joint Commission on Commerce and Trade to significantly reduce piracy rates.

This is a serious problem for American entrepreneurs, as the extent to which promising new technologies are fully realized is a function of return on investment, and piracy seriously increases the risk and reduces the potential return. Protecting intellectual property is now the number one concern for American companies who establish joint ventures in China, for the more we outsource to China, the more counterfeiting occurs. In fact, the problem has become so pervasive that some firms have started to consider moving their operations out of China to countries like Mexico and Eastern Europe. Relocating, however, is no guarantee of protection, for China is certainly not the only country guilty of piracy. Over fifty countries are on the International Intellectual Property Association's watch list, with Russia, Brazil, India, Pakistan, and Ukraine joining China as the worst offenders.

Theoretically, the United States should be able to exert pressure on these countries, or at least those that are members of the World Trade Organization (WTO), to address the piracy issue. Under an annex to the WTO charter known as Trade Related Aspects of Intellectual Property Rights (TRIPs), all WTO members must enforce minimum intellectual property standards and give equal treatment to foreign intellectual property holders; otherwise, the WTO can authorize trade sanctions. There are also several treaties which have been negotiated through the United Nation's World Intellectual Property Organization that have helped raise these standards. Unfortunately, the organization has no enforcement mechanism, and in most cases the problem isn't the lack of standards but rather the enforcement of those standards. Even when apprehended, the punishment for pirating often constitutes little more than a slap on the wrist, as Eric Smith, the president of the International Intellectual Property Alliance, noted in a report to the U.S. Senate Judiciary Subcommittee on Intellectual Property in May of 2005:[14]

> Rampant piracy in most of the countries highlighted in this report constitutes the copyright industries' greatest barrier to trade, costing U.S. jobs and contributions to the U.S. economy. This subcommittee is aware that part of this damage is due to inadequate laws on the books in some countries, including effective legal protection for copyrighted material transmitted over the Internet. Today, however, unlike in the 1980s and 1990s, the problem has less to do with inadequate laws and more with ineffective and non-deterrent enforcement systems.

Recognizing that enforcement is the critical issue, the White House has created a Strategy Targeting Organized Piracy (STOP) campaign, touted as a comprehensive effort to stop the trade in pirated goods. The plan is to update United States intellectual property statutes and strengthen criminal penalties here in the United States, as well as working with foreign governments on enforcement issues. The U.S. Department of Homeland Security has already conducted a joint enforcement action with China that resulted in the seizure of 210,000 pirated DVDs early in 2004, but this was a drop in the bucket that had little substantive impact.[15]

The real problem is that developing countries have very little incentive to enforce intellectual property rights because they don't create much intellectual property themselves and have few recognizable brand names. While trade sanctions may pressure them to cooperate with the United States, they often don't have the financial resources for effective enforcement. Developing nations also have problems enforcing intellectual property rights because their citizens are new to the concept and don't agree with it. In China, for example, intellectual property rights are only twenty years old, and many Chinese citizens see piracy as benefiting consumers. In fact, there are numerous towns throughout the developing world, particularly in China and Pakistan, where the local economy is completely based around counterfeiting products like Prada handbags or Callaway golf clubs. If the government shuts down these operations, entire towns will be put out of work.

Unless these places can create legitimate, well-paying jobs, piracy will undoubtedly continue.

This is a problem with no easy solution, as economic studies have found that trade sanctions are not a sufficient deterrent and only result in trade distortions unrelated to the original issue. There are also legitimate debates as to how intellectual property protection should be structured. For example, India has traditionally protected the process by which drugs are made, while the United States protects the content, a difference that reflects India's preference for keeping the cost of drugs low while the United States prefers to foster breakthrough innovation. The application and interpretation of intellectual property laws is not an open-and-shut case, as the debate over Napster and peer-to-peer file sharing has shown. Moral standards regarding this issue vary widely within the United States, and even more so internationally.

The real problem is that developing countries have very little incentive to enforce intellectual property rights because they don't create much intellectual property themselves.

To some extent, globalization should help to force compromise and agreement on standards. Countries like India and Brazil, which in the past had largely isolated domestic economies, are now opting into the global economy and have more to lose from trade sanctions. Taiwan, for example, used to be a hotbed of piracy, but is now less of a threat, because thanks to globalization its economy is prospering. As the Taiwanese people's standard of living has risen, they have started creating their own intellectual property, and with that has come respect for intellectual property rights. Eventually, China is likely to undergo the same transformation, but in all likelihood this simply means that counterfeiting will move elsewhere. As long as there are developing countries where technological expertise runs ahead of the standard of living and property rights, there will continue to be piracy.

Patent Wars

Given how important it is for the United States to be the world leader in innovation, it is only natural there has been pressure to strengthen intellectual property rights and define them more broadly in recent years. Yet while intellectual property rights play a critical role in the development of new inventions and technologies, there has always been a trade-off between the benefits and the drawbacks. Patents, for example, are intended to provide inventors and entrepreneurs with an incentive to bring new innovations to market by establishing limited monopolies. This is necessary to offset the financial risks, particularly the risk that counterfeiters will copy a new invention without having borne the brunt of the development effort and costs.

Patent protection and enforcement are especially critical for products like pharmaceuticals, which require extensive research and development budgets. Free-riding, the practice of other companies utilizing research without bearing any of the development costs, can lead companies to shy away from developing breakthrough products because they can't recoup their investment. Poor quality knock-offs also serve as a deterrent to innovation for drug companies due to potential legal liability. Even in situations where piracy and counterfeiting aren't as pronounced, patents provide a financial incentive that encourages more innovation than there would be otherwise.

On the other hand, patents can also work against the public good. They create an environment where self-interested competitors jealously guard their secrets rather than sharing information. This can slow the advancement of entire fields of knowledge and research, sometimes even delaying the introduction of important new products. Patenting can be particularly detrimental in a university setting, as it restricts other scientists' access to research results whose primary application may be as a basis for further research. Corporations funding research generally insist on making university researchers sign confidentiality agreements despite a long scientific tradition of sharing research results. In a 1997 nationwide survey of biomedical researchers, 79 percent admitted to refraining from sharing research with colleagues in order to secure patents first.[16] Scientists and doctors are becoming increasingly reluctant to share advancements with their colleagues either because they want to secure a patent first, or because they fear they will be subjected to frivolous infringement lawsuits. These developments are disturbing, because science and medicine used to be fields of endeavor dedicated to the public good rather than being focused on profit or liability exposure.

"The incentives are working against each other," explains Dr. Jimmy Clark, a retired genetics professor from the University of Kentucky. "On the one hand, people are talking about trying to encourage more collaboration and multi-disciplinary research. But on the other hand, universities have really been pushing for greater commercialization through patenting and licensing in order to generate revenue, and that encourages secrecy and competition. It used to be that very few scientists patented anything, and when they did, they didn't use it for their own financial gain. The mycologists who patented the first antifungal, for example, used the proceeds from their patent to help fund other research. Nowadays, universities are much more focused on profit-oriented research, and you can't have it both ways. While people are paying lip-service to multidisciplinary research, if a project has the potential for financial gain from licensing, it generally tips the scales in favor of secrecy."

In the past, university professors and medical practitioners used to consider patenting a discovery or procedure to be beneath them. When Dr. Jonas Salk developed the polio vaccine in 1954, he said the discovery belonged to the public. Since that time, however, it has become routine to patent vaccines, drugs, and even medical and scientific techniques. Despite the fact that research projects at universities and national laboratories are funded with federal tax dollars, the results of those projects are now being patented by a few individuals, rather than being made part of the public domain. The new trend of conducting research that is jointly funded by universities and large corporations has made the issue even murkier. While patenting and secrecy is undeniably in the best interests of the corporations funding the research, vital medical and scientific knowledge is being withheld from the research community, impeding the historical free flow of information that has been the strength of the American university research system.

Secrecy isn't the only problem. Patents create limited monopolies, and patent holders often use them to do much more than just recoup their investment, exploiting the monopoly for all it is worth. Companies are now seeking patents earlier in the development process to gain broader protection, and the exclusive rights granted by patents can be used to block the development of competitors' products. Even if the patent holder chooses to grant access through licensing, this raises competitors' costs and lowers their profit margins, and the proliferation of licensing fees often has the effect of discriminating against small companies. Fees that are minor expenses to multi-national corporations can exhaust an entrepreneur's capital, and as the number of licensing fees grows, the cost of doing business rises accordingly.

> In a knowledge economy, however, patents, copyrights, and trademarks are frequently considered to be a company's most important assets.

These problems have become more pronounced in the information age because intellectual property rights are now more important than ever before. In the industrial era, the foundations of wealth creation were land, capital, and labor. Intellectual property rights were intangible and considered to be of lesser importance. In a knowledge economy, however, patents, copyrights, and trademarks are frequently considered to be a company's most important assets. It is now estimated that approximately two-thirds of American manufacturing companies' assets are intangible.

As intellectual property rights have increased in importance, our ideas about what is patentable have changed as well. The standard used to be that people could patent only tangible innovations, a particular application of an idea rather than the idea itself. Yet that standard is eroding as we transition to the information age, where value comes not from the tangible products we produce but rather from the information we possess. In the early 1990s, for example, a medical researcher who performed the first successful ex-vivo gene therapy for a rare genetic disorder successfully filed for a patent that gave him exclusive rights to all ex-vivo gene therapy. This grant was most likely the result of a patent examiner who knew little about biomedicine and did not understand what an incredibly broad claim that was. As technology becomes more complex, it is harder for patent examiners to determine the validity of the applications they review. Thus, some incredibly broad patents have been issued over the past fifteen years that allow the patent holders to charge dubious licensing fees that essentially amount to a tax on knowledge.

In addition, the non-obviousness standard, which requires that an invention being patented should not be obvious to a person with ordinary skill in the field, is eroding as well. "There clearly has been a degradation of the non-obviousness standard, and it's particularly troublesome in areas of new technology," says law scholar Charles McManis. "The U.S. Patent Office is very dependent on the patent record as the first place it checks for obviousness, and the problem is that when a new technology is recognized and starts being patented, there's not a lot in the patent record the examiners can refer to in order to make their decisions. Only when examiners develop enough experience in granting and rejecting patent applications in the new field does the patent office build up its own database of what is and isn't obvious. Furthermore, a lot of new technologies are subject to very random decisions because patent examiners don't have all that long to do their examinations. They have something like fifteen working hours to examine each patent, and that doesn't give them a whole lot of time to look outside the patent record to see whether or not an invention is non-obvious. As a practical matter, many of those decisions only get fine-tuned when somebody secures a patent and sues somebody else for infringement. Then the evidence starts coming in as to obviousness or non-obviousness."

These challenges, and some dubious decisions by the intellectual property courts and patent examiners, have led to a proliferation of opportunistic intellectual property claims in recent years. It is not uncommon for companies to now be formed for the express purpose of exploiting a patent by winning infringement suits, and many of the companies that are sued acquiesce because it is cheaper to pay licensing fees than to defend their case in court. The cost of litigation does not provide a similar deterrent for predatory plaintiffs, because once they successfully win the first case, much of the legal documentation can be used to prosecute additional cases. Defendants who lose, meanwhile, can be forced to pay punitive damages three times the amount of economic harm caused to the plaintiff. This has led to an explosion in frivolous intellectual property claims and suits—the number of patent lawsuits filed annually grew 111 percent from 1991 to 2000.[17] In other Western nations where plaintiffs who lose are responsible for paying the defendants' legal fees, frivolous lawsuits are far less common.

Even if a competitor develops their own product independently, a patent-holder can sue and win a preliminary injunction against that competitor, blocking sales of their product until the case is settled. In 2000, for example, Amazon.com successfully filed a patent on its one-click ordering feature and promptly sued BarnesandNoble.com for infringement, winning a preliminary injunction. This practice is particularly problematic for small entrepreneurial firms whose revenue stream, and continued existence, may be dependent on one product, creating cash flow and credit problems if they are sued. By the time the litigation has been worked out, the window of opportunity has often closed. As a result, preliminary injunctions are most often sought by large corporations who are attempting to eliminate smaller rivals. According to the American Intellectual Property Law Association, the median cost of patent lawsuits that go to trial is $500,000; in cases where over $25 million is at risk the average cost is $4 million.[18] The difficulty of raising funds to finance the litigation usually forces small firms to either submit to licensing or cease using particular design features. In this era, the right patent, coupled with litigation, can lock out small startups from entire niche markets.

Some of the worst cases of predatory litigation have involved software companies, which have led the way in adapting patent law to the demands of an information economy. In the past, software could only be copyrighted, but in the 1990s software companies began to apply for and be awarded design patents, which offer a stronger level of protection. They also pushed for patenting of business methods and processes, which used to be protected by the rules governing trade secrets. "Many academics, myself included, were somewhat skeptical of the recent federal court of appeals decision that business methods were patentable," McManis notes. "In order for that ruling to make sense, you have to believe that without the protection of patents, business methods wouldn't be developed, and of course that is utterly counter-intuitive.

"Another argument you could make is that patent protection will lead to the public disclosure of those business methods, which in the long term benefits the public. Otherwise, the way business methods are developed is in the back room, subject to trade secret protection. Now that's a more plausible argument, but only if you assume that it is better for society to have public disclosure of certain innovations such as business methods. At a certain point, however, you're inevitably going to have trade secrets if companies think they can make more money doing it that way than by getting a patent. It is not at all clear that a disclosure policy will in fact put any business methods in the public domain that wouldn't have been available without patent protection. Thus, the evidence is inconclusive as to whether business method patents are really necessary, and if they're not necessary, the question becomes are they socially desirable?"

The recognition of business method patents, the erosion of the non-obviousness standard, and a rash of overly broad claims has turned the patent system into a lottery in which the winner takes all, while the losers are locked out of the game or must purchase the right to participate. In fact, the intellectual property gold rush is creating monopolies that far eclipse those of the nineteenth century robber barons, and it isn't just patenting that is out of hand. There has been a disturbing trend of people rushing to claim exclusive copyrights and charge licensing fees for information that has long been considered part of the public domain. Perhaps the most notorious example is writer Ashleigh Brilliant, who has copyrighted over 7500 well-known aphorisms and won over a hundred lawsuits for copyright infringement. This has led an increasing number of people to wonder if the benefits of strong intellectual property protection have been overstated.

"Obviously some industries and fields of innovation are very dependent on the patent system, such as the pharmaceutical and biotechnology industries," says McManis. "In both cases, the up-front investment required to develop technology is so high that without some promise of exclusivity down the line, new technologies simply wouldn't be developed. On the other hand, there are other areas of innovation where a strong argument could be made that patent protection is not only not essential and not necessary, but indeed counterproductive."

The question is, where do we draw the line, and how do we argue effectively for stronger intellectual property protection abroad when we have yet to find the right balance at home? In most cases, the thorny issues surrounding intellectual property disputes, at home and abroad, come down to balancing financial gain against ethics and integrity. The balance that is struck varies from one culture to another, and we would be wise to clean up our act at home if we intend to push harder for enforcement abroad. American entrepreneurs must learn to judge the difference between bending and breaking the rules, and realize that when in doubt, it's always better to be safe than sorry when your integrity is on the line. As the former Chancellor of Washington University William Danforth once told me, "When you look back on your life, you have to be able to do so with pride. These people who practice business in a questionable ethical manner will ultimately pay a high price for their choices." Unfortunately, our country will pay a high price as well if we allow predatory patent wars to continue.

The Open Source Debate

The idea that perhaps intellectual property rights are being taken too far is one of the factors driving the "open source" movement in software. Open source relies on volunteers to write source code which is then peer reviewed, and there are two basic approaches. One is the model used by the developers of the Apache web server, which allows companies to create proprietary commercial software that is built on top of the open source Apache server. The other model, utilized by the developers of the open source operating system Linux, uses what is called a general public license. It is structured so that if a company creates a software product based on their code, they are obligated to make that software available for free as well.

"I think that it is perfectly consistent with proprietary intellectual property protection that innovators should be able to decide that rather than exclude people from using their innovation, they want to make the use of their innovation contingent on users making derivative innovations available on the same terms," says McManis. "In effect it's just a novel use of licensing schemes for a purpose that creates a cooperative innovative team rather than a proprietary innovative team. Many people argue that has resulted in a real improvement in quality of software, because when the proprietary software producers hide the source code, they're keeping too many eyes and ears off the quality problems. The open source movement is succeeding to the extent that it is because there are simply more innovators at the workbench looking at the product and suggesting solutions. So I don't think there's anything antithetical to intellectual property protection in the development of open source software. In fact, it's all built on the assumption that people have proprietary claims to innovation, and they can condition other people's use of innovation any way they want to. If they choose to do it in an open source manner, that's their choice."

For commercial software companies, whether or not they favor open source generally depends on what type of open source they are dealing with. IBM, for example, embraced the open source model when it decided to discontinue its own proprietary web server in favor of using the open source Apache server, which had much greater market share. IBM created a nonprofit Apache Software Foundation, and worked out all of the legal issues so that it could build proprietary software systems on top of the Apache server. Then in 1998 it incorporated Apache—which powers about two-thirds of all the web servers in the world—into its WebSphere web server product, with the result that IBM is now the leader in that software category.

Microsoft, on the other hand, has to compete head-to-head with Linux, and thus has a decidedly negative view of open source. They, and other opponents of open source, point out that while free software sounds nice in theory, there are a number of dangers and drawbacks for companies that base their products on an open source operating system like Linux. First, there is risk of copyright infringement, as one has to be very careful about building a proprietary application on top of source code covered by a general public license. There is also the risk that one of the contributors to the open source code might incorporate someone else's proprietary intellectual property, thus subjecting anyone utilizing the free source code to litigation.

"There is a legitimate argument over general public licenses, because they are contracts only in the most general sense," explains McManis. "Supporters of the free software movement are using public licenses to say, 'Here are the terms and you're obliged to follow them.' Yet when software developers who want to assert proprietary rights do the same thing, there are protests from consumers that it isn't a real contract because they didn't specifically agree to it. So there is a question of what really counts as a contract, and how far can you use it. The term that's used in the trade is a reach-through contract, and the question is, how far can you use a license to condition a person's permission to use your intellectual property on sharing the benefits for some downstream innovation they make, one that may not even be related to what you have licensed them to do? I think there have to be limits on the scope of reach-through licenses.

"Let's say I create a research tool, and I patent my research tool and you want to use it to run an experiment on a new pharmaceutical. I say fine, but I want not only X percent royalties every time you use my research tool, but I'd also like Y percent of the royalties on the invention you invent with my research tool. When you do that you're beginning to leverage your patent to reach through and tax another person's invention, and there's at least some argument that if your invention is just an improvement on my invention, I should have a right to do that. But if your invention is really completely different, and you just happen to use my patented tool to come up with your patented invention, then that's reaching too far.

"The same thing would be true for an open source reach-through contract. If the licensee of an open source license improved what was the subject of the open source license, you could legitimately argue that they should be obliged to make it equally open source. But what if they use the open source license to come up with an invention that really had no bearing and was not directly related to the initial open source technology at all? I think you could argue that trying to force somebody to disclose and make publicly available an invention that used open source technology, but really wasn't an improvement of that particular technology, is overreaching. In that case you're trying to go too far out into the field of innovation to claim for open source what you really shouldn't be able to claim."

Admittedly, a big part of the challenge with open source is how to keep track of who owns what, how to determine what is free and what is proprietary. But perhaps even more important, many opponents of open source argue, is the question of how to foster innovation in a society where commercial companies are required to compete with people who provide software for free. Open source may be able to support incremental advances, but where will companies get the money to fund the research and development necessary to create the next big breakthrough?

The open source debate is one of the most contentious issues surrounding innovation, for while intellectual property rights are clearly essential to innovation, people differ on some of the very specific and intricate ways in which those rights should be managed. We need to find ways to get industries to agree on standards that are public and can be shared so that companies can be more innovative, yet still allow everyone to own intellectual property and build proprietary systems on top of it. That requires better practices within industries for making sure all of the right players come to the table to agree on procedures and don't get bogged down in litigation afterwards.

> The open source debate is one of the most contentious issues surrounding innovation.

American industry needs to address these issues, because open source is not only here to stay in the software industry, but is spreading to other industries like biotechnology as well. Indeed, if we can come up with appropriate incentives to reward and motivate collaborative behavior, the open source model may be the key to fostering more multidisciplinary research. As author James Surowiecki has argued in the best-selling *The Wisdom of Crowds,* decentralized groups with a diversity of independent opinions that can come up with a way to aggregate those opinions generally produce very high quality results. The challenge is to find a way to use the open source model for basic research and development, while reserving the traditional commercial model for development activities that create differentiated products of high value and foster jobs and economic growth.

Reforming the Intellectual Property System

As America transitions to a global knowledge economy where intellectual property is increasingly important, it is crucial to look at the intellectual property system holistically and evaluate its effectiveness.

Does it suit our current needs? Is it appropriately balancing the need to reward inventors for innovation while encouraging the speedy dissemination of that knowledge for the public good? Are we defining patents too broadly and rewarding incremental innovation too richly? Are we properly protecting and rewarding breakthrough innovation? In a world where patents, trademarks, and copyrights may be the most valuable assets American companies own, these are important questions, and there is a fine line between creating an intellectual property system that encourages innovation and one that stifles it.

A critical step in the right direction would be to revamp the U.S. Patent and Trademark Office (USPTO), and to make sure it has the appropriate resources to function effectively. The dramatic increase in patent filings has placed a huge strain on the system, and the Patent Office estimates that their workload is growing at a rate of 20 to 30 percent annually.[19] This has led to a number of questionable patents being issued. For example, although scientific theories are supposed to be excluded from patent consideration, a computer programmer who wanted to test the system filed, and successfully won, a patent on Kirchoff's Law, a scientific theory originally proposed in 1845.[20] This is an indication that patent examiners do not have the time, resources, and training necessary to do a good job reviewing and issuing patents. The Patent Office also lacks a clear ideology on how to deal with new technologies, like computer programs and gene therapy, which are very different from traditional manufacturing inventions. As a result, significant mistakes are being made, and broad patents are being granted which extend intellectual property rights beyond the meaning of the law.

The USPTO is aware of these problems, and it has created a 21st Century Strategic Plan to address them. While this is a good start, the USPTO needs more than a strategic plan, it needs sufficient funding. At current budget levels, the Patent Office estimates that it will take at least a decade to achieve their target goal of eighteen months to process patent applications, and has actually cut back the number of patent examiners they plan to hire. The irony is that due to user fees from patent and trademark filings, the Patent Office is actually a revenue center for the federal government. An increase in staff and additional training could easily be funded from these fees, but the federal government has chosen to spend this revenue elsewhere. In fact, from 1992 through 2004, the federal government diverted $750 million from the Patent Office to other government programs.[21] In May 2005, the Senate introduced legislation to prevent the reallocation of user fees, but as of press time it had not yet been approved.

In addition to re-engineering the USPTO, the federal government and business community need to revisit some basic issues regarding our intellectual property system. One is the legitimacy of business process patents. Certainly, business process and methods patents are problematic, and Jeff Bezos, the CEO of Amazon.com, has suggested that the duration of software and business process patents should be limited to three to five years instead of the standard seventeen years, as unlike pharmaceuticals they do not require extensive capital expenditures or clinical trials to develop. But the real problem is the scope, not the duration, of these patents. Should anyone really be able to obtain exclusive rights to anything as broad as one-click ordering or a surgical technique? It is time to reexamine the issue of business method patents and discuss whether they are appropriate.

> It is time to reexamine the issue of business method patents and discuss whether they are appropriate.

Another issue currently under consideration by the U.S. House Judiciary Subcommittee on Courts is whether we should adopt a post-grant opposition process that would enable third parties and members of the public to challenge the validity of a patent and request reconsideration. This would be an important step in ensuring that unreasonably broad or questionable patents are not issued. "There is a lot of scholarly argument, and I tend to agree with it, that there ought to be a limited post-grant opposition feature," says McManis. "The Patent Office currently has a limited re-examination procedure, and while it was recently modified to make it more comprehensive, it still hasn't been utilized as much as it should be. Thus, there have been some strong arguments in favor of a more comprehensive post-grant opposition procedure, which would be open for a limited period time after the grant of the patent, during which people could file oppositions to amend the record and make sure the patent office didn't make a mistake."

We also need to reform how the legal system handles intellectual property issues in order to reduce costly lawsuits. The first step is to make the scope of intellectual property rights and the standards for infringement clearer. The standard for trademark infringement, for example, depends on the likelihood of confusion on the part of the consumer—a fuzzy and highly subjective assessment. The standard for copyright infringement is similarly subjective, resting on whether the defendant "unlawfully appropriated the plaintiff's expressive work."[22] Thanks to digital media and Napster, the concept of fair use, which includes making copies of copyrighted material for educational purposes, has also become problematic and requires a fresh look in light of modern technology.

In addition, the legal profession also needs to examine whether judicial restraint is in order to control predatory litigation. Infringement lawsuits are profitable because the plaintiff can use the work product from the first litigation in subsequent litigation, and the threat of triple damages is enough to prompt many defendants to settle opportunistic claims out of court. The profession needs to reconsider whether triple damages, which are seldom awarded anyway, are really appropriate. Also, judges need to be more cautious and consistent about awarding long-term and potentially crippling preliminary injunctions.

The need to reform the intellectual property system at home is great and needs to be addressed immediately, for a number of reasons. Wall Street, for example, is currently reviewing ways to do leasebacks of intangible assets in order to free more cash for research, but this would require improved intellectual property protection before it could be implemented. More generally, the system simply needs to be adapted to the demands of the information age and the global economy.

Despite the need for various reforms at home, however, the most pressing issue the United States has to deal with is still how to enforce our intellectual property rights abroad. The question of how to protect our rights in a global economy, without creating the perception of American imperialism, is one that has no easy answer. With our attention focused on the War on Terror, we may have to accept that golf clubs and handbags are going to be counterfeited. This is the price we pay for our foreign policy. Yet when it comes to cutting-edge technology like pharmaceuticals, biomedicine, and nanotechnology, we cannot afford to be lax. These new technologies require millions in research and development spending, and have the potential to create entire new industries full of well-paying jobs. As long as American scientists and entrepreneurs are closely involved in their development, most of those new jobs will be kept here in the United States, at least for a while. If we allow promising new high-tech products to be counterfeited, however, return on investment will decline and innovation will grind to a halt. There will be fewer breakthrough products, and fewer American jobs.

The damage being done to U.S. intellectual property owners—particularly by counterfeiters in China, Russia, Ukraine, India, Pakistan, and Brazil—must be dealt with, if not through sanctions, then through some other method. The global playing field has to be fair and even, and if these countries can not, or will not, enforce intellectual property standards, then the United States will have to rethink its stance on global intellectual property rights. So far, we have respected other countries' patents in an effort to encourage widespread global recognition of intellectual property rights. If piracy continues to spread and starts affecting our high-tech industries, however, we won't be able to afford this moral stance. We may have to play hardball and engage in a war of attrition, refusing to recognize other countries' intellectual property rights until they clean up their act. That could lead to quite a backlash, especially since we are moving an increasing proportion of our manufacturing to developing countries. Unfortunately, in a global knowledge economy where innovation is crucial to winning the game, there may simply be no other alternative.

7

THE MOTIVATION FOR INNOVATION— INCENTIVE COMPENSATION

◇◇◇

The allure of wealth is generally not the primary motivating factor for most successful entrepreneurs, who tend to be driven by the challenge of developing a new product or a vision of the world they want to fulfill. Nevertheless, the possibility of becoming wealthy certainly provides an important incentive to pursue entrepreneurship. In fact, entrepreneurship is the most common path to wealth in the United States, for while most entrepreneurs are not millionaires, approximately half of millionaires are entrepreneurs.[1] Half of Forbes *magazine's top ten richest Americans in 2005—Bill Gates, Warren Buffett, Paul Allen, Michael Dell, and Lawrence Ellison—are entrepreneurs, and the other five were all direct heirs of Sam Walton, arguably the most successful entrepreneur in recent history.*

Bill Gates is currently the richest man in America, and most people would probably assume that he is the richest entrepreneur of all time. Yet wealth, like success, is a matter of perception, and there is always someone richer or with a different perspective of what being rich means. When J.P. Morgan died in 1913, he reportedly left an estate of $69.6 million, which was a huge amount of money at that time. Upon discovering that Mr. Morgan left only $700,000 of his wealth to charity, the general public was outraged, but not Andrew Carnegie. When he read of the size of J.P. Morgan's estate, Carnegie said, "And to think—he wasn't even a rich man!"[2] Obviously, most of society disagreed.

Gates is certainly the wealthiest entrepreneur of all time in absolute terms, with a net worth of $48 billion, but a dollar today does not have the same purchasing power as a dollar one hundred years ago. If you were to compare America's most famous entrepreneurs on a relative basis rather than an absolute one, who would be the wealthiest? The answer, surprisingly, is that the entrepreneurs who made their fortunes in the eighteenth and nineteenth centuries were comparatively wealthier than today's current billionaires. In The Wealthy 100, authors Michael Klepper and Robert Gunther compared entrepreneurs according to their wealth divided by the gross domestic product at the time of their death. They found that John D. Rockefeller, Cornelius Vanderbilt, John Jacob Astor, Stephen Girard, and Andrew Carnegie were the five wealthiest entrepreneurs in American history.[3]

The question of who was the first to be worth a billion dollars is an interesting one as well. Most sources credit Rockefeller, whose estimated wealth at the time of his death was $1.4 billion, but without the Securities and Exchange Commission filings required today, it is hard to be certain. In absolute terms, Rockefeller is certainly a good bet, but again, there is the issue of purchasing power across generations, and in relative terms many of the founding fathers were actually billionaires. John Hancock was worth $350,000 at the time of his death in 1793, which translates to $14 billion in today's dollars. George Washington had an estate worth $530,000 when he died a few years later in 1799, the equivalent of $12.7 billion. And Benjamin Franklin, the quintessential American entrepreneur, amassed a fortune that would be worth roughly $7.5 billion today.[4]

Franklin, Hancock, and Washington were not entrepreneurs in the sense that Vanderbilt, Carnegie, and Rockefeller were. The founding fathers' fortunes were made from real estate, although Franklin did first rise to the middle class by becoming a publisher. Nevertheless, their financial success was a testament to the incentive power of ownership. The difference between *the haves and the have-nots during America's early years was that the poor worked for a living, while the wealthy owned assets. Comparatively few people could rise to a middle class life, much less an upper class one, merely by working for other people. The dream of working class citizens and immigrants was to own their own farm or business, for ownership was the path to a better life and financial freedom.*

The wages and job security offered by American companies after World War II changed that mindset, altering the American Dream from owning your own farm or business to obtaining a good, steady job that would allow you to buy a nice house. Yet the true American Dream is alive and well in Silicon Valley, where thousands of information technology workers have become not just employees, but owners, through incentives such as stock options. Many employees at Microsoft, Google, and a number of other high-tech companies have become millionaires while making Silicon Valley the world's foremost hotspot for innovation. The lesson is clear—the incentive to innovate comes from having the opportunity to own a piece of the action and reap the rewards, for as Woody Allen once said, "Money is better than poverty, if only for financial reasons."

One of the key factors to the success of an entrepreneurial firm, be it large or small, is attracting and then motivating good employees. The media likes to attribute the success of great companies to the talent of their entrepreneurial founders—the stories of how John D. Rockefeller created Standard Oil and how Bill Gates started Microsoft are as good as any Hollywood tale—but no entrepreneur succeeds entirely due to their own efforts. Great companies require great employees, talented individuals who help to make the entrepreneur's dream a reality. Entrepreneurial success is a team effort, and while entrepreneurs certainly deserve credit for leading that effort, without a highly motivated workforce, their vision would never materialize.

The question of how to foster an innovative workforce is one of the more difficult problems that leaders of entrepreneurial companies have to solve. In the 1950s, most employees devoted their lifetime to a single company, trading company loyalty for job security. But in today's world lifetime employment is rare, and the typical college student will have up to fifteen jobs and several careers during his or her lifetime. Companies now essentially rent employees, almost as if they were contract workers, for a short period of time. While American corporations have gained workforce flexibility, not to mention significant leverage in their ability to hold down wages through the threat of massive layoffs, in the process something important has been lost. Company loyalty has become an outdated concept, and while professional pride and fear of termination keeps many employees hard at work, some only put in the minimum level of effort required in order to avoid getting fired, especially those who sense their contributions are not valued.

While this attitude is the result of decades of prosperity and entitlement, it is also the result of corporate America reneging on the loyalty-for-security pact. Employees today are suspicious of management, so they want things in writing, want to understand the impact of changes on their individual situation, and don't want to do more than they are being paid for. This puts the United States at an enormous disadvantage in comparison to Asian countries, where the workforce arguably has a much stronger work ethic and people are willing to work for far less.

Employee motivation is in many ways a question of effective leadership, and entrepreneurs aren't always the best leaders. While it is certainly possible for people to modify their leadership style and improve their understanding of how to motivate people, natural ability plays an important role, as Mike Pressler, the highly successful lacrosse coach at Duke University, can attest. "Leadership is like speed, size, or IQ—either God gave it to you or he didn't," says Pressler. "Just because you're a great athlete, scientist, or entrepreneur doesn't mean you're a great leader. Some of the best players I've known had zero leadership skills, because talent is different than leadership. Effective leaders have to be honest, trustworthy, loyal, and absolutely genuine, because a phony in a position of power can bring harm to his team.

A great leader must have the ability to know what it takes to motivate each individual. He must reward his people for a job well done."

Figuring out how to reward and motivate people effectively is critical to entrepreneurship, and what the entrepreneurial community in Silicon Valley discovered during the 1990s was that incentive compensation was a strong motivating force, not just for executives, but for the average employee as well. In a developed nation, the proportion of people who are willing to completely forego the security of steady employment will always be a comparatively small minority—car payments and mortgages demand a steady stream of income. The proportion who are willing to risk some of their income and be compensated in the form of equity, however, is much larger. When offered more broadly, incentives can generate a great deal of innovative activity not just from entrepreneurs, but from employees. This is a critical factor behind the incredible productivity levels of Silicon Valley startups, and a potentially important tool in redressing the balance of power between shareholders and labor in a global economy.

> **Figuring out how to reward and motivate people effectively is critical to entrepreneurship.**

Over the past ten years, CEO pay has increased by over 150 percent, and corporate profits are up more than 75 percent. Yet pay for the average employee has increased less than 40 percent, barely keeping pace with inflation. In today's transitioning global economy, there is an excess of labor that is exerting strong downward pressure on American wages, while at the same time allowing shareholders and executives to reap incredible rewards. The increasingly free market economy worldwide has tipped the scales decisively in favor of the owners of capital rather than labor. In this environment, where company executives are focused solely on shareholder value, the only way the American middle class is going to continue to raise its standard of living is by becoming shareholders themselves.

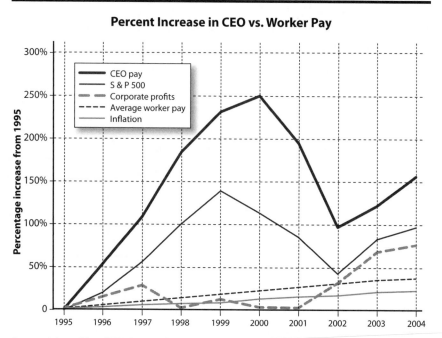

Percent Increase in CEO vs. Worker Pay

Source: Adapted from "CEO Pay, Stock Prices, Corporate Profits, Worker Pay, and Inflation, 1990-2003," www.faireconomy.org/research/income_charts.html (accessed September 1, 2005).[5]

The Legacy of the Organization Man

One of the rites of passage in American society is to obtain a good job with a steady paycheck. It is a sign that one has become, in the eyes of society at least, a mature, responsible adult. This attitude towards employment is so pervasive and unquestioned that many people don't realize just how recent a phenomenon it is. In the days before the industrial revolution, the idea of a secure job and a steady paycheck would have been a highly unusual notion. Before 1800, most people grew up on family farms and were generally self-employed as farmers, craftsmen, or merchants. One might start out as a farmhand, an apprentice, or a shop clerk, but the goal was not a lifetime of employment. Even after the industrial revolution made factory jobs common, most workers viewed these jobs as temporary.

To own your own farm or small business used to be the quintessential American dream. Having a job as a member of the working class was often deemed necessary, but was certainly not preferred. Americans wanted to be their own boss.

Over time, the industrial revolution produced a gradual change in attitude. Increasing agricultural productivity lowered prices and made it harder for people to make a living as small farmers, but thousands of new jobs were being created in factories. At first they paid notoriously low wages, but slowly organized labor and increasing productivity changed that. By the 1920s, the average worker's standard of living had improved considerably. In fact, a study commissioned by Henry Ford of one hundred Detroit workers found that most families lived in homes with an average of one room per person. All of the families surveyed had electricity, and a good number had central heating, indoor plumbing, and washing machines. Workers' lives were further improved with the passage of the Fair Labor Standards Act in 1938, which established a minimum wage, prohibited child labor, and set provisions for overtime pay, effectively creating the forty-hour work week. With these provisions in place, lifelong employment became a lot more attractive. In fact, business was so good after World War II that it was possible to earn a steady paycheck with large bonuses and regular promotions merely by being a decent, loyal employee.

It was the era of the "organization man," when millions of middle class Americans joined the ranks of middle management and traded unquestioning company loyalty for job security. Life was good for organization men and women, and for a generation their standard of living rose rapidly. They soon had the disposable income to buy a nice house in the suburbs, two cars, yearly vacations, and sometimes even a summer home. Once they were accustomed to this standard of living, however, organization men and women were reluctant to do anything to jeopardize it. People tended to find a job in a large company and stick with it, cementing company loyalty, but this loyalty was tested during the mass corporate layoffs of the 1980s. The loyalty-for-security pact that had sustained organization men and women slowly started to disintegrate, and by the early 1990s even IBM, which had maintained a full-employment policy for fifty years, laid off 120,000 workers. Suddenly, the organization man's attitude towards work had become obsolete.

As a result, young Americans developed an entirely different attitude towards employment. They had seen that company loyalty did not pay off, and motivation plummeted as employees' trust in management evaporated. As the American workforce has been asked to work longer, harder, and smarter in response to foreign competition, with no guarantee of a job tomorrow, commitment has waned. Gallup research indicates that only 25 percent of working Americans are truly engaged in and passionate about their work, while 55 percent are just going through the motions, and 20 percent are actively disengaged and are looking for a different job.[6] That's a tremendous amount of disinterest and dissatisfaction on the part of American workers, and it is very hard for entrepreneurs to recruit, motivate, and retain talented employees in such an environment. Yet at the same time, finding a rewarding job has become extremely important to most Americans, to some extent even overshadowing the importance of family and community. According to James Clifton, the chairman and CEO of the Gallup Organization, "A major sociological shift has taken place in the last decade. Today, most Americans define themselves by their job title and the brand image of their employer . . . The great new American dream is having a good job."[7]

Rekindling Motivation through Incentives

How do American entrepreneurs who are strapped for cash recruit top notch employees, particularly when giant corporations can offer higher salaries, better benefits, and a recognizable brand name to add to an employee's resume? How do they energize employees in an era when people are extremely suspicious of management? How do they retain their best people in a culture of job hopping? Silicon Valley's answer to these questions has been to use stock options to create motivation and loyalty.

Stock options are a form of incentive compensation, which means that pay is contingent on some measure of company performance. Anyone who has held a job for a significant period of time knows that after a while, the motivational power of a steady paycheck begins to wane. Most people are not slackers, and they will make a sincere effort to do what is required. But after the initial honeymoon phase is over and people feel that their job is somewhat secure, many will look around at the level of effort everybody else is putting in, consider their potential for advancement, and then adjust their own effort accordingly. The great majority will do enough to produce decent work and maintain their position, but rarely will they do more without additional incentives.

> **Performance-based incentives help mitigate the problem of scarce managerial resources, which is common in small firms.**

Performance-based incentives help mitigate the problem of scarce managerial resources, which is common in small firms. Good managerial talent is expensive, and people that are attracted to entrepreneurial firms tend to be independent and don't like being excessively managed anyway. One of the problems associated with a lack of management, however, is that sometimes even the best of employees get a bit lazy, especially if there are no pressing deadlines and their jobs have become boring or repetitive. In today's office environment, it is all too easy to hide in a cubicle and waste time. Corporate bureaucracies deal with this by using managers partially as watchdogs, but this is expensive for the company, wastes valuable managerial time, and is annoying to employees—three things an entrepreneurial firm can't afford.

Most corporations ask their best employees to perform the most difficult and greatest amount of work. Generally, companies accept less from mediocre employees, yet their performance reviews do not identify them to be mediocre. If they are loyal employees and stay with the company for many years, their regular increases in base pay compensate them as if they were outstanding employees. Meanwhile, this same system usually fails to identify and compensate the best employees for their performance and contribution over and above the mediocre employee. What Silicon Valley entrepreneurs have realized is that to keep their best employees, they have to design compensation plans which identify and reward their most talented staff members for being what they are—superior contributors to success.

Dan Maher, a tax partner at the accounting firm of Deloitte and Touche, understands this well. He has more than twenty-five years worth of experience working with both large and small entrepreneurial companies, and notes, "It's easy to fall into the trap of thinking that it's tough to motivate certain behaviors. At Deloitte and Touche, we help companies create a corporate mission statement and a five-year plan, and many times, half way through the process we sit back and say, 'Boy is it hard to change people's behavior!' But I don't think that's necessarily true. I've seen and experienced a variety of incentive-based compensation plans, and I've got a healthy respect for the ability of those plans to motivate people."

Incentive compensation motivates employees to regulate their own behavior, and successful entrepreneurial firms generally make 10 to 50 percent of employee compensation contingent upon performance. When employees are partial owners, they have an incentive when their regular work is done to find other ways to maximize their earnings. They have far more reason to spend down time working on back-burner projects that, while not urgent, can result in cost savings or innovations. Incentives encourage employees to look beyond their immediate job description and consider the big picture. By linking pay to the overall success of the company, it allows employees to share the wealth if the firm is doing well, while bringing wages more in line with global market rates.

Critics of incentive compensation argue that it is ultimately either ineffective or destructive. Linking compensation to achievement of individual goals, on one hand, can create an incentive to pursue that one goal to the detriment of all others. Tying an individual's compensation to a measure of company-wide performance like stock price, on the other hand, can be frustrating because there is no clear link between a single employee's actions and their effect on the overall company goals. Critics also point to studies which indicate that employee satisfaction is much more closely tied to autonomy and a challenging work environment than compensation as evidence that incentive-based pay is not an effective motivational tool. In addition, employees who have been drawing a fixed salary plus a percentage bonus for years may be less than thrilled by the idea of a significant portion of their pay becoming variable.

The critics make some valid points. Good incentive plans are hard to design, and incentive compensation has its downsides, first and foremost being that it involves greater risk. Employees at small entrepreneurial companies who have incentives such as stock options as a large component of their compensation won't reap the benefits if the company fails; those at larger companies who are forced to take stock as part of their compensation or retirement package can be in big trouble if the company is mismanaged and goes bankrupt, as did Enron and WorldCom. Incentive compensation demands that employees learn how to accept and manage variability and risk, as there are fewer safety nets with such a system. Yet it has the potential to elicit much greater rewards, and in a global marketplace it presents one of the few options for employees to enhance their earnings and net worth in an environment where wages are falling. The challenge is designing and implementing incentives that effectively motivate innovative and entrepreneurial behavior, rewarding success without subjecting employees to an unacceptable amount of risk.

According to Christopher Morin, president and CEO of Noble International, implementing an effective incentive compensation program is no easy task, but if done well, the results can be outstanding. "In our organization, we have incentive plans put in place at almost every level, so even team members who are part of the core manufacturing process are eligible to be part of an incentive program. We were amazed at how initiating incentive programs caused some really surprising changes in behavior, not out of everybody, but certainly out of a lot of people that historically we never would have expected to see perform as they did. We've been impressed with the usefulness of these plans and their ability to direct change and enhance profitability."

To remain competitive in the global economy, American companies need to elicit greater creativity and innovative effort from their employees while paying internationally competitive wages. Meanwhile, American workers need to find a way to reap a greater portion of the wealth they help to create without resorting to outdated and ultimately destructive labor practices. The way to accomplish this is to adopt a system where every employee has an ownership stake in their company and earns a significant portion of their income through profits rather than just regular wages. We have to let go of the entitlement mindset of the organization man era and return to an ownership culture with a greater reliance on variable compensation tied to results. This is going to require a more entrepreneurial attitude, a willingness on the part of employees to accept greater risk and uncertainty in their income, and a willingness on the part of employers to share ownership with those who help to create their wealth. Entrepreneurs in Silicon Valley have embraced this idea. Now, entrepreneurs across the country, as well as executives at larger, established firms, need to realize that incentive compensation could play just as important a role in making their companies more innovative as well.

The Role of Stock Options in the Success of Silicon Valley

Incentive compensation is not new, as employers have developed a wide variety of methods over the years to elicit greater performance from their employees. Factories, for example, have often used piece-rate systems where workers are paid according to how many pieces they produce rather than by the hour (an incentive that encourages employees to work faster, although quality generally declines as a result). It is stock options, however, that have generated the most debate over the past decade, and which are widely credited as having a major role in the success of Silicon Valley during the 1990s. A stock option is a contract that gives an employee the right to purchase stock from the employer, after a certain vesting period, at a set price which is generally at or below the market price on the grant date. Broad-based stock options can play a critical role in fostering a more innovative, entrepreneurial economy.

As early as 1919, Harvey Firestone had instituted a stock purchase program where shares were sold to employees at below market cost, an experiment he introduced along with the eight-hour day in his Akron rubber factories. Stock options as we know them today, however, originally became popular in the 1950s as a tax shelter for top executives. At the time, the personal tax rate for those in the highest bracket was 91 percent, but in 1950 Congress passed a law that allowed stock options to be taxed at the capital gains rate, which was only 25 percent.[8] This loophole allowed executives to keep a greater portion of earnings resulting from improved stock performance, which had the additional benefit of aligning executives' interests with those of shareholders more closely. Over the next several decades, however, that loophole was reduced, and in 1976 Congress eliminated the tax shelter status of stock options completely.

> We have to let go of the entitlement mindset of the organization man era and return to an ownership culture with a greater reliance on variable compensation tied to results.

While the popularity of stock options with top executives was waning in traditional corporate America, it was being used more often to compensate entrepreneurs in Silicon Valley. In 1957, eight young employees at Shockley Semiconductor Laboratories left to start their own company, and went to Fairchild Camera and Instrument for startup capital. They got it, on the condition that Fairchild would have the right to buy out the startup's founders if the new company was successful. It was, and Fairchild bought out the founders in exchange for $250,000 each in Fairchild Semiconductor stock. Their success created a new financial model for entrepreneurship, one where founders planned to be with the company for only a few years in exchange for potentially large equity gains upon buyout or initial public offering (IPO). This soon inspired many other Silicon Valley employees to start their own companies.

In order to stop the brain drain, companies throughout Silicon Valley started offering stock options to help retain their employees, and they offered them not just to executives but to scientists, engineers, programmers, and many other white collar employees. Yet the practice failed to spread to mainstream corporate America, which continued to see stock options as an executive perk unsuitable for the average employee. When President Ronald Reagan's tax cuts lowered the top personal income tax rate to 28 percent, stock options became much more valuable as people were allowed to retain a greater portion of their earnings. Those who had exercised and held on to their options throughout the 1970s cashed them in for a handsome profit.

The stock options bonanza did not go unnoticed. By the late 1980s, there was a mass exodus of talented employees from blue-chip corporations to high-tech companies with their options and high growth potential. As a result, productivity in the Valley soared, while mainstream corporate America struggled to compete in the global marketplace. By 2001, Silicon Valley employed 1.35 million people, its productivity and income levels were approximately double the national average, and it was responsible for one out of every twelve new patents in the United States.[9] Slowly, some mainstream companies began to follow suit and offer stock options to employees below the executive level, but the practice was never as pervasive and egalitarian as in Silicon Valley. The perception of lower-level employees as simply cogs in a wheel was too entrenched, and today relatively few public companies offer stock options to non-management employees. This is a missed opportunity, for stock options offer a number of advantages to employers and employees that can foster greater innovation and entrepreneurship.

"Stock options are useful because they tie managers' and employees' pay to the financial success of the company's owners and investors, as measured by stock price," says Morin. "By giving people a stake in the ultimate success or failure of the company, it helps them think like owners instead of employees, aligning their interests with that of investors." In recent years, management teams and employees in high-tech companies have generally been granted a stake of 5 to 10 percent of the company, depending on the nature of the business and the plans for a spin-off, IPO or other equity transaction. Often, equity packages produce a value that is two, five, or even ten times the value of annual base pay, with the multiple depending on the ultimate success of the enterprise. Stock options have even made millionaires out of employees at companies like Microsoft and Google.

Incentives such as stock options are crucial in an entrepreneurial economy, because one of the problems for small, growing firms is that they cannot afford to pay the high salaries and plentiful benefits that are the norm at larger, established companies. In a fast-growing company, stock options offer employees the possibility of significant, unlimited gains far beyond what they would earn in base pay at a larger, established company, while at the same time preserving the company's liquidity. Stock options are an effective way to postpone compensation and, to some extent, fund it through future expectations. In a sense they are a mortgage on future earnings, and they receive favorable tax treatment as well.

"At Noble, we've found that stock options have been a great way to share the wealth with employees," says Morin. "We've offered them far beyond the core executive group, and there are people in, for example, administrative positions who never would have been able to earn what they've been earning simply through regular wages. Stock options have really allowed them to share in that upside potential, and as a result it's been great for employee morale and retention."

The retention power is due to the so-called "golden handcuffs" effect, as options generally have a significant vesting period of several years and are not transferable. If employees leave before the options can be exercised, they lose the value of the unvested options. Most companies continue to offer more stock options on a rolling schedule so employees always have some options that have not yet vested, giving them an incentive to remain with the company. Options help to stimulate continued good performance, conserve cash, and ensure that the firm pays employees only what it can afford, while at the same time offering the opportunity for significant gains if the company does well.

In the larger picture, the use of stock options as part of an overall compensation package helps to bring base wages more in line with global market rates, while at the same time creating the potential for employees to increase their earnings through investment income. If they were used more widely, they would have the potential to redress the balance of power between labor and owners of capital, which since the dot-com crash has increasingly favored the latter. Wages for non-managerial employees have stagnated, while corporate profits and shareholder value have increased significantly; in 2003, professional and technology workers' real wages increased less than 1 percent, while corporate profits were up almost 25 percent.[10] In an environment where the labor market is increasingly global, there will be continued downward pressure on American wages. Over the long run, American workers will most likely be better off if a greater portion of their compensation is based on equity.

The Drawbacks of Stock Incentives

For all their advantages, stock options do have some significant drawbacks. One problem is that, once exercised, options create more shares and thus dilute the value of the existing stock. In effect, this transfers wealth from investors to employees, and whether or not you think that is a good thing depends on your perspective. Young entrepreneurial companies count on fast growth to overpower the effect of dilution, but more mature companies with slower growth cannot count on this effect. Therefore, they often choose to buy back shares of their own stock in order to prevent dilution, but this diverts cash away from capital investment activities such as research and development. This can lead to a situation where companies have to borrow to finance stock buybacks even through they have plenty of cash on the books.

Another problem with stock options is that, once employees exercise their option to buy, they tend to sell the stock immediately to pay for the exercise price and any tax on the subsequent increase in value. After the stock has been sold, the program loses its incentive power, although this problem can be addressed by continuing to award new options. Stock options can also lose their motivational power if the options go underwater (meaning the stock price trades below the exercise price). A common practice has been to re-price the options at a lower price, but that in essence rewards employees for poor company performance and thwarts the purpose of the incentive. Re-pricing also diminishes shareholder value and incurs additional expenses, as it requires canceling the old options and reissuing them at a new price. A recent change to accounting standards also requires that companies recognize the difference in fair value when they reissue options, which makes re-pricing far less attractive.

> In an environment where the labor market is increasingly global, there will be continued downward pressure on American wages.

If stock options go underwater and the company chooses not to re-price the options, however, they generally turn into a disincentive, and talented employees frequently leave the company for another opportunity where the market price of the options is greater than the exercise price. Furthermore, stock performance has as much to do with market swings, interest rates, and inflation as it does with the actual performance of the company, and a bear market can send options underwater even when employers are hard working, highly motivated, and doing everything right. If employees feel that options have been driven underwater by circumstances beyond their control, the worthless options become extremely demoralizing.

"I think some stock ownership is a good thing," notes Dan Maher. "It's very consistent with making people feel like they have a stake in the overall success or failure of the company. However, I really do think some moderation is appropriate, because there just isn't a strong cause-and-effect link between an individual manager or employee's performance and the performance of the stock in the market. It's very difficult for someone who does a great job to feel that the performance of the company's stock reflects their performance. I've worked with a lot of companies where the company is performing well, and it would appear that their people are really motivated, doing all the right things and making progress toward all of the goals they have. Yet for reasons nobody can explain, the stock price just cannot get into the money, and that's not a very strong motivational tool.

"Alternatively, for stocks that really take off out of nowhere, often times it's hard to ascribe that to a particular behavior, as opposed to luck or being in the right place at the right time. So I think it's appropriate to allow employees to share somewhat in that, and it's also appropriate to give them a good reason why they should care about the performance of the stock. But I think you have to be careful about making stock the centerpiece of any kind of compensation plan. I'm much more in favor of a compensation program built around the things an employee or a manager can realistically accomplish, and where their actions can specifically support the strategies and goals of the organization."

Some of these problems can be addressed by using alternate forms of stock incentives such as stock grants, where the company gives the employee shares outright at no cost, and discount stock purchase plans, which are similar but require the employee to contribute at least some of their own money to buy the shares. Stock grants and stock purchase programs have the benefit of providing actual ownership in the company, rather than just the option of ownership. Supporters of these types of programs argue that stock options that aren't exercised don't represent a real loss, while falling stock value does. Thus, stock has a stronger psychological impact than stock options, especially if the employee actually bought the shares or traded a portion of their salary for equity. (Some argue the opposite is true—stock still retains some of its value even if the price is falling, while underwater options are worth nothing and therefore represent a greater loss.) A major drawback to both stock grants and stock purchase plans is that the threat of real losses can encourage a short-term outlook. Also, as with options, issuing new shares to employees as compensation dilutes the value of the existing shares for the owners.

"The dilution problem can be addressed by using stock appreciation rights (also known as phantom stock), which fluctuate in tandem with the value of the real stock," says Anthony Tersigni, the president of Ascension Health and a person intimately familiar with the challenges of an entrepreneurial business. "This mimics the value of real shares without diluting them because it isn't actual stock, and is a good option for privately held companies that don't have actual stock to award. The problem with phantom stock is how to fund the eventual payout to the employee. The payout must come either from retained earnings, which would lower the value of the remaining stock, from reduced dividends, or from bank borrowings. One way or another, investors are effected even if the shares aren't diluted."

On the other hand, one of the benefits of phantom stock is that it can easily be indexed to downswings and upswings in the market. This way, employees' compensation is insulated from shifts in the stock price that have nothing to do with changes in the actual value of the company—a major problem with other forms of stock incentives. Even with indexing, however, the single biggest drawback to stock incentives from an employer's perspective is that the average employee has no sense of how their day-to-day performance affects stock price. The connection, often referred to as "line of sight," is simply too weak.

From the employees' perspective, the biggest drawback is that stock incentives require them to assume much greater compensation risk than traditional methods such as merit pay and annual bonuses. It exposes them to the cyclical nature of the market much more so than ever before, and requires them to be much better educated about investing, which is a complex and often intimidating subject for many. Stock grants and options also have the potential to increase volatility and exacerbate market downturns, as when the company's stock starts to fall, employees will be tempted to sell in order to lock in some gains, pushing down the value of the stock even further.

Nevertheless, if a company is publicly traded or its financial strategy involves a spin-off or IPO, then stock incentives can be a very effective motivational tool. Stock options in particular are useful for young entrepreneurial firms because they provide more leverage than real stock, as it enables companies to award a greater number of shares. If a company is likely to remain private or closely held, however, options may not be a good device to use because they can only be valued by formula or independent appraisal. In such cases, a phantom plan, or even a formula-based plan tied to some financial valuation, may be more effective than options.

The Stock Option Expensing Debate

When the dot-com bubble burst, the use of stock options came under fire for several reasons. One, entrepreneurs and employees who had not exercised and cashed in their options before the bubble burst saw their sweat equity disappear overnight. Many who had been millionaires on paper were left far worse off than they would have been if they had received a steady paycheck from a Fortune 500 company for all those years. In addition, the fact that stock options were not required to be expensed, and therefore did not show up directly on a company's income statement, was one of the factors blamed for the over-valuation of high-tech companies, which led to the bubble in the first place. This rekindled a longstanding and contentious debate as to whether stock options should be expensed and how.

In the past, the Financial Accounting Standards Board (FASB) had not required that stock options be included as an expense on the income statement. While intuitively stock options are a form of compensation, and should therefore show up as an expense on the income statement, the problem is how to value them appropriately. For many years, the agreed-upon method was to value options on the day they were issued by subtracting the exercise price from the day's current market price. Yet this did not reflect the true value, as options have an intrinsic value people will pay for even if the future market price is equal to the present price. This problem led the accounting community to sidestep the issue and not require options to be expensed for many years.

As the popularity of options grew in the 1980s, however, the FASB proposed that options should be expensed based on what is called the Black-Scholes model for valuing call options. But the FASB encountered fierce resistance from high-tech companies in Silicon Valley that used stock options extensively. They feared the reduction in earnings would create a huge drop in their stock prices, which among other problems would drive their options underwater. After extensive lobbying of Congress, the FASB backed down, and in 1995 it ruled that while it preferred options to be expensed, it was not required.

This decision created an accounting problem, for while stock options were not expensed, they were credited to shareholders' equity on the balance sheet, which inflated earnings per share. Stock options were required to be noted in footnotes, and professional analysts accounted for the distortion in their evaluations. Nevertheless, the overstatement of earnings made it hard to compare companies' relative performance. One study found that because of stock options, the hundred largest companies in the United States overstated their profits by as much as 50 percent in 1998, when the dot-com bubble was growing most rapidly.[11]

Since the dot-com crash and the scandals at WorldCom and Enron, there has been increasing pressure to expense stock options, and in December 2004, the FASB revised its accounting standards. While this undoubtedly creates a more accurate assessment of earnings, it will have a decidedly negative effect on small companies. Requiring the expensing of stock options will most likely result in companies issuing fewer of them, once again reserving options for a more elite group of managers and executives rather than expanding them to all employees. This change will be extremely counterproductive to America's long-term economic interests in encouraging innovation and entrepreneurial activity.

> **Requiring the expensing of stock options will most likely result in companies issuing fewer of them.**

The expensing debate is certainly an important question, but in our zeal to protect American employees and investors, we must be careful not to throw the baby out with the bathwater. Whether or not stock options are being handled in the best possible way from an accounting standpoint should not call into question the soundness and importance of stock options as a compensation method in general. The productivity level of Silicon Valley during the 1990s speaks for itself, and while stock options weren't the only factor contributing to that productivity, the power of incentive compensation certainly played a critical role.

Alternate Methods of Incentive Compensation

While stock incentives are an important form of performance-based compensation, they are by no means the only effective method for eliciting greater innovation and overall performance. There are several other types of incentive compensation which can also be extremely effective, including profit sharing, gain sharing, and performance bonuses. The nature of the performance goals in incentive plans will vary based on the type and size of the firm, long or short-term orientation, and emphasis on achievement of group or individual goals, as well as the mission and strategy of the business. For example, a business that is being built to be sold or spun off might have different performance measures than one that is meant to be managed and operated as a private business. An effective incentive compensation plan should provide a mix of elements that emphasize the achievement of strategic goals.

Profit Sharing

Profit sharing is a form of group incentive that can be very useful in both large and small companies, because it is one step removed from the stock market. The concept of profit sharing is simple: a percentage of the company's quarterly or yearly profits are redistributed to employees. The company awards the extra compensation only when it is merited (and thus only when it can afford to), and the ongoing distribution at regular intervals provides continuous motivation. "Profit sharing is a great alternative or supplement to stock incentives because it's very understandable," explains Dan Maher. "More conservative employees often like profit sharing because they feel they can impact profitability far more easily than stock price. It doesn't seem as arbitrary."

In a small company where the entrepreneur is trying to create a sense of shared commitment, profit sharing can be extremely effective. It allows management to keep base pay at a somewhat conservative level and pay a year-end bonus based on profitability. If used properly, profit sharing can also become the focus of various events to celebrate business success and the achievement of certain key business plan milestones. As a company grows, an individual employee's ability to impact the bottom line is weakened, and the motivational power of profit sharing plans along with it. But while companies remain small, profit sharing plans can be particularly effective.

I personally have a preference for profit-sharing plans over stock incentives because they are more tangible to employees. People believe they understand what helps make a company more or less profitable. They can relate what they do on a day-to-day basis to profitability, so there's a stronger link between performance and profitability, as opposed to performance and stock price. Dan Maher agrees. "There are many times when a company seems to be performing well profit-wise, but because of the peer group it's in, the market just will not push up the value of the stock. That can be a real source of frustration for employees with stock incentives. With profit sharing, certainly they're frustrated if the company doesn't make money and they don't get a bonus, but at least they understand why."

Profit sharing can be linked to a variety of different measures, from earnings growth to economic value added (EVA) to shareholder return. The problem is selecting the right metric, says Anthony Tersigni. "EVA, for example, is sometimes problematic. If you use it to manage the business and make alternative investment decisions, then it can be an excellent tool to use in the incentive plan. But if you are not making business decisions based on EVA, and your managers do not think and plan in those terms, then it is probably not a good incentive measure. Earnings growth is always effective. It is plain, simple, easy to calculate, and typically correlated with the growth in company value. Total shareholder return is another good measure, combining appreciation in stock value plus dividends paid to shareholders."

If the metrics become too complicated, the factors influencing profit sharing can seem just as mysterious and arbitrary as those that affect stock price, but when kept simple it can be very effective. Nevertheless, there are drawbacks. "In many situations, profit sharing plans might be more effective than equity-based compensation plans because they are simpler," says Tersigni. "However, the downside of profit sharing is that it may take several years in a startup company to produce a profit and fund such a program. Profit sharing payouts may consume cash that would otherwise be needed to fund the growth of the business, and if paid in cash, they have no power to enhance retention." As with stock incentives, profit sharing should generally be used in combination with other forms of incentive compensation.

Gain Sharing

Gain sharing is often confused with profit sharing, but it is actually quite different. Profit sharing focuses on overall profitability, and is generally distributed among the company as a whole; gain sharing focuses on cost-cutting and production efficiencies within work groups, and rewards employees by sharing the gains from any savings. In gain sharing programs, monthly or quarterly performance goals are set for various work groups. The performance metrics and goals are different for each group depending on the nature of their work and the key value drivers in their area. For example, a manufacturing production work group might have performance goals based on parts per hour, scrap, defects, timeliness, and safety incidents. Performance is compared to the goals in order to quantify the benefit to the company, and a percentage of the gains are shared with the employees in the work group.

Gain sharing has many of the positive benefits of profit sharing, but with improved line of sight, as the performance metrics are tailored to the employees' work. This gives them a much greater sense that they can affect the performance metric in question. Thus, gain sharing is an excellent method for focusing on short-term goals, while profit sharing can be used to focus on long-term goals. For this reason, gain sharing incentives should be distributed on a monthly or, at most, quarterly basis so that the reward is closely linked in time to the behavior. One of the primary goals of gain sharing is to tap into the wealth of knowledge and ideas that employees possess and encourage them to apply those ideas to improve performance. Therefore, it is important for gain sharing to be an open process where goals are set collaboratively to ensure acceptance on the part of employees.

"Gain-sharing plans can be very effective if they are well designed," says Tersigni. "This means good line of sight, with performance measures that employees understand and believe they can impact in a positive way. In some ways, this is easier to do in a small company, simply because of size. The employees usually feel a common commitment to the business objectives of a startup company, tend to all work in a single location, and may simply feel more connected to the business. I think it is easier to create this culture in a small, young company."

One point of contention with gain sharing is whether managers or administrative staff should share in the gains for the work group.

Current management thinking appears to be leaning towards not including these subgroups. Rather, administrative staff should be part of a separate administrative group for gain sharing, and managers should receive their gains based on overall company performance. This helps to eliminate some of the perception of free-riding on the benefits derived from others' work. Of course, free-riding can be a problem within the work group itself, but if the group is small enough peer pressure is often effective in reducing this problem, and if not it can be addressed in performance reviews.

Merit Bonuses

While it is important to base some rewards on company-wide and group performance, rewards for individual performance are also critical, and bonuses are generally the easiest and most effective way to reward individual performance. Unlike incentives based on stock price or profitability, bonuses can be tied to very specific actions or concrete measures of performance. This allows employees to see a direct link between their individual performance, its impact on the metric, and the resulting bonus. Tying bonuses to the appropriate metrics can achieve stunning results.

Entrepreneurial managers like bonuses because of the strong cause-and-effect link between individual behavior and rewards. However, the selection of behaviors to be measured is critical, warns Dan Maher. It has to be very quantitative. "If you tell somebody that if their sales exceed a million dollars their commission gets adjusted from 2 percent to 5 percent, then you're going to see people doing anything and everything within their power to exceed a million dollars, because it means real money and it's very tangible. When you get into areas that are fuzzier and very subjective, particularly where 'good' or 'bad' is in the eye of the beholder, bonuses are far less effective. It becomes more a matter of what the boss thinks, and it's hard for employees to figure out what is driving the boss's assessment. If you can break performance down into measurable behaviors, then bonuses work well to reward those behaviors. They're not as effective when it becomes relatively or very subjective."

Bonuses can be funded in several ways. Merit bonuses are funded out of payroll and are substitutes for merit increases in base pay. Essentially, they are part of the base salary that the entrepreneur can afford to pay but holds back and makes contingent upon performance. For example, an employer that can afford to pay a particular employee a $100,000 salary might offer base pay of $80,000 and up to $20,000 in merit bonuses. Another example would be a tiered commission structure where salespeople are rewarded with a greater commission percentage once they achieve a particular sales target.

One-time performance bonuses are essentially individual profit sharing bonuses awarded for performance beyond what is expected. A key component to these types of bonuses is to determine the contribution expected from the employee in exchange for his or her base pay. One-time bonuses should compensate for performance over-and-above an expected norm, not for mere good performance. Landing a key contract, developing a way to streamline a process, or successfully launching a new product are all examples of situations where one-time performance bonuses are appropriate. One-time bonuses work particularly well in situations where entrepreneurs want to immediately reward employees who take initiative, and encourage them to stay with the company.

Employee award programs are also an example of incentive bonuses. These are generally company-wide programs that give a small financial reward to employees who achieve a particular goal seen as critical to the company's success. For example, retail stores often award bonuses to employees that provide excellent customer service. Award programs are generally found in larger companies, but they can work just as well in smaller firms. Entrepreneurial companies often offer awards for suggested improvements, and a few of the more enterprising ones even offer rewards for mistakes and failures to encourage risk-taking. The cash awards do not have to be large, and are a good way of highlighting and encouraging specific behaviors, especially new behaviors that are part of a change-management effort.

One hotly debated issue is whether bonuses should be linked to multiple performance measures or just one. Those who oppose multiple measures claim they are confusing and diminish goal clarity, while those who support multiple measures say they are necessary to ensure that one goal is not pursued to the detriment of all others. In reality, it's probably best to compromise and use somewhere in the range of three to five priorities per employee, says Anthony Tersigni. "I tend to like plans with multiple measures, but this also depends on the plan's participants. Plans for senior executives can be more focused or limited in terms of the number of measures. If you are focused on growth, then you may use growth in revenues, earnings or in earnings per share. However, an earnings measure alone does not reflect the efficient use of capital to achieve the earnings or the growth, so you may want to blend an earnings measure with a return on equity or return on assets measure. Much of this links back to business strategy. Are you trying to start a business and build volume or market position at any cost, or are you trying to start a company that you can quickly spin off for a quick financial gain? I have also found that plans which include mid-level managers and non-management personnel tend to have more measures; this is where you use measures such as quality, cycle time, unit cost, and other similar measures that tend to be operational or tactical in nature."

While bonus plans are one of the most effective ways of rewarding individual performance, they're also a good way of rewarding achievement of group milestones. Annual incentive plans tend to be somewhat discretionary in a small, entrepreneurial company, because the business is dynamic and it is relatively challenging to develop appropriate annual operating goals. Thus, some younger, growing companies use business milestone incentives, where bonuses are paid when certain goals are achieved—such as a specific sales level, breakeven financial performance, or a successful secondary placement—as opposed to being paid on a regular annual cycle.

Group bonuses help to reinforce the milestone achievement and create greater commitment and loyalty within the firm.

Employee Recognition Programs

In some cases, rewards do not have to be monetary to be effective motivational tools. Often the psychological reward of being formally recognized for one's contribution is even more important and powerful than a small monetary award. "Recognition for employees is really neglected," says Maher. "The value it has in terms of providing satisfaction to employees is just not appreciated by most managers. I guess managers believe that highlighting good performance and giving people a public pat on the back is not really appreciated by employees. Their view tends to be that if it's going to mean anything, there's got to be money attached to it. I know in our company, it surprises me the degree to which people are motivated just by the fact that a manager made it clear they are actually paying attention to what an employee is doing, and that they value what the employee is contributing. I don't think it's possible to do too much of that."

> Often the psychological reward of being formally recognized for one's contribution is even more important and powerful than a small monetary award.

There are a number of creative and highly effective ways to recognize employees, some of which have a direct or indirect cost to the company while others do not. For example, smaller entrepreneurial firms can leverage their size and flexibility to offer rewards such as extra vacation or flex-time. Other forms of recognition such as employee trips, holiday parties, clothing allowances, and family events provide additional benefits in that they can be used not only to reward behavior, but to strengthen the bonds between employees and help create a positive attitude towards the company as a whole.

"It is not always necessary to pay cash awards," agrees Tersigni. "There are a lot of effective programs that use prizes, premiums, extra time off, internal recognition, and other non-financial rewards—additional paid time off usually ranks high on the list of non-cash rewards that are preferred by employees. Another good reward is gift certificates that can be used by the employee and a spouse or significant other. It's also important to avoid getting into a rut; keep changing the reward opportunity, so people don't get complacent or bored with the program."

While financial incentives can be very effective in motivating employees to achieve specific goals, it would be a mistake to believe that employees are merely motivated by money. For today's younger workers, challenging work, autonomy, and flexibility are often just as important—and some would claim more important—than money. This change in attitude underscores the dissatisfaction many American employees feel and offers important clues as to how to rekindle motivation. Most of today's office workers long for a job that requires creativity and offers the freedom to do things their own way. Successful entrepreneurs will figure out how to give it to them and reward them, both financially and psychologically, for their efforts.

Putting It All Together

How should entrepreneurial firms mix stock incentives, profit sharing, gain sharing, and bonuses to achieve maximum performance and innovation? There is no perfect formula for designing incentive plans, as every firm is different, but the selection of performance measures is critical. Every company should have a vision statement, a set of strategies, and an action plan to achieve its goals. Entrepreneurs and managers need to be able to take the company's overall strategy and somehow link each individual's personal goals to this strategy.

When designing an incentive compensation plan, reward contingency is crucial, as employees need to be able to discern a direct link between actions and rewards. This calls for an emphasis on individual and small group rewards that are linked to performance measures over which the employee has direct control. In small firms, that may require designing different performance measures for each and every employee. Good design is critical. If employees don't understand how their decisions impact the incentive, then there's a very good chance their decisions *won't* have a clear impact on the goals that have been laid out for them, and so the incentives will not be effective.

One common mistake in designing incentive plans is linking rewards to achieving budgeted objectives. This is a prime example of tying incentives to the wrong metric, as it leads to a major conflict of interest. Any reasonable person who knows their bonus is tied to staying within a cost line in a budget will submit an inflated budget, and inflated budgets destroy the usefulness of aggregate planning. Incentives should never be linked to staying within budget, but rather to creating value.

When designing an incentive compensation plan, reward contingency is crucial, as employees need to be able to discern a direct link between actions and rewards.

Another mistake is ignoring the long term. There are some activities, such as investing in employee training, that don't necessarily show up in the quarterly bottom line, but which add to a company's value over time. It is important to provide different incentives that reward both short-term and long-term results. Unless specifically designed otherwise, most incentives lead people to maximize gains in the short term, while ignoring or even cannibalizing long-term results.

"If you're just starting out and everything is a three-year goal, that's not tangible enough for most managers or employees," says Maher. "On the other hand, certain behaviors by their nature will never provide short-term payback, and yet they can be critical. For example, the kind of people you recruit to the organization, the sort of morale you are able to foster, and the values you try and instill in your people are behaviors you can't measure in the short term.

Entrepreneurs need to use a well-balanced blend of short-term and long-term incentives, tied to the business strategy."

A final, and sometimes deadly, mistake is failing to think through all of the possible behaviors a particular incentive might lead to, warns Maher. "Don't underestimate the power of incentives to motivate behavior. Make sure you have studied the consequences of excessive, potentially negative behaviors. If everything is geared to profit, then you've got to make sure you understand how people might respond to that in order to generate the highest level of profit, and make sure you anticipate issues around reporting and accounting. You have to recognize the ability of incentives to impact behavior, and anticipate all the different kinds of negative behavior that might achieve the goal or incentive you've laid out. That doesn't mean you don't put incentives in place, but it means you have to communicate and put in place some checks and balances as well. You've really got to think through and anticipate all the sorts of things people will do in order to achieve those incentives."

Despite the potential dangers and drawbacks, incentive compensation plans are an essential tool for entrepreneurial firms in both attracting talented employees and keeping them motivated. In fact, talent and motivation are key to a new venture's survival, and also to the continuing success of larger, more established companies. Just look at Southwest, which remains one of the few consistently profitable airlines. Southwest starts employees with below-average base pay, but rewards them with stock purchase plans and profit sharing, as well as a number of rewards such as books, gift certificates, t-shirts, extra time off, tickets to special events, and other forms of monetary and non-monetary recognition. The result is a highly committed work force that provides sustainable competitive advantage for Southwest Airlines.

Ultimately, maintaining the commitment and motivation of the middle class, and the greater workforce at large, is going to require redesigning the American job. Companies are going to have to tear down hierarchies and offer greater flexibility and autonomy in exchange for greater responsibility and risk. Whether this is possible in traditional corporate America is questionable, but small entrepreneurial firms certainly have the ability to create this environment without having to overcome an established corporate culture. To win the innovation race and compete on the world stage, American employees need to think like owners, feel a vested interest in the success of their companies, and reap a greater percentage of their income from equity rather than wages. Entrepreneurial managers, on the other hand, need to stop thinking of employees as mere workers, and start seeing them as creators, innovators, and partners in the enterprise.

q

8

THE FUTURE OF INNOVATION— COLLABORATION AND INTRAPRENEURSHIP

◇◇◇

One of the greatest collaborative innovations in history was the Apollo lunar spacecraft that landed a man on the moon. As early as 1898, when H.G. Wells published The War of the Worlds, *people were dreaming of other worlds and interplanetary travel. For most, this was a fantasy, but for some visionary scientists it was a dream they were determined to make a reality. Among them was Robert Goddard, who in 1926 became the first person to successfully launch a rocket at his aunt's farm in Massachusetts. The rocket reached an altitude of 41 feet and flew for 2.5 seconds, landing 184 feet from its launch site. It was the first step on a long and difficult road to the moon that required the combined efforts of thousands of individuals to achieve.*

The next step came when none other than Charles Lindberg went to multimillionaire Daniel Guggenheim to ask for $100,000 in research funding on Goddard's behalf. He got it, and by 1935 Goddard was testing much larger rockets that were reaching altitudes of a mile and a quarter. Goddard was not alone in his quest—the space dream was advanced during the 1920s and 30s by various societies of amateurs, including the American

Interplanetary Society in the United States, the British Interplanetary Society in England, and the Society for Space Travel in Germany. Soon, however, rocketry had advanced to the point where it was too expensive for individuals or even societies to pursue. It was national governments that had the money to fund research, but they were interested in military applications, not space travel.

The Germans took the lead just before World War II by hiring Wernher von Braun and several other promising scientists and engineers from the civilian Society for Space Travel to lead their government rocket program. By the end of 1934, von Braun and his team had successfully launched a rocket that reached an altitude of five thousand feet, and by 1939, the Germans had developed a rocket-powered aircraft. Back in the United States, Goddard tried to get the Army and Navy interested in funding work on missiles and rocket-propelled aircraft, but to no avail. With the war and the success of the Germans, however, the U.S. Army finally took notice. They founded a Rocket Development Branch in 1943 and started experimenting with using rocket engines to propel ballistic missiles. Goddard died just as World War II was ending, but when the Germans surrendered, the Americans moved quickly to replace him. They spirited away Wernher von Braun, his team, and most of the German rocket technology to the United States, just before the Soviets arrived.

The next logical step in the progression towards space was launching a satellite into Earth's orbit. While the United States worked on this project in the 1950s, it was much more interested in developing long-range intercontinental ballistic missiles. In fact, the only reason there was a satellite program at all was because of its obvious military applications it terms of surveillance and reconnaissance. Yet political infighting between the Navy and the Air Force stalled the satellite project, and the Soviets beat the United States to orbit with their launch of Sputnik I on October 5th, 1957. This event was a jolt to both the federal government and the American public, which firmly believed the United States was the greatest nation on Earth. In response, Congress created the National Aeronautics and Space Administration less than a year later, but the United States needed more than a space agency. It needed a goal, one with more substance than simply staying ahead of the Soviets.

It was President John F. Kennedy who finally stepped forward and fulfilled the role of the visionary entrepreneur by setting the audacious goal of landing a man on the moon by the end of the 1960s. His vision finally catalyzed the American public into focusing on science and technology in an all-out effort to win not only the arms race, but the space race, a vision he set out in an address at Rice University in Houston, Texas on September 12, 1962:

"Those who came before us made certain that this country rode the first waves of the industrial revolution, the first waves of modern invention, and the first wave of nuclear power, and this generation does not intend to founder in the backwash of the coming age of space. We mean to be a part of it—we mean to lead it. For the eyes of the world now look into space, to the moon and to the planets beyond, and we have vowed that we shall not see it governed by a hostile flag of conquest, but by a banner of freedom and peace. We have vowed that we shall not see space filled with weapons of mass destruction, but with instruments of knowledge and understanding. Yet the vows of this Nation can only be fulfilled if we in this Nation are first, and, therefore, we intend to be first. In short, our leadership in science and in industry, our hopes for peace and security, our obligations to ourselves as well as others, all require us to make this effort, to solve these mysteries, to solve them for the good of all men, and to become the world's leading space-faring nation . . . We choose to go to the moon. We choose to go to the moon in this decade and do the other things, not because they are easy, but because they are hard, because that goal will serve to organize and measure the best of our energies and skills, because that challenge is one that we are willing to accept, one we are unwilling to postpone, and one which we intend to win."[1]

The achievement of this goal would require collaboration between thousands of individuals in the federal government, the military, industry, and academia. Over one thousand representatives from three hundred companies and various government agencies attended the initial NASA-Industry Apollo Technical Conference, including major defense contractors such as Martin Marietta, General Dynamics, North American, General Electric, and McDonnell, as well as subcontractors like Honeywell, Hughes, Raytheon, RCA, and Westinghouse. By the time Neil Armstrong and Buzz Aldrin landed on the moon on July 20th, 1969, thousands of contracts worth tens of billons of dollars had been awarded. It was a stunning technological achievement that required the effective collaboration not just of scientists and astronauts, but of welders, fitters, technicians, draftsmen, secretaries, managers, and many others on an unprecedented scale. Looking back, the fulfillment of Kennedy's vision is a reminder of what the United States can accomplish when it focuses on a goal and collaborates effectively.[2]

Thus far we have focused on the essential building blocks of the American innovation system—research and development, entrepreneurship education, venture capital, intellectual property rights, and incentive compensation. Economic success in the twenty-first century, however, requires more than just updating and fixing the cracks in these systems. It also requires integrating the various pieces of the American innovation system more fully and improving communication between all of the various people and organizations that participate in the innovation process. The changes created by globalization and information technology have created an environment where the old paradigm for innovation no longer applies. Today, innovation requires a more collaborative approach.

In the debate over restoring American jobs and competitiveness, there has been a lot of focus on supporting small entrepreneurial businesses as a way of revitalizing the American economy, and indeed small businesses play a very important role. They account for about half of private sector gross domestic product, and new firms create 10.5 million new jobs annually.[3] Yet an annual assessment of global entrepreneurial activity called the Global Entrepreneurship Monitor (GEM) project showed that two-thirds of new business owners expect to have little or no innovative impact on the market, and to create no more than two jobs in their first five years. Only 3 percent were classified as being potentially high impact, meaning they intend to use state-of-the-art technology to bring innovations to markets with few competitors.[4]

Small business alone will not sustain the growth we need to support the American economy. The world is becoming ever more complex, and the kind of entrepreneurial ventures that have the potential to create significant growth increasingly require a depth and breadth of expertise beyond the capabilities of a small venture. In a global knowledge economy, it is not going to be possible for any one company, small or large, to keep pace with the vast amount of information and new discoveries being made every day. A global economy requires a more open process of innovation, where the multitude of research done by startups, multinational corporations, research laboratories, and universities is exchanged in a knowledge brokering process that allows new ideas to be shared across various industries, institutions, and disciplines.

> **Small business alone will not sustain the growth we need to support the American economy.**

Collaboration has always been important, but the complexity and speed of innovation has increased so much that no single organization can realistically invent everything it needs internally. Successful companies are not going to be those that make a particular discovery and commercialize it first, but rather those that are able to combine breakthroughs and insights from various sources in a way that creates significant added value for their customers. Large companies need to become more entrepreneurial, to figure out how to leverage all of their intellectual property to its fullest potential. They also need to learn how to tap into the unutilized creative talents of their employees and respect the contributions they have to offer.

This applies not just to corporations, but to universities as well. We now rely upon universities to perform the majority of our basic research, and while researchers are patenting more and more technologies, very few are ever licensed and commercialized. Academia needs to do a better job of collaborating with industry and government to transfer technology into the marketplace. Meanwhile, small companies need to more fully utilize the local economic development resources at their disposal, like business incubators and technology centers, in order to improve their chances of success. All of this requires collaboration within the entrepreneurial community on an unprecedented scale, but that is exactly what is required in an ultra-competitive environment where we must extract maximum value from each and every innovation.

The Role of Large Companies in Innovation

Today, we're used to thinking of breakthrough innovation as the specialty of high-tech startups, but this was not always the case. During the golden age of research and development following World War II, corporate giants like IBM, General Electric, and DuPont were the leaders in creating innovative new products. As discussed previously, these companies invested heavily in research and development at a time when American industry was highly vertically integrated. They were incredibly self-sufficient, and there was little movement of people or information between various competitors and suppliers within industries. As a result, it was easy for corporations to maintain control over their research discoveries and to prevent them from leaking out, allowing these companies to capture significant value from their research investments. The investment in research and development worked so well in the era of vertical integration that it led to a continuous stream of new and improved products, and a fair number of breakthrough innovations as well.

Tom Anderson, a former manager in the global research and development activity at General Motors, remembers this era well. "When I started at General Motors in the late 1970s, GM was highly profitable and had a good share of the marketplace, and at that time the research center functioned like a university," says Anderson. "We had over twenty departments, and we did a lot of basic research. The

R&D function was driven by business-related problems—for example, we might have needed a stronger magnet for our electric motors so they could be smaller and lighter—but the science that went on was at a pretty fundamental level. In the case of the magnets, that research resulted in a whole new metal chemistry and a new alloy for magnets that was orders of magnitude stronger than what was previously available. This actually led to the development of a new plant in the General Motors hierarchy that made those magnets so we could use them in our motors."

Companies like General Motors were able to invest a tremendous amount in research and development because, when successful, it led to breakthrough products and entirely new lines of business. This generated revenue, which could then be invested in the next generation of research and development, creating a virtuous cycle. But this process also generated a large number of technologies that were simply shelved, caught in limbo between corporate research and development departments. From the company's perspective, this was fine so long as the technology remained within the company. But as the venture capital industry grew, employees with a talent for innovation left big companies to start new ones based around these ignored technologies. Essentially, these startups were free-riding on the R&D investment of larger companies, and while many of them failed, a few turned into the next generation of industry leaders.

When combined with the emergence of foreign competition from Japan, Germany, and elsewhere, the result was a stunning shift in the corporate landscape as some of America's oldest and most established firms took a beating from new competitors, both at home and abroad. By 2000, half of the one hundred biggest manufacturing and industrial firms from the 1970s had ceased to exist due to takeovers or bankruptcy, and their share of the nation's workforce had been cut in half.[5] While firms in the S&P 100 continued to employ about 7 percent of the civilian population, an increasing number of those jobs were supplied by relatively new companies like Microsoft.

So what happened? The answer is that the American business environment underwent a number of changes starting in the 1970s that made it difficult for market-leading firms to continue the virtuous cycle of innovation. First, the bigger-is-better philosophy that had prevailed in American business for the previous century was taken to extremes when corporations started forming conglomerates. When synergies failed to develop, their stock prices fell, and corporate raiders started using leveraged buyouts to dismantle overly large corporations, breaking up vertical integration. Inflation, rising oil prices, and the rising cost of American labor also put multinational companies on the defensive, making them vulnerable to foreign competitors. Big business started to respond to these competitors by becoming less hierarchical, returning to core competencies, and cutting their workforce, and when millions of workers lost their jobs, the loyalty-for-security pact was broken. The research and development knowledge that had been

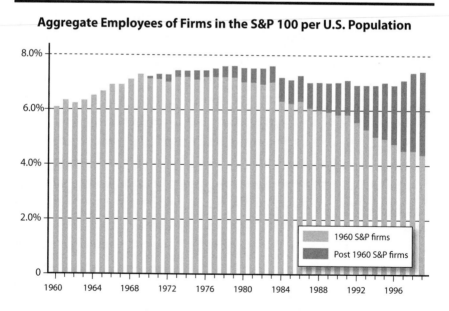

Aggregate Employees of Firms in the S&P 100 per U.S. Population

Legend:
1960 S&P firms
Post 1960 S&P firms

Source: Reprinted by permission from Ken Harrington, the Skandalaris Center for Entrepreneurial Studies. Data from Standard and Poor's.

so well protected previously began to spread among competitors, vendors, and suppliers as skilled labor became more mobile, and the increase in availability of venture capital made it easier to found high-tech startups.

As a result, the rate of new business incorporations quadrupled as the high-tech industry in Silicon Valley gained momentum, and with it came a transfer of power away from manufacturing giants to high-tech startups. A number of factors contributed to this change, allowing smaller entrepreneurial companies to challenge larger corporations. Free trade agreements and increasingly sophisticated communications technology had made it easier for small companies to sell products in foreign countries without the need for an actual foreign presence, and the deregulation of capital markets also allowed small companies to borrow money more easily. In addition, new manufacturing techniques such as flexible batch sizes, just-in-time production, and mass customization had emerged that could be employed more easily by small companies, and transportation and communications costs were falling. All of these developments reduced barriers to entry in many industries and opened the door for smaller firms. By 2001, a staggering 17 percent of working-age Americans were engaged in starting or running a new business, an unprecedented level of entrepreneurial activity for a post-industrial economy, and today small business accounts for two thirds of private sector job growth.[6]

The fact that most of the job growth in the last quarter of the century came from smaller firms implies that, among other factors, they were better able to capitalize on technological innovation. This is surprising, given the many natural advantages of large established firms. Yet as Clayton Christensen argued in his bestselling book, *The Innovator's Dilemma*, it is a consistent pattern for the market leader to falter and be replaced by a younger, hungrier competitor. While large companies are good at capitalizing on sustaining innovations that build incrementally on existing technologies, they often struggle when dealing with breakthrough technologies that require an entirely different market and business model.

According to Christensen, big companies excel at conducting the research to produce sustaining technologies, ones that have the potential to enhance their existing products and better serve their current customers, and in such cases they are good at pushing through and commercializing that innovation. When faced with a disruptive technology, however, one that requires a different business model and target market, they typically stumble. Mature companies succeed by listening to their customers and giving them what they want, but disruptive technologies tend to appeal to new markets, which are generally hard to identify through formal marketing research with current customers. Even when a big company can identify a suitable market for a new disruptive technology, it is generally small and not profitable enough to be of interest. Established companies whose growth is tapering off can only sustain their growth by serving large markets with good profit margins, and there is often significant pressure from stockholders and analysts to focus on the core business rather than branching out into something new.

Small companies, on the other hand, find it much easier to justify investments in new technologies than do companies whose growth has slowed. Small markets that are inconsequential to big firms are large enough to sustain and even fuel significant growth for a small company, allowing it to survive until the technology improves enough to move up-market. Because survival is on the line, employees in small firms are more likely to be excited and motivated by small successes and to take personal pride in these achievements. The startup culture is generally more relaxed, more tolerant of mistakes, and more flexible in responding to failure and change. The culture of a more mature company, on the other hand, is designed to discourage mistakes, and to control costs and quality through checks and balances. Unfortunately, this works against creativity and innovation, so as the growth of venture capital funds allowed more people to found companies to commercialize new technologies, startups took the lead in bringing innovative products to market in the 1990s.[7]

While startups have often succeeded where more mature companies have failed in commercializing breakthrough technologies in recent years, it would be wrong to assume that mature firms cannot innovate successfully. Small firms often have an advantage in commercializing disruptive technologies, but they have a hard time supporting the early-stage basic research necessary to create those breakthrough innovations. While federal research funding is four times more likely to be used for basic research at a small firm than a large one,[8] many of the fundamental basic research questions that are being worked on at the frontiers of research today require the joint efforts of a large group of mixed, multidisciplinary talent. It can take large investments of time, money, and human capital to do this fundamental research effectively.

"A large firm can do a lot more capital and labor-intensive research," says Tom Anderson. "They can invest in university-based research more effectively. It is more difficult for small firms, since contract research at a university can have a long time horizon. While a large corporation can be patient and invest in a research program that might take five to seven years to pay off, this is usually not an option for a small, entrepreneurial company working to put their first product on the market. That same small company can, however, effectively employ university-based research and development to provide advanced development resources that would be prohibitively expensive to attempt to create internally."

Small entrepreneurial companies generally don't have the resources to do early stage basic research. In fact, as technology becomes more advanced and complex, it's going to be increasingly difficult for small companies to do later-stage applications research as well. A hundred years ago, Henry Ford could invent the car in his garage, but the leading-edge technologies of today include gene splicing, nanotechnology, alternate fuel sources, and advanced satellites. These aren't things that inventors tinker with in the basement. Without sophisticated laboratories and large amounts of research capital, it is very difficult for small companies, with a handful of scientists and engineers, to develop advanced technologies.

Large firms also have a huge advantage over small ventures in regards to technological innovation because they have integrated learning bases. In addition to well-funded research and development facilities, they have varying product lines that appeal to a wide range of markets, and their knowledge of one market or product can be applied to another. Market leaders have the advantages not just of size, but of scope. They have fingers in many different pies along the supply chain, and the opportunity to leverage knowledge from a broad array of suppliers in various sectors and markets. To quote the famous business historian Alfred Chandler, "If the U.S. thinks it is going to regain global competitiveness through small business, it is fooling itself."[9]

Mature American businesses have an important role to play in fostering innovation and economic competitiveness.

Mature American businesses have an important role to play in fostering innovation and economic competitiveness, but they are not going to succeed by using the same approaches that they have in the past. For America to remain competitive in the innovation race, our multinationals are going to have to become more innovative and entrepreneurial, because entrepreneurship is not just carried out by young firms. Existing businesses also create innovative new products, services, and processes that create jobs and economic growth, and in this category one would expect American companies with their huge research and development budgets to lead the way. Yet the United States ranks a mere tenth in entrepreneurial activity by established firms, notably behind nations such as Chile, South Korea, New Zealand, Hong Kong, and China.[10]

Overall, the United States is part of a middling group of countries with average rates of entrepreneurship by mature companies—a far cry from being the global leader.

Firm Entrepreneurial Activity Index (95% confidence intervals)

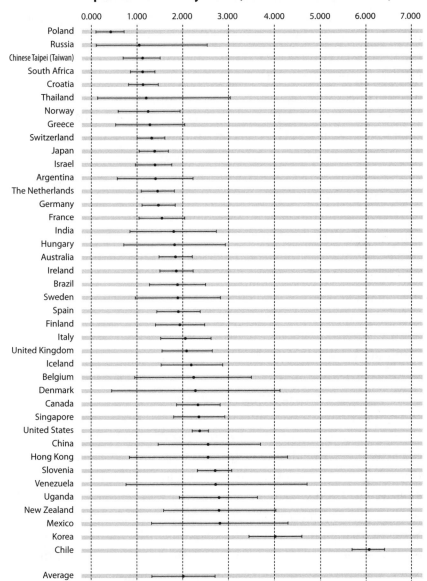

Source: Global Entrepreneurship Monitor 2003 Executive Report. © 2003 Paul D. Reynolds, William D. Bygrave, Erkko Autio, and Babson College.

American CEOs know they need to make their companies more innovative, but they're having a hard time translating that knowledge into action. According to the 2003 Global Entrepreneurship Monitor Executive Report, over 95 percent of mature firms worldwide are content to simply replicate their existing activities.[11] The main reason is that the organizational culture necessary to foster innovation is in many ways diametrically opposed to the command-and-control structure of corporate America. Twentieth century scientific management has taught business leaders to cut costs, streamline operations, and reduce risk. A big part of this has been making jobs worker-proof, thus reducing the possibility of error and inefficiency by reducing the need for the average employee to solve problems, interact with others, and make decisions. Although innovation is recognized as necessary, it is parceled off to those chosen few who are deemed worthy of doing creative work. This has squelched the innovative potential of the American workforce at large, and the tendency towards functional specialization has discouraged the kind of collaboration that is going to be so essential to success in the global economy.

Corporate Intrapreneurship

So how can senior managers make a large, multinational corporation with hundreds of business units and thousands of employees more entrepreneurial? This is the question that faces General Motors chairman and CEO Rick Wagoner, as well as every other American CEO, as they consider how to play the game in an environment where innovation is critical, yet difficult to control. Indeed, the auto industry has been wrestling with this question for decades as they've struggled to respond to foreign competition. While there are no easy answers, an important part of the solution will be for the auto industry to reinvent itself based on new technologies. The changes this will entail are going to be hard for many auto industry executives, but Wagoner is not an old-school Detroit auto guy, and thus he brings a fresh view to why General Motors succeeded in the past, and how it can succeed in the future.

"At General Motors, we built our position atop the global auto industry because one of our early leaders, Alfred Sloan, rejected the prevailing notion in 1920 that customers could buy any color they wanted, so long as it was black," explains Wagoner. "Sloan's revolutionary idea was to offer, as he put it, 'a car for every purse and purpose,' and to offer it as part of a price ladder of distinct brands, with Chevrolet at the bottom, and Cadillac at the top. That innovative strategy was very successful, and General Motors went on to become the largest automaker in the world. Now, Sloan may have blazed the trail, but there were a lot of people right behind him over the years, both inside and outside of General Motors, and it's been their job to improve on Sloan's ideas. We've done that within GM, and that's why we retain our global leadership position today. But a lot of other companies have done that as well, in countries and companies around the world, and that's why GM's lead is not as great as it was 40 years ago.

"This pattern, in which the pioneer in a given field enjoys tremendous initial success, followed by fierce competition when others catch up, is a pattern we see repeated throughout history, in many different disciplines. From events as important as the women's suffrage movement, as pivotal as Jackie Robinson breaking the major league baseball color barrier, or as utilitarian as deregulation of the long-distance telephone industry, when you broaden the field or open the game, you drive innovation, you promote growth, and you typically improve the game, whatever that game might be. Well, today, around the world, the game is economics, and free-market capitalism looks like the big winner. We in the United States may have pioneered it, but now the other players are catching up fast. That creates new opportunities and challenges for us. Going forward, as more of the world adopts the systems and strategies that the United States helped pioneer, we're going to see competition increase. We're going to see much more innovation, and much more growth, and the people of the world will be better off. On the whole, a better game, but we in the United States are going to have to play the best we ever have if we're going to continue growing, especially if we're going to remain leaders."

The importance of innovation to playing well in that game is obvious, so why don't large companies try to encourage more of it? When I talk to CEOs of mature companies, most claim that they do. Innovation is high on the list of current management buzzwords, and management gurus are pushing the idea that companies have to become faster, more flexible, encourage creativity, empower employees, and foster a culture of innovation. Companies have tried a variety of methods to accomplish this, such as cross-functional teams, creativity training, and employee empowerment programs, just to name a few. Unfortunately, the real problem for large firms isn't generating new ideas, but rather implementing them. According to Gifford Pinchot, the author of *Intrapreneuring in Action,* the missing link in the implementation and commercialization process at mature firms is the entrepreneur. In a study of fifty new product development projects at Texas Instruments, Pinchot found that the key difference between success and failure was whether the project had a "zealous volunteer champion" who took the lead, recruited others, focused on the details of implementation, and pushed the project through all the red tape to completion. Every successful project had one; every failed project didn't.[12] The problem is that senior managers are failing to identify and support people within their organizations who are capable of successfully driving innovation.

> **The missing link in the implementation and commercialization process at mature firms is the entrepreneur.**

The word entrepreneur tends to invoke the image of a lone pioneer with a small startup, not an employee within a Fortune 500 company. In the twenty-first century, however, "intrapreneurs" with the resources of a multinational corporation at their disposal may actually play just as important of a role in the fate of America as small business entrepreneurs. The concept of intrapreneurship got its start in 1976 when Pinchot coined the term intrapreneur. He used it to define his vision of an intra-corporate entrepreneur, a person who would fill the entrepreneurial role within a mature company by developing new business models to commercialize breakthrough technologies. In his vision of intrapreneurship, the intrapreneur would trade a portion of their salary in exchange for "intracapital" and a financial stake in the project. He established a school for intrapreneurs and within a few years, the concept had spread amongst the academic and business community. Entrepreneur Steve Jobs even described the development of the Macintosh computer as an intrapreneurial venture.

Over time, however, the idea of intrapreneurship faded into the background like so many other management fads, primarily because CEOs found they couldn't implement it successfully. Yet the problem wasn't the concept of intrapreneurship itself, but rather that its implementation was routinely undermined by ingrained corporate cultures. Despite all the management initiatives, even at the most innovative companies it is still very difficult to get a new idea through the layers of red tape designed for analysis, approval, and control. Senior management, while sincerely desiring innovation, seemingly cannot let go of the overwhelming urge to plan and control it. Corporate culture is the single greatest barrier to intrapreneurship, for the command-and-control bureaucracy typical of most large companies tends to sideline any projects that are risky and reprimand those employees who step beyond the boundaries of their job description.

In order to succeed, many intrapreneurs have to bootleg funds from other projects, work on their own time, and sometimes defy direct orders from their superiors—all without any promise of a reward for their successful innovations. Pinchot saw this repeatedly in the course of his work studying intrapreneurship, and developed a list of ten commandments for intrapreneurs that includes "remember it is easier to ask for forgiveness than for permission," "circumvent any orders aimed at stopping your dream," "work underground as long as you can," and "come to work each day willing to be fired."[13]

Come to work each day willing to be fired? No wonder American companies have so much trouble innovating! If intrapreneurship is so difficult, unappreciated, and frustrating, and if the financial rewards are limited, why would anyone want to be an intrapreneur? Managers in big companies do not see the development of new products as a strong career path, since it can take years to generate a positive return on investment, and if the project fails their career can be negatively impacted. Thus, the best managers tend to avoid these opportunities.

Mature companies are desperately short of intrapreneurs because the bureaucracy in corporate America is, quite frankly, hostile to them. In a corporate environment these people are viewed as loose cannons, and often times as a liability, because they make mistakes. It's a difficult path to take, and when intrapreneurs feel they're not being listened to or allowed to follow through on their ideas, then they start their own companies and become the new competition. In fact, a study done by researchers at the Massachusetts Institute of Technology, which followed thirty-nine employees who left one company to start their own businesses, found that after five years their combined sales volume was two-and-a-half times greater than the company they had left.[14] Frustrated intrapreneurs often leave to become entrepreneurs, and the fallout doesn't stop there. When a number of the best and brightest employees leave, the rest of the good employees take notice, and some of the top talent follows them out the door. The result is that very few employees are willing to take on the intrapreneurial role in large organizations, because the most creative, innovative people have fled for more welcoming environments in smaller companies, the non-profit sector, or self-employment.

The question now facing big companies is how to stop the brain drain of their top creative talent and foster more intrapreneurship. This is no easy task. Making a large company more innovative and intrapreneurial is a tall order, and while most CEOs understand the importance of doing so, the majority have no idea how to effectively bring it about. When executives talk about making their companies more innovative, they often ask how they can make employees more self-directed and creative, but according to Pinchot, this is the wrong question. The right question is, how can senior management create a corporate culture that supports employees' innovative activities rather than killing them? Making a large company more intrapreneurial poses many challenges, because the bureaucracies that allow large organizations to function effectively tend to stifle creativity and high-risk projects. The answer lies in tapping the entrepreneurial talent that exists within companies, and creating an environment where that talent can thrive.

> The question now facing big companies is how to stop the brain drain of their top creative talent and foster more intrapreneurship.

"One of my personal favorite quotes from General Motors' most famous leader, Alfred Sloan, is that 'Each generation must meet changes—in the automotive market, in the general administration of the enterprise, and in the involvement of the corporation in a changing world. The work of creating goes on.'" says Wagoner. "At GM, much of that work is continued by what have been called intrapreneurs, who are the entrepreneurs within large organizations, the people who take responsibility for turning an idea into a profitable product through assertive risk-taking and innovation.

"One example of intrapreneurship within General Motors was the development of the Pontiac Solstice, a roadster for which we have very high hopes. It debuted as a concept car a few years ago, as a result of a challenge to our design studios to see who could come up with the best idea the fastest. The original concept went from sketch to show floor in a matter of months, and it was a huge hit. Based on the enormously positive response it got, we green-lighted it for production, but the biggest contribution it has made to GM might just be the way it inspired us to revamp our entire product development process. That aspect of competition in its development proved so successful that it became the way we do cars and trucks now, period. We have instituted what we call a "9:3:1 bakeoff," which means every new car or truck program starts with nine designs from our different design studios around the globe. The best three are chosen to go to the next stage of development, and from there we select the final design. The spark of competition lights the match of creativity and innovation among our design staff, and really brings out the best in them. It involves more people in the creative process, and encourages them to do things in ways that might not have occurred to them otherwise."

General Motors' new approach to product development is a significant step along the path to involving a greater number of employees in the innovative process, one that other companies would do well to imitate. One of the main reasons that intrapreneurship initiatives fail is that managers can't quite bring themselves to trust their subordinates to innovate and think for themselves. The scientific management movement in many ways was an attempt to simplify jobs in order to make them "worker-proof," and to restrict problem solving, creativity, and decision making to a small, elite class of workers. But the notion that innovation should be left to a select group of properly educated and trained individuals is short-sighted. All human beings are creative, and to leave manufacturing, administrative, and sales workers out of the innovation process not only demeans those workers, it cuts them off from performing the kind of work that might add value for the company and create more engaging and satisfying jobs. Only if corporate America taps the creative and innovative potential of all its employees and fosters greater intrapreneurship will it be able to compete long-term in the global knowledge economy.

In addition to fostering intrapreneurship on the part of their employees, America's leading companies also need to be more open to taking more calculated risks when it comes to innovation. At General Motors, the company's long-term strategy can be summed up in one phrase—hydrogen fuel cells—and Wagoner knows that while betting on this new technology is risky, it is exactly the kind of strategic move that is required to stay ahead of the global competition. "For the automotive industry, the hydrogen fuel cell represents a new platform for innovation, and really, a chance to revolutionize our business," says Wagoner." Over the last several years, we've made what former CBC Evening News anchor Dan Rather called GM's 'billion dollar bet' on hydrogen-powered vehicles. Our investment has been substantial, and today we are the leaders in developing fuel-cell powered vehicles, but we're not alone in this race. Other companies, and other countries like China and Japan, are also very interested in developing fuel cells, and they're moving forward quickly. While it's not going to be easy or without some risk, fuel-cell technology has the potential to reinvent the automobile as we know it. The companies and countries that do so will shape the global auto industry for years to come, much as GM and Alfred Sloan did eighty years ago by offering 'a car for every purse and purpose.' Are there risks in committing so many resources to a project that might never come to pass? Of course, but to my way of thinking, there are even greater risks in failing to pursue a technology that could change the auto business, and the world, as we know it. In many respects, the hydrogen fuel cell vehicle represents our industry's 'moon shot,' and we at GM are committed to playing a leading role in making this vision a reality."

For General Motors to be successful, it is going to need to support intrapreneurs at every level within the organization who can drive hydrogen fuel-cell technology forward, and it is by no means alone. Every leading company that faces global competition is going to need to take its own moon shot, and will need to support intrapreneurs who can turn those strategic visions into reality. Right now, unfortunately, there is a limited career path for intrapreneurs, but in the future, opportunities for entrepreneurs are likely to come increasingly from within big companies. As technology becomes more sophisticated and development times decrease, it's going to take the resources of a large corporation to facilitate changes as quickly as they need to happen, and the vision of an intrapreneur to make sure that innovative projects see the light of day. Corporations are going to need to create jobs for intrapreneurs where they can work side by side with scientists and engineers, developing the product and then handing it back over to the corporations to be managed only after it is launched.

If American companies are serious about wanting to foster innovation—and they should be—their managements need to accept that the creative process is unpredictable and requires a great deal of freedom and flexibility. Executives need to lift the restrictions and red tape, watch to see what ideas and intrapreneurs emerge, and then give those employees the opportunity and resources to run with their ideas. This is easier said than done, and the issue of whether intrapreneurship can really be successful in large, established corporations is certainly open to debate. While some companies have harnessed the power of intrapreneurship quite successfully, they tend to be younger, high-tech companies that did not exist a hundred years ago. There is deep skepticism as to whether traditional, blue-chip companies can really become more entrepreneurial. Yet Wagoner, while acknowledging that General Motors will never be as flexible and entrepreneurial as a startup, nevertheless believes that intrapreneurship within large corporations is not only possible, but essential.

"One of the qualities that has contributed to America's productivity is our ability to innovate, to take risks, to act as entrepreneurs, even within big companies," says Wagoner. "Often, our inclination in uncertain times is to hunker down and avoid risk. But entrepreneurs resist that urge, and do what they do best: search for opportunities, move aggressively, stake out the lead. History shows us that one of the few constraints in our world is change, and unless you keep up with it, you'll be history yourself. At General Motors, we think the answer to keeping up with change—or better, staying ahead of it—lies in the entrepreneurial spirit. We look for and promote that spirit within our own company by taking calculated risks. We understand that, in order to survive, we have to evolve, to change, as the world and the needs of our consumers change. To do that, we need entrepreneurs, both inside and outside of our company."

Knowledge Brokering

While it is important for all firms to be innovative if they want to survive in the global economy, the degree of control necessary at mature firms is diametrically opposed to the type of culture required to nurture a true breakthrough innovation, and most have a dismal record of commercializing the type of breakthrough innovations that drive economic growth. Although many CEOs have attempted to make their companies more open and innovative, very few have truly managed to create an innovative, entrepreneurial culture. There is too much ingrained resistance to risk and change from within their companies, and too much relentless pressure for consistent short-term results from Wall Street. This is why, in many instances, the best path to market for a breakthrough technology is one that is outside of the company that originally invented it.

One of the keys to managing innovation in the twenty-first century is to adopt a strategy of knowledge brokering so that companies can reap greater financial benefits from their intellectual property. Information technology has brought the research monopolies of the big companies to an end, because there is too much information that is easily accessible online and at universities for industrial labs to be able to maintain secrecy and control. Thus, companies need to sell what they don't need on the market so that they can buy what they do need to be successful. Admittedly, allowing intellectual property out of the organization and into the hands of competitors by selling or licensing it is a huge strategic shift for executives. Yet in an environment where the diffusion of information is impossible to totally control, this is an effective way to use intellectual property to generate revenue.

Company executives who are managing their intellectual property successfully realize there is an increasing amount of information being

> One of the keys to managing innovation in the twenty-first century is to adopt a strategy of knowledge brokering.

generated outside their company, and in some cases it is more cost efficient to buy it than to create it themselves. In fact, according to Henry Chesbrough, the author of *Open Innovation,* the best strategy for large firms may be to minimize the amount of research they do internally and instead buy as much research from others as possible. In the coming decades, he argues, multinational corporations will not be able to support comprehensive research and development programs where they invent everything internally as they did in the past. Instead, they will need to spend much of their time staying informed about all of the advances in their field made by startups and universities, using internal research and development to fill in the gaps.

In a knowledge economy, information is no longer a scarce resource, and power comes from combining knowledge from various sources in useful ways, rather than by maintaining secrecy and exclusive control. Instead of viewing intellectual property as something to be created and used internally, putting it on the shelf if there isn't an immediate need for it, companies need to either incorporate the intellectual property resulting from their research, license it for external use, or launch new ventures around it. While the goal of most industrial research programs is to develop and utilize patents and other intellectual property internally, in some cases the best use of intellectual property is to sell or license it to another company that can use it more effectively. This requires an entirely different approach to the research and commercialization process, one that is far more dependent on collaboration, not only within organizations, but between organizations.

Supporting what Chesbrough calls "open innovation" requires finding ways to encourage greater cooperation between large and small companies by creating intellectual property networks and markets to exchange intellectual property. Small firms have come to play an increasingly important role in conducting breakthrough research over the past several decades; patents awarded to small firms tend to be technically more important and twice as likely to be among the top one percent of high-impact patents.[15] For America to fully utilize its research potential, large and small firms need to overcome their traditional adversarial roles and learn how to form strategic alliances to their mutual advantage.

> Big and small companies have increasingly complementary roles in technology development . . . Frequently, small companies have deep expertise in niche skills, but little skill or experience in working in large teams or managing complex projects. Large companies often have very broad technology portfolios, but insufficient depth in specific technical areas. They are often expert at managing complex projects and can link up teams of people with disparate cultures, languages, skills, and business approaches. Small companies may be able to respond more quickly to customer needs or quick market changes, while large firms can offer very broad supplier and customer networks. As a result, technology partnerships and collaborations between large and small companies make good partners because the strengths of one are the weaknesses of the other... The different roles taken on by small and large firms together create more technological progress, innovation, and growth than either category could have achieved by itself.[16]
>
> —*Innovate America* report,
> Council on Competitiveness

In general, large and small companies have been moving towards more collaborative relationships since the 1980s. Microsoft, for example, has an Intellectual Property Ventures program through which it licenses internally developed technologies to high-tech startups, an increasingly popular business model. Information technology companies like Microsoft and Intel and pharmaceutical companies like Pfizer and Merck also have hundreds of research partnerships. They increasingly rely on small firms to do early stage research and development, licensing the technologies or buying the companies outright as they mature.

Nevertheless, collaboration between large and small firms is still difficult, as the debate over open source and standards reveals. David

Attis, director of policy studies for the Council on Competitiveness, notes that in their National Innovation Initiative meetings, "We had a lot of representatives from both big companies and small companies in many of our working groups, and I think they both realize the degree to which they need each other. IBM, for example, like all large, innovative companies, realizes they absolutely need small companies to come to them with new technologies and partner with them for all kinds of experiments. At the same time, both large and small firms recognize there's an incredible amount of bureaucracy and regulation that gets in the way when partnering. Leaders of small firms don't know whom to call at IBM, and there are all kinds of contracts that have to be signed before they can talk and a lot of questions about intellectual property rights. They all agree that there are some steps that could be taken, such as figuring out what best practices are and coming up with model agreements, so that both sides feel more comfortable when they sit down at the table to share ideas and collaborate. It can be done, but for now, it is still really challenging for small and large entities to collaborate."

As a result, when a startup firm proves the commercial viability of a new technology, mature firms with extra cash often take the easy way out and simply acquire the company rather than forming strategic partnerships or licensing their technology. Unfortunately, trying to merge two different corporate cultures also presents formidable problems, especially when one is a small, entrepreneurial venture being forced to adopt the more formal, controlled culture of the acquiring firm. In many cases the best employees from the acquired firm leave, and much of what made the small firm valuable and innovative is lost with them. Furthermore, the acquiring firm generally increases its debt burden in order to finance the purchase of the other company, which makes it essential that they realize efficiencies and cut costs as quickly as possible. The debt burden shifts the focus from long-term growth and innovation to cost-cutting and short-term results. While this may make sense from the acquiring firms' standpoint, it often smothers the entrepreneurial spirit of smaller, acquired firms, destroying their potential for further innovation. In the process, much of their innovative potential is lost.

Mature firms' desire to maintain control also tends to work against corporate venturing, which is another important option for managing intellectual property. Research is by nature unpredictable, and not everything discovered will be profitable if used only internally. That does not, however, mean that it isn't valuable, and in a country with a well-developed venture capital system, new discoveries that sit on the corporate shelf have a way of leaking out. Therefore, the best approach is often for companies to spin off new ventures around promising new technologies themselves. By allowing ideas and innovations to flow outside of the company into small startups, CEOs of mature firms can free the entrepreneurial team from the constraints of the established corporate culture, while still keeping a financial stake in the company as well as some control over the technology.

"We did a bit of corporate venturing when I was at General Motors," relates Tom Anderson. "We had technologies the Research and Development Center created to meet an internal need, but they weren't really core business items for us, so we worked to find a partner that could commercialize and support those technologies externally. One example was a software tool for circuit design that optimized the physical size of the circuit. We needed it for our own use, but it wasn't something we wanted to support continued development of, so we found a circuit design company that was interested in rolling it into their offering. They provided the support and continued development, and we got the benefit of being able to use the technology and have it continue to improve."

In the past, a number of companies have attempted to set up internal corporate venture groups rather than spinning off external companies, but this can be very tricky to do well. The parent company has a way of forcing its culture upon the startup group, which defeats the purpose of creating the spin-off in the first place. The instinct of a manager in a large, established company is to control uncertainty, but developing a business model around a new technology requires the flexibility of a small, entrepreneurial culture. Support for internal venture groups also tends to wax and wane depending on the return on capital investment, which is influenced by external market factors. It can also be difficult to show financially how the value of new ventures that are created accrues to investors of the parent company.

How do we encourage mature companies to license or spin off more of their technologies and partner with startups rather than acquiring them? One way would be to provide large corporations with tax credits or other incentives to make their non-core technologies available to individual or small-enterprise entrepreneurs. In many instances, innovations and opportunities lie dormant in large companies because they are not critical to the profits of the company. With the right incentives, large corporations might be more willing to sell unused technology, or to develop joint ventures with small business entrepreneurs in order to commercialize that technology. If executives see a financial benefit to partnering with smaller firms, that will go a long way towards changing attitudes towards letting intellectual property out of their organizations.

Technology Transfer

In addition to encouraging greater collaboration between large and small firms, we also need to improve cooperation between universities and industry in regards to research and development. In an open innovation environment, one of the most pressing issues is how to adequately fund basic research. Under the old system, industrial R&D laboratories used to do basic research internally as part of their total research efforts; in fact, a number of research scientists from industrial labs actually won Nobel Prizes. In an environment where large companies can't retain control of the information they produce, however, funding basic research isn't profitable. Yet without it there will be no foundation for future breakthrough innovations.

"As profitability has been declining at American corporations, there has been a move to make sure that research is more directly coupled to products and profitability issues," says Anderson. "There's a much stronger coupling now between research, development, and manufacturing than in the past, and that's kind of a doubled-edged sword. On one hand, you get a quicker flow-through from research to product, and that's important for larger programs like developing fuel-cell vehicles. On the other hand, what you lose is some of the basic research that might lead to an innovation that you wouldn't have thought of, that you wouldn't have planned for initially." As a result, the role of universities in the commercial research process has become critically important. In the United States, 60 percent of basic research is performed by universities, yet with the proposed cuts in federal funding for research, that critical piece of the American innovation system is in jeopardy.[17]

It is clear that in an innovation economy, universities play a central role in basic research, and that universities and private industry are going to have to collaborate ever more closely if we hope to maintain our research base and technological leadership. The companies that grow and prosper are going to be the ones that effectively utilize the research resources and human capital in our leading universities. A key part of this process is technology transfer, the movement of promising technologies from university laboratories to private industry. In fact, Congress' desire to stimulate greater technology transfer was the motivation behind the passage of the Bayh-Dole University and Small Business Patent Act in 1980. The act sought to strengthen the connection between academia and industry by creating a uniform federal policy granting universities the right to retain control of intellectual property resulting from federally funded research. It supported the negotiation of exclusive licenses between universities and private enterprise regarding such rights, in the hopes that this would result in increased technology

> **Universities and private industry are going to have to collaborate ever more closely if we hope to maintain our research base and technological leadership.**

transfer between university laboratories and industry and greater commercialization. Indeed, the Bayh-Dole Act is widely credited as the reason patenting and commercialization of university research has increased significantly over the past three decades.

Yet according to Lesa Mitchell, vice president of Advancing Innovation at the Kauffman Foundation, the apparent link is not that straightforward. "Because of the point in time when the Bayh-Dole Act was approved, one could lay all credit on Bayh-Dole, but there were many contributing factors to the increase in university innovation," says Mitchell. "At the time, there was a movement away from big corporate research budgets, and in parallel there was a movement toward increasing federal funding of research in universities. Neither Israel nor the United Kingdom has a similar policy in place, yet both locations have prolific university innovators evidenced by the high number of patents and startup companies in their countries."

Opponents of Bayh-Dole have argued that the unintended consequences of the act have been detrimental to basic research, because it introduces an element of commercialism to universities. Many industry leaders also believe that focusing on revenue generation has influenced universities to not only patent too much, but also too early. There is an assumption that platform technologies in computer science and engineering should remain part of the public domain, and that universities often resist open source models because they are assuming a "protect, patent, and profit" stance. Yet all of these views are too black and white to represent reality. Despite the school of thought that universities are over-commercializing, the reality is much different in many universities.

"The Foundation's interest in university innovation stems from our belief that innovation represents the knowledge creation, or front end, of the entrepreneurial pipeline," says Mitchell. "Universities have the capability of enabling a virtuous cycle, and to propagate innovation we must enable the alternative pathways of innovation. Many fear that our campuses are becoming research factories for private industry, yet a great deal of promising innovation consistently fails to be developed and brought to market for practical use. This includes research in the life sciences that could lead to vital new drugs and medical therapies, as well as research in computing and engineering that could lead to useful new products and job-creating new firms. In short, despite the belief in rampant commercialization, there are very few institutions that have the resources to enable their innovations."

The problem, ironically, is tied to the implementation of the Bayh-Dole Act. While the act eliminated a major roadblock to ownership of university innovation, there was no planning surrounding how this policy would impact practices and resource allocation within American universities. While there were less than one hundred university technology transfer offices in place in 1980, universities with offices already in place, such as Stanford and MIT, had a rich history of innovation and a high level of research funding to support expansion. Today, the other institutions that receive federal dollars are left with the impression that they need to replicate this technology transfer office model, but most don't have the resources to support it.

While the last twenty-five years have brought about a substantial increase in knowledge transfer, patenting, and licensing, there are many universities who receive federal funding that do not have the resources to enable faculty innovations. "Within universities with a small patent budget and insufficient human resources, you will find that patents sit on the shelf due to the lack of university outreach or industry in-reach," says Mitchell. "In too many cases, innovations are caught in limbo between universities, entrepreneurs, and industry, and are left to languish." Industry leaders understand the difficulty of portfolio evaluation and managing innovations through their research and development pipeline. While these same difficulties apply when moving innovations to market, it is much more complex through a distributed system of university research funding.

Mitchell, however, does not believe that the answer lies in replicating technology transfer offices at every university. "There are other alternatives to the patent-license pathway," says Mitchell. "There are tools that can enable a more open environment between researchers, entrepreneurs, and faculty researchers. There are also multi-university collaborative models that could aid in the facilitation of new knowledge. At the Kauffman Foundation, we do not assume a silver bullet or a one-size-fits-all model. The complexities of university innovation and enabling the virtuous cycle have not been broadly recognized. As a researcher in a large corporation understands, a novel innovation isn't necessarily ready for the commercial market." Good ideas have to be identified and evaluated, and an appropriate commercialization plan developed—a patent file sitting on a university shelf is far from being a marketable product. Innovations generally need to be developed into a working prototype and have an identified market before any investor will be interested. As a result, the overwhelming majority of successfully patented and licensed innovations come from a small number of elite universities.

Government and industry have enormous potential to assist universities in the process of commercializing innovations, but an unintended consequence of this focus is that it has placed pressure on universities to spark economic growth in local communities. This pressure, coupled with a reduction of funding to state universities, has created a focus on revenue generation from university technology transfer offices. Often, the universities' licensing and entrepreneurial startup expectations are unrealistic, and many of them have limited resources. This increases the drive to identify a few high-priority innovations, while ignoring the vast majority of what could be licensed.

At universities like Stanford and MIT, the interest in technology transfer is an outgrowth of excellence in education and research. "For those schools, advancing innovation is a by-product of a much bigger mission," says Mitchell. "The moment a university focuses on revenue generation as a primary motivator, it creates an insurmountable barrier with research faculty. At any university, education and research should be the primary mission. Outcomes of good research require codified pathways to facilitate the next steps of innovation."

Innovation Zones

One way to help support the transfer of technology from both universities and large corporations to startups is through innovation zones, which are collaborative efforts between state government, universities, industry, and private investors. Essentially, they are industry clusters of high-tech businesses, research institutions, and startup incubators that build on regional infrastructure and expertise. The purpose of an innovation zone is to help commercialize and build local businesses around intellectual property that is developed at nearby universities and other research institutions. State and local governments generally provide tax breaks and other financial incentives to young businesses that choose to operate within the zone, thus encouraging local economic development. The zone concept also promotes clustering of related businesses, as innovation zones often designate a few key technology areas as their focus. Innovation zones are now being created in states across the nation to develop a more multifaceted approach to commercial research and development.

> The purpose of an innovation zone is to help commercialize and build local businesses around intellectual property that is developed at nearby universities and other research institutions.

Michigan, for example, has ten innovation "SmartZones," including Automation Alley in Troy. Tom Anderson is now the director of the Technology Center at Automation Alley, which leverages businesses, educators, and government to bring new technologies to market more quickly and efficiently. "The purpose of the technology center is two-fold," Anderson told me. "One is to help transform technology innovations into solutions for the market. Even when I was working at General Motors in their corporate research center, I experienced that technologists, scientists, and engineers who are in the business of discovery often wind up being enamored of the technology. They think it will sell itself and that the benefits are apparent, but if you have a technology that doesn't map to a marketplace need, then all you have is a really cool science project. It's not a new business. So the first thing we do when we are presented with a new technology is to make sure it has the underpinnings for a new business, and we do that in conjunction with our membership, which is really a group of technology consumers.

"The second thing we do is to help build a plan for going to market by determining what the path to profitability is, getting commercial validation of that technology, and creating focus for the entrepreneur. For example, we had one company that had a data-mining approach that would pull together information from a number of different sources through a web-based portal and consolidate it all in one place. This had applications in automotive and electronics design, in health care, in financial management, all of these different market verticals. We helped them pick the one where their team had enough domain expertise that they could actually move forward as a successful business, with the plan that they would eventually expand into these other market verticals. You need to have a focus when you start a business, and we help entrepreneurs to find that focus."

Technology centers give a focal point to innovation zones by providing an actual, physical building where collaboration can take place. The point of a technology center is to aggregate high-tech startups in one place and to provide shared access to high-tech development facilities, as well as providing mentoring and business incubator services to startup companies that are accepted into the center. Even for those companies that are not accepted, the technology center generally provides assistance to entrepreneurs by hosting educational and networking events. The goal is to bring together the right people and resources in order to facilitate commercialization, and this is particularly helpful for high-tech ventures where business advice and access to venture capital is critical. By giving the innovation zone a focal point, technology centers and incubators help promote collaboration between local researchers, entrepreneurs, and venture capitalists.

Most entrepreneurs come to the technology center at a stage when they already have a patented or copyrighted technology. "The ones that we typically see have technology that is protected one way or another, so it's proprietary. It's been demonstrated to work, and in some cases has a little bit of market traction. In others we provide some seed funding to get customer validation that it will actually work. With the company that developed the data-mining technique, for example, we provided them enough funding to develop a prototype that would cover one small segment of the information they were gathering. That allowed them to build a working prototype that they could take out to customers at Ford, General Motors, and Daimler Chrysler, and they were able to show them how the web portal worked. The customer could actually do inquiries and see the level and depth of information that they could get back and how quickly, so they could see the benefit they might have if all of the automotive electronics information were populated into this one portal."

By assisting entrepreneurs with this customer validation process, technology centers help to move discoveries out of university technology transfer offices and develop them to a point where venture capitalists are willing to invest. In fact, most innovation zones include at least one research university within their borders, because they recognize the central role that universities play in today's commercial research and development process. Some technology centers are sponsored by the universities themselves, and almost all work closely with universities to help identify and develop promising technologies.

"All of the major research institutions across the country are really looking for ways to better commercialize the research they have ongoing," says Anderson. "They're investing to be able to go a little further down the development path and provide incubator support to take those discoveries out of the lab and into the marketplace. While only a small portion of the inventions at a university really fit and can support the development of a new business or a new industry, they're helping to provide additional resources and support to take those innovations forward. This is where a university can combine its business acumen with its scientific advancements to create a viable venture."

Technology centers and innovation zones are more than just a means to transfer technology from universities to the marketplace, however. They encourage collaboration with local businesses as well, because innovation zones are designed to create industry clusters—high concentrations of related manufacturers, suppliers, and service providers in the same industry. Original equipment manufacturers, like the big three automakers in Detroit, have a vested interest in developing high-tech suppliers and service providers that can meet their industry needs. Technology centers give industry leaders a place to go with non-core technologies that they would like to spin off or license, without having to develop it themselves.

"At the Automation Alley Tech Center, we have worked with a couple of opportunities that have been spin-offs from larger corporations, cases where a technology that they were going to use for one piece of their business had broader implications, so they wanted to spin it off as a separate and new business," says Anderson. "Technology transfer, whether it is coming from universities or corporations or somewhere else, really is a contact sport. It's a matter of the numbers of people that you know and talk to, and the relationships that you cultivate. The key is to be able to listen to what each partner in that relationship has, needs, and wants, and to structure the interaction in a way that there's some benefit for all of the participants. It has to be a win-win for everybody, and that's a matter of understanding what drives all of the participants and how they can each benefit. That's another one of the things we do at the technology center; we help facilitate those relationships."

Innovation zones are an excellent example of the community-based, collaborative approach that American government, academia, and industry need to adopt in order to foster innovation and economic development. For years, we have left innovation to its own devices, and in too many cases promising technologies have been left to languish in companies or universities because they did not fit a profile, or because there weren't resources to develop them. While we have been very successful at innovating in the past, unless we adapt our approach to innovation to the demands of the twenty-first century, we will lose our competitive edge. Ultimately, our leadership in the global economy is going to depend on collaboration between large and small firms as well as universities, private labs, non-profit organizations, and all levels of government. We will need to transfer knowledge and intellectual property far more effectively if we are going to optimize our innovative and entrepreneurial potential.

> **Innovation zones are an excellent example of the community-based, collaborative approach that American government, academia, and industry need to adopt in order to foster innovation and economic development.**

"The challenges of the global economy are great," warns Rick Wagoner. "Around the world, the twentieth century was known by many as the American Century. Well, I believe the twenty-first century will be a 'global century,' a grand opportunity for those countries and those companies that are prepared to reach beyond their traditional borders to embrace new opportunities for growth in a global economy. Here in the United States, to remain competitive, to create jobs, to improve our standard of living, to promote economic growth in a competitive global economy, government and business really need to work constructively together like never before, and let me be perfectly clear on what I mean by that. Representatives of business, large and small, as well as those from government and academia, often come at global competitiveness issues from different perspectives. All too often, our positions place us at odds, and we don't accomplish as much as we could and should when we finally do sit down together to get things done. Well, it's time to recognize that when it comes to today's global economy, and specifically to our ability to compete and win in this changing U.S. economy, we no longer have the luxury of being able to argue and debate among ourselves, wasting time, and not addressing the key issues affecting the competitiveness of our economy.

"The United States pioneered free-market capitalism, and that has put us on top for a long, long time, but now, other competitors around the world are catching up fast. We need to come together and proactively and seriously address some real issues affecting the long-term competitiveness of our country and our state. We need to work together, at all levels, collaboratively, with one vision—to keep our economy, our nation, our state, our communities, and our industries competitive on a global level. In tomorrow's economy, investors will have an even wider range of investment options, all around the world, and one thing we know is that these investors will place their investment bets in the most competitive locations, and the most competitive industries. It's our responsibility, along with our counterparts in the federal government, to ensure that the United States remains the place where people choose to invest in this emerging global economy. What we have to accomplish is not impossible, but the time to act is now, and it is up to all of us."

9

THE POLITICS OF INNOVATION—ECONOMIC DEVELOPMENT

◇◇

In the seventeenth century, the world's leading economic power was Holland, and its emergence as the center of world manufacturing created a relatively large and prosperous middle class. The Dutch had risen to prominence based on the strength of their fishing, shipbuilding, mining, and textile industries, and the numerous jobs in the shipyards, mills, mines, and sea lanes formed the basis for their widespread prosperity. Technological innovation and leadership had propelled the Dutch far ahead of their competitors, and their products dominated sales in world markets. Dutch products were in high demand, and exports far exceeded imports.

By the eighteenth century, however, the Dutch were struggling. They became less innovative, failed to maintain their infrastructure, and ran up debt financing the War of the Spanish Succession. As Holland's manufacturing prowess began to fade, the increasing competitiveness of its European rivals turned Holland's trade surplus into a massive trade deficit, eliminating thousands of jobs in the process. The Dutch investor class, however, cared little about falling exports and rising unemployment. They had turned increasingly to finance to sustain their fortunes, particularly by investing overseas. As Holland began to produce less and collect more rent and interest, wealth became increasingly polarized. The standard of living of the middle class fell steadily, and by 1778, an editorial in a Dutch newspaper asserted that "the body of the Commonwealth would shortly consist of little more than rentiers and beggars—the two kinds of people who are least useful to the country."[1]

Sound familiar? It should have to the British after World War I. As the Dutch faded, the British had supplanted them as the world's leading economic power starting in the mid-1800s. A century of technological innovation and ingenuity during the early years of the Industrial Revolution coalesced, catapulting Britain's steel, textile, coal, and shipbuilding industries into prominence. Once again, an increasingly large and prosperous middle class developed thanks to an abundance of well-paying manufacturing jobs, and by 1860 Britain controlled 45 percent of the world's industries, 40 percent of its manufacturing trade, and a third of its shipping. By the 1890s, however, its industrial output was growing by a mere 1.5 percent annually, outpaced by both the United States and Germany with their newer factories and cheaper labor. As the trade surplus turned into a trade deficit, unemployment rose, the cost of living increased, and real wages fell.

As the national debate raged over what was happening and what to do about it, World War I briefly revived British manufacturing and once again increased the standard of living for the middle class, strengthening the traditionalists' arguments that everything was just fine. Unfortunately it wasn't. The boost from the war was temporary, and starting in the 1920s, Britain entered a steady decline that eventually reduced it to the status of a former world power. Unlike the Dutch, who adopted an increasingly regressive tax system as they fell into decline, the British opted for progressive taxation that cushioned the middle class for a while, but which punished the upper middle class entrepreneurs who might have revitalized British industry. Polarization of wealth was reduced, but this did nothing to address the underlying problem of Britain's lack of competitiveness in manufacturing. World War II devastated the economy and its infrastructure, and food rationing for the British continued until 1954—nine years after the end of the war! The once mighty British Empire had been reduced to a country that could not even feed its own people.

What was bad for the British, however, was great for the United States. American technological innovation and ingenuity helped our industries to leapfrog the declining British, and by the start of the twentieth century, American manufacturing output was greater than that of England, France, and Germany combined. Westward expansion had created an ever-larger domestic market, immigration provided an ongoing supply of cheap labor, and the land offered a seemingly inexhaustible supply of natural resources. Innovations such as the moving assembly line changed the nature of manufacturing and allowed it to be conducted on an unprecedented scale, adding thousands of factory jobs as well as middle management and administrative positions. The Great Depression turned out to be a temporary setback on the way to increasing prosperity, as wartime production put the economy back on track.

The zenith of the American economy occurred during the two decades after World War II, when American manufacturing reigned supreme and foreign competition was muted. Almost all other leading industrial nations in Europe and Asia had been ravaged by the war, and their infrastructure took years to recover. There was a new world order in which the United States, still a young country with vast natural resources and its infrastructure intact, emerged as the dominant player. This allowed America to grab a huge piece of the world economic pie, and it dominated world trade and exports. Thanks to an ever-increasing number of well-paying blue collar, administrative, and management-related manufacturing jobs, the middle class soon swelled to include the majority of Americans, making this nation the most prosperous and powerful in history.[2]

The question now is, for how long?

The United States of America is a country that was built by entrepreneurs. From the start, America has attracted hard-working people with vision, initiative, and incredible determination. Immigrants came to this country in waves, not just because it offered personal liberty and freedom of religious worship, but because it was a place where people could pursue their dreams. Only in America, it was felt, could people set foot on shore without a penny to their name and, through hard work and ingenuity, rise to success and prosperity. The harshness of frontier life and the possibility of a better one was a strong incentive that spurred a tremendous amount of innovation, and over time our entrepreneurial spirit has become a defining element of our national character.

> At the start of the twenty-first century, the United States needs to take a good, hard look at the state of our entrepreneurial economy.

At the start of the twenty-first century, the United States needs to take a good, hard look at the state of our entrepreneurial economy. While we have many natural advantages that have allowed us to win the global innovation race for over a century, our long history of success has bred a dangerous complacency about our future. The triumph of capitalism over communism has taught us to place an almost blind faith in the power of free and open markets. We seem to believe that if the world plays the game according to our rules, we will win due to an innate superiority. When it comes to economic success in a global economy, however, nothing could be further from the truth.

Free and open markets are essential to economic growth—they are the field on which the game of capitalism is played. We are naïve, however, if we think that the playing field is even or that the rest of the world will play by American rules. The United States, as the dominant force behind the World Trade Organization, has certainly written the trade rules in its favor. But there is plenty of cheating going on, such as theft of intellectual property, backdoor subsidies, pegged currencies, lack of adherence to international labor and environmental standards, and bribes for companies that build plants overseas. While multinational corporations may benefit from some of these tactics, for American entrepreneurs, the playing field is anything but fair.

What concerns me even more, however, is that the United States is playing the game without a coherent and discernible national strategy. Our national pride is so great, and our faith in free markets so strong, that we seem to think we can continue winning without a game plan. Yet as the defeat of the American Olympic basketball team in Athens shows, the team that has the best talent, most money, and longest history of success does not always win. Training, preparation, and strategy matter; in fact, they can topple giants and transform underdogs into winners.

In the global economic game of the twenty-first century, countries like China, India, Japan, Ireland, and others have well-developed economic strategies that they are implementing with single-minded determination. They are upgrading the skills of their workforces; they are investing in education, physical infrastructure, and research; they are working hard to retain and attract top science, engineering, and business talent; and they are targeting key, strategic industries where they intend to be at the cutting edge of innovation and thus dominate world markets.

The United States, by contrast, has very little in the way of a coordinated national innovation policy. We are taking the field with a deep bench of star players but no coaching, no teamwork, and no plan of attack. We grant subsidies to old agricultural and manufacturing industries, while doing little to secure our dominance in important future industries like stem cell therapy and nanotechnology. We name strategic priorities in research and development, while simultaneously cutting federal funding. We pass initiatives to increase the number of students pursuing math and science degrees, yet fail to fund the programs. We consistently refuse to reform the health care system even though American business is clearly struggling under the weight of escalating health care costs. And while much of our attention is focused on the War on Terror, the countries with national economic strategies are fast catching up, and in some areas they have already surpassed us.

If we Americans want to maintain our standard of living and our large and prosperous middle class, then we have to have a strategy to win the innovation race. We need a plan and an overarching vision that starts at the national level and permeates down through state and local governments, businesses, academic institutions, and even individual families. We stand at a critical turning point in history, and while it is often considered un-American to suggest that we have peaked economically, every expansion has a contraction. It is unrealistic to think that we can keep the growth trajectory of either the post-World War II boom or the Internet bubble going forever, or at least, not by sitting back and doing the same things we've done before. We have to remake and reshape our economy to suit the needs of the twenty-first century.

> If we Americans want to maintain our standard of living and our large and prosperous middle class, then we have to have a strategy to win the innovation race.

Regional Economic Development

In the offices of Ardesta on South Main Street in Ann Arbor, Michigan, reshaping the local economy is exactly what Rick Snyder has in mind. Snyder is the current chairman and former COO of Gateway Computers as well as the founder of Ardesta, a venture capital firm that specializes in microtechnology. While juggling duties as chairman of a multinational corporation and CEO of a venture capital firm would be more than enough to keep most people occupied, Snyder has also taken on the responsibility for chairing a new innovation-focused economic development organization called Ann Arbor Spark.

"Typically, local economic development organizations are focused on broad attraction and retention of businesses in the community," explains Snyder, "but Spark is focused on innovation-oriented organizations, and the type of services Spark provides are geared towards that. We've identified five areas in which we plan to be active in our community—business acceleration services, technology and entrepreneurial talent development, early stage funding, business outreach, and marketing and events. Because of our innovation focus, I think we probably have a broader range of services or activities than a normal economic development organization, and our goal is to double the number of technology-based businesses and triple the number of technology jobs in the next five years."

In many ways Spark is similar to other small business incubators around the country in that it provides business planning and consulting assistance to local entrepreneurs. It also works to build relationships with angel investors and venture capitalists in order to provide early stage funding for local high-tech ventures, as well as encouraging technology transfer from local research institutions. "I view Spark as an important complement to technology transfer at the University of Michigan," says Snyder. "University technology transfer offices have a responsibility up to a certain level, but their mandate does not including taking technologies beyond the point when they are sent out of the university either through a license or an equity deal. Spark provides a local handoff, and we now have a way to actually complement technology transfer and work closely with the university at the local level. We want to convince people that there are advantages in creating new businesses locally compared to other locations in the country. In my view, that's better for the community, because it is a lot easier to retain companies than to attract them."

What makes Ann Arbor Spark unique, however, is that its founders are focusing on innovation as a way to create high-tech jobs in the local community. They want to work with local businesses, large and small, to help meet their innovation and talent needs. They also plan to market the Ann Arbor entrepreneurial community on a national level in order to attract more venture capital and generate high-tech jobs. "Basically, we want to create good-paying jobs here that people will be excited about, and innovation-focused jobs tend to be better than average in terms of compensation," says Snyder. "We don't have enough of those kinds of jobs in Ann Arbor, and so we need to expand the number of positions we have available at that pay level. There are a lot of people who grew up here and went to an Ann Arbor high school, or who came to the University of Michigan and graduated and would like to stay, but we don't have enough high-tech jobs to support them all. They can find a job, but that job's not going to pay enough for them to have a reasonable lifestyle, particularly in light of their education, and these people aren't going to go work at Wal-Mart just so they can stay in town. Without organizations like Spark working to create more high-paying jobs, we're going to lose that talent to other cities that will utilize their skills."

For Ann Arbor, the critical problem is not finding a way to attract highly skilled professionals, which it already has in abundance. The hard part is to attract and train entrepreneurs who can build companies and generate high-paying jobs to keep those skilled professionals in the community. "In Ann Arbor, we have a lot of great researchers and technologists because of the university," notes Snyder, "so we have a strong core already, and we're graduating more every year. The problem is that people often think you can just take these technologists and turn them into entrepreneurs, but that's not how you build a good company. What you really need to do is marry technologists with business people who have practical product experience in order to build a team of people whose talents complement one another. Unfortunately, in Ann Arbor we have more technologists than we have business people, so we're losing the technology and talent that we generate at the university to other parts of the country. As a community, we need to figure out how to attract experienced CEOs for young companies, as well as experts in marketing and finance, to come in and be the early management teams for these companies."

While Ann Arbor Spark is just getting started, its founders already have a number of ideas as to how to tackle this issue. "One idea we have is to create boot camps for experienced business people coming from big companies who want to be entrepreneurs," explains Snyder.

"We need to train and counsel people about the cultural issues of moving from a big company to a small company and help them understand if it's appropriate for them to make that jump. You don't want to lose good people because they're afraid to make that leap, but neither do you want people leaping without having the right background. You want someone who has enough experience to be an effective entrepreneur. What you find quite often with senior managers is that they may be the right people for a certain stage, but when they get to the next stage, they should really hand the company off to other people who have different experiences and expertise. That's not to say that they would necessarily fail, it's more that they are specialists at building a certain stage of company." Given the high failure rate for startups, having the right person shepherding the company at the right time is crucial.

Another unique idea that Snyder has is to establish entrepreneur-in-residence programs at local universities. "This is just an idea that we're considering, but I'd like to see if we can work with the University of Michigan and Eastern Michigan University on offering adjunct professorships to experienced CEOs. We could have them come teach entrepreneurship classes, but only give them a half-time teaching load so they spend the other half of their time giving advice to local startups. I view that as an alternative to places like Silicon Valley, where big venture capital funds will have an entrepreneur in residence who works with the companies they fund. The challenge to doing that here is that an Ann Arbor venture capital fund is not going to attract an executive from the West Coast to come be an entrepreneur in residence when they can do it in Silicon Valley without moving. We have to offer something different, and I think the opportunity to be an adjunct professor at Eastern Michigan University or the University of Michigan is pretty appealing, because that's not something they can do in the Valley."

This is only the tip of the iceberg, for Spark's founders have an abundance of interesting ideas regarding how to attract entrepreneurs and deal with many other issues, such as trailing spouses and the loss of talent graduating from the university. They have zeroed in on the fact that it takes more than just connecting technologists with investors to build a company, it takes trained entrepreneurs as well. They have also recognized the key role that collaboration between government, universities, and local businesses plays in the innovation process, and they're aware of the fact that they have to compete with other cities around the country and around the world to retain their talent and technology. The unanswered question, however, is even if they do succeed in tripling the number of high-tech jobs in the community, how can they prevent those new jobs from being outsourced?

"You never know for sure that the jobs created by these economic development programs won't be outsourced, but usually what you'll find is if the company is really headquartered here and their center of activity is in the local community, then those jobs will stay," says Snyder. "From a practical standpoint, when you first start a company, even if you employ as many as twenty or thirty people, you don't want to have them in a lot of different locations. You have enough problems and challenges just getting that group to work really well together, and learning how to be cost effective and efficient, without taking half of your company and putting it in another location. What normally happens if you're building a product is that you want to get the prototypes, samples, and even the early manufacturing done locally. Then quite often you find that if there's more than one component to the product line that you're creating, you'll look to outsource the non-core piece of what that is. You're probably going to outsource manufacturing, because to do it yourself you're going to end up building a $20 million fabrication facility. So you outsource that, but then you'll have the assembly and the key components done locally, close to your headquarters. Outsourcing works well for some functions, but if you get down to the core parts of the business, the benefits of good communication and having people physically here in person outweigh the labor differential. That's how you have to deal with the outsourcing issue, by making jobs really sticky in terms of great communication, responsiveness, and speed of innovation. All of those features are how you address the fact that you can get a cheaper solution somewhere else. You have to argue the quality of the product or service is higher locally, and that justifies the price."

Ann Arbor Spark has the potential to be a role model for community-based economic development in the coming decades. With $3 million in funding from the University of Michigan and other sources, as well as an experienced board comprised of a cross-section of individuals from local businesses, universities, and government, the group clearly has broad-based community support, and is exactly the type of approach that the federal government needs to encourage. As the Council on Competitiveness' vice president for regional innovation Randall Kempner notes, "Our belief at the Council is that economic development should be driven by regions, metropolitan areas that have recognized the need to transfer from a traditional economic model to an innovation-based economic model. We think the federal government should play a complementary role by making initial planning support widely available, and then providing matching funds to regions that have developed an innovation-based strategy to transform their economies. The matching funds would provide these regions with additional financial support to implement some of the initiatives that they have developed. The point is not for the federal government to go pick hot spots and say 'I anoint you,' but to support regions that are committed to making these transitions."

The American Workforce

The type of regional economic development that Ann Arbor Spark is pursuing is a great example of what local communities need to do to restore American competitiveness and retain American jobs, and the federal government needs to support them in that effort. All of this economic development work is going to be wasted, however, if we fail to train and educate the kind of workforce that we need to fill the high-tech positions groups like Spark are working so hard to create. Ann Arbor is lucky in that it has an overabundance of skilled professionals because it is home to the University of Michigan. Many other American communities are not so fortunate, and with high school graduation rates falling, they lack not only entrepreneurs but skilled labor in general. In its *Innovate America* report, the Council on Competitiveness' National Innovation Initiative has highlighted talent, investment, and infrastructure as the three key areas we need to focus on in order to improve American competitiveness. All are critical, but it is ultimately the talent factor which we need to pay attention to developing most of all.

> Anyone who expects to maintain a middle class lifestyle is going to need solid quantitative and technical skills in order to secure a good job.

"We believe that talent is this country's most important asset. Human capital is the basis of innovation—much more so than financial or physical infrastructure," says Kempner. "Right now the United States is home to very skilled human resources and we are still the best configured country to leverage those human resources in the majority of the industries in which we compete. However, Council members are very concerned about the declining number of scientists and engineers in the training pipeline, the lack of mathematical expertise, and the lack of skilled labor generally. It's not just high-tech firms, but manufacturers who complain they don't have access to skilled labor. That's a real problem today, and it may get significantly worse over time if we're not able to graduate high-level technically skilled people. We've very concerned that we're going to have a massive class of Americans without the college or community college educations necessary to obtain decent-paying jobs."

While most students will not need to become scientists or engineers, anyone who expects to maintain a middle class lifestyle is going to need solid quantitative and technical skills in order to secure a good job. Unfortunately, the vast majority of American students appear to lose interest in math and science around middle school. In fourth grade, U.S. students actually score near the top internationally in science and math tests. By eighth grade, however, they fall to the middle of the pack, and by twelfth grade they score near the bottom compared to other developed countries.[3] Clearly, science and math performance is falling off drastically as American teenagers go through our middle and high schools, and there's a real lack of interest in pursuing any field that is remotely quantitative in college. Either they don't think it's cool, they don't think they're going to make money that way, or they think math and science are just way too hard.

Dr. Jimmy Clark, a retired biology professor from the University of Kentucky, has watched this apathy towards math and science on the part of incoming college students develop over the past three decades. Interestingly, he doesn't believe the problem has to do with the quality of instruction at American high schools, which he thinks in many ways has improved. "The top domestic American students in science and engineering are actually really good," says Clark. "They're well educated, they can think critically, and they have a strong work ethic. In fact, the quality of their education coming into the university has actually gotten a little better over the past thirty years, because they've had more difficult classes and better preparation in high school. Those students are, in some sense of the word, geniuses, and unfortunately there's a very small number of them. What a good high school should do is not only give you the geniuses, but also another ten or fifteen percent of students who are what you might call imitation geniuses.

"That's what the Asian schools do. Their students are trained well and educated well in an environment that fosters a strong work ethic, and those that are a little less able work extremely hard to make up for it, whereas the American students in that second tier don't work nearly as hard. They don't have the natural quantitative ability of the top students, and they aren't willing to work to develop it. As a result, almost all of the international students come to our universities significantly better prepared than most of the American students in terms of math and science, and their work ethic is phenomenal. They're not necessarily superior to American students in terms of natural ability, but when it comes to working hard, that second tier of American students can't, or won't, match them."

What is driving this difference, Clark argues, is that Asian parents are pushing their children hard academically in order to achieve a better economic future, a future American parents take more for granted. "Asian kids just don't have as many options in life. So the problem for American kids is that whatever they do, the Asian students are going to do more, because their parents are really pushing them to climb that economic ladder. One Chinese student told me that if he fell asleep at the table while he was studying, his mother didn't wake him up and say 'go to bed now,' she said, 'stand up,' because that way if he fell asleep he would hit the floor and wake himself up. Another student told me that in his little town the street lights were on late, so they would take their schoolbooks and go stand under the street lights to study. Can you imagine an American student doing that? Parents in Asia are pushing their children really hard, and they don't accept any excuses. Not studying is not an option."

The great irony of the golden age of the American middle class in the 1950s is that the good life was perhaps a little too easy to achieve. American parents who grew up during that period remember high school as a place of football games, debate clubs, and band practices, with a liberal dose of high school dances and parties mixed in. For those who weren't going on to college, subjects like algebra were often dismissed as having little value in the real world. Indeed, many of those 1950s high school graduates went out and got jobs, bought houses, and raised families just fine without algebra. Today, parents know that a college education is important, even a requirement, in a way that it wasn't back then. But their reaction to that knowledge, and the emphasis they place on academic excellence, varies greatly.

Some parents want their children to have a balanced life, one full of social activities, and they don't see the need to push for achievement in math and science. If their children's grades are mediocre they are likely to blame the teachers, which is one of the factors behind today's rampant grade inflation. Other parents who are more conscious of just how important going to the right college can be will push sports more than academics because they see it as the best way for their child to get a scholarship. Unfortunately, those students are frequently unprepared for the academic demands of higher education as a result. Meanwhile, for those parents who want their children to go to elite universities, academic achievement is not enough, and excellence in a wide variety of extracurricular activities can be the difference between being accepted at Harvard or not. Thus at all levels, the emphasis on extracurricular activities is increasingly pulling the focus away from academics at a time when it should be increasing in importance.

"American parents have different priorities," says Clark. "They want their children to go to college and get a good job, but they want them to enjoy school as well, and many place more emphasis on sports than academics. It's not that American kids won't work hard. Many of them work extremely hard, hours a day, doing sports and other extracurricular activities, and the kids like those activities because they get a lot of immediate rewards from fellow students and parents. As a result, you have American kids who put five or ten times as much effort into sports as academics, and when you have students who do twenty minutes a day of homework and three hours of sports, they are going to be unprepared academically. There are a few American kids who do everything well, but not many, and those who do have a highly disciplined life and are very smart.

"In the United States, we should have a tremendous advantage academically, because quality public education is universally available all the way through high school, unlike in rural China or India. Yet because it is universally available, we take it for granted. In Asia, the kids who are lucky enough to go to high school don't have a life other than school, it's all academics. If there's an exam coming, you have to do well on it, because if you don't, you have to stop going to school and start working with your hands instead. In American high schools, on the other hand, our teenagers have this whole social life with dating, sports, and parties, and all of that academic stuff is just a nuisance to them. For the most part, our high schools are now a disaster.

"We have a culture problem in our high schools, and it needs a cultural fix, which is profoundly difficult. It requires switching where those students get their sense of self-esteem away from their peer group and sports to adults and academics. That's what you have to do to make the high schools work. There are other technical things too, but the fundamental problem is the social situation and the overall culture. A surprising number of students who do poorly academically in high school actually go on to community college and do quite well. They have the ability, and they can succeed once they're out of that high school environment and are serious about how to make a living. But some of them don't recover, and will be hampered by a lack of quantitative and technical skills and a mediocre work ethic for the rest of their lives. I'm afraid those students just aren't going to be able to compete in the world that's in store for them."

Middle class American parents are showering their children with every possible economic advantage, and their children are taking it for granted. It never occurs to most young Americans that it might be in any way difficult for them to maintain the standard of living to which they are accustomed. They may be having a wonderful time in high school, and American parents may shake their heads in disapproval at how hard Asian parents are pushing their children, believing that they are robbing them of a happy childhood. In truth, parents on both sides of the world just want their children to be successful and happy. What is different is their perception of how difficult that dream is going to be to achieve and the best way to go about it.

National Innovation Policy

Our country desperately needs a national innovation policy to inspire us, give us priorities, and lay out a plan of action to continue achieving the American Dream, because support for innovation is anything but certain despite all of the arguments that it is central to our economic prosperity. "Today, the United States is the most innovative country in the world, period," says Randall Kempner, "but that lead is declining, and there is no guarantee that the United States will maintain its leadership position unless we quickly start taking actions to develop a national innovation strategy."

At the federal level, we need to consider issues like immigration, heath care, tort reform, and regulation from the perspective of what is best for innovation and economic growth, with the end goal of raising the standard of living for all Americans, not just the investor class. We need to decide whether we are going to let other countries continue to steal our intellectual property, keep the exchange rate for the dollar artificially high, and lure our industries out of the country with tax breaks and other financial incentives. Perhaps most important of all, we need to seriously consider whether we are willing to continue losing our domestic manufacturing in the naïve belief that we will retain research and development and related services.

> **Our country desperately needs a national innovation policy to inspire us, give us priorities, and lay out a plan of action to continue achieving the American Dream.**

"American manufacturing has an essential role in America's future," argues Rick Wagoner. "Some people may think of American manufacturing as dying, but I prefer to paraphrase Mark Twain's famous quote: Rumors of our death have been greatly exaggerated. In fact, the comeback of American manufacturing in the last two decades has been a remarkable story. In the early 1980s, American business, and particularly American manufacturing, was described by many as inefficient and ineffective—in a word, uncompetitive. The United States was losing its credibility as an industrial power. But American business and American manufacturers worked hard to fix what was wrong, and the United States has emerged, once again, as the most productive and competitive economy in the world. America's manufacturers have made dramatic improvements in their competitiveness, with big strides in productivity and quality while continuing to bring outstanding new products to market, and our impact on the U.S. economy is enormous. Manufacturing generates two-thirds of America's R&D investment and three-fourths of our exports, not to mention about 15 million American jobs.

"While there's been, and will continue to be, lots of growth in the service sector of our economy, we need to keep in mind that many of these jobs are tied directly to the manufacturing base. They provide their services to manufacturers. In addition, our manufacturing base has led to accompanying investments in our technology base. Do you think General Motors' huge Technology Center would be in Warren, Michigan, if we didn't have a massive manufacturing base here in the United States? So in addition to the direct benefits, a strong manufacturing base provides critical ballast to our economy, and to our future economic growth. That's why so many other countries around the world are interested in developing and growing their own manufacturing bases, and that's why the U.S. manufacturing sector needs to keep pushing and raising the bar if we are to remain the leader.

"The competition in manufacturing is increasingly global, and it gets a lot tougher every year. If we want to maintain the manufacturing and economic leadership that we worked so hard to reclaim, if we want to remain competitive in the global marketplace, if we want to keep our economy growing robustly, then America must be the best place in the world to do business, and must maintain a competitive manufacturing base. As business leaders, we need to begin by helping ourselves, ensuring that our own houses, our own businesses, are in order in everything from R&D investments to quality systems to cost structures. That's essential. That's the first step. But that is not sufficient. To put it bluntly, in addition to businesses helping themselves, business and government need to work together to address a number of important issues that put U.S. manufacturers at a severe disadvantage to overseas competition. We must address the cumulative effect of many well-intentioned policies that now harm American manufacturing and our nation's ability to compete effectively in the global market place."

The threat to U.S. manufacturing is one of many issues that we need to consider at the national level, and then shape a national strategy in response. The National Innovation Initiative has called for the Executive Office of the President to enact a formal federal innovation strategy, which they hope will build support for innovation-driven growth and implementation of pro-innovation policies at the national level. They are also working with allies on Capitol Hill to shape national policy in Congress, but without a definitive economic crisis, it is in many ways an uphill battle. Because we have so many other critical issues competing for our time, money, and attention, support for innovation is likely to keep shifting depending on what we perceive as the most pressing demands and crises of our time. It is therefore hard to predict exactly what may happen over the course of the next several decades, as there are many different possible scenarios that could play out.

Scenario # 1: Death by a Thousand Cuts

One scenario is that America will continue on its present course without realizing just how level the global playing field has become, and how much of a threat that poses to the middle class. In this scenario, the economic changes wrought by globalization would fly under the radar, their effects diffused and gradual enough that they never provoke widespread opposition. The lack of a definitive economic crisis would lull the country into complacency, so that we never make optimizing for innovation a priority. Such a scenario could result from the continuation of the government's current policy of putting unquestioning faith in the power of free markets, ignoring the fact that multinationals will act in their own best interests—which will increasingly diverge from America's national interests—as China and India become the new economic superpowers. It is a likely outcome in an entitlement culture that takes our economic prosperity and leadership for granted.

In this scenario, the resilience of the American economy would allow a sufficient number of new jobs to be created so that opposition to globalization never reaches a boiling point. Yet the United States would increasingly battle with India for supremacy in high-tech services, while China solidified its position as the world's leading manufacturer. With the latter's ongoing failure to enforce intellectual property rights, American companies would have an increasingly hard time justifying investment in breakthrough innovation and the development of new technologies. As a result, American multinationals would outsource more and more of their research and development to Asian countries, a development that these countries would be only too happy to encourage. This would enable China and India to build R&D bases that would allow them to compete effectively in high-technology industries, turning Asia into the center of world innovation.

Over time, the center of gravity in the global business world would shift to Asia as consumers continued to lose respect for American brands. American venture capital and direct foreign investment would increasingly flow overseas to build businesses in emerging countries, rather than in the United States. American multinationals would squeeze suppliers for every penny, outsource, and viciously defend patent rights at home, while making significant concessions to the Chinese abroad. To better serve Asian markets, multinationals would start relocating not just manufacturing, but research and development, marketing, and even their headquarters to China and India, seeing themselves as global companies with global interests rather than American companies with American interests. The world's top science, engineering, and entrepreneurial talent would be drawn away from the United States and towards the growing opportunities in Asia, and fewer American students would pursue science and engineering due to a lack of opportunities at home.

Middle class Americans who had grown up with the expectation of going to college and getting a steady job would be unprepared for the rate of job churn and technical demands of the global knowledge economy. Overall, there would be increasing disparity in earnings power between high school and college graduates, and the public education system would struggle to turn out vocationally skilled workers from American high schools. Many four-year colleges would also fail to prepare students adequately for the demands of a highly technical knowledge economy, and people with advanced degrees would increasingly turn to community colleges in order to obtain the technical certifications they needed to obtain a well-paying job.

In the coming decades, American workers would be forced to take significant cuts in base pay in order for American companies to remain competitive with Asia, although some knowledge workers could make up the difference and more as a result of increasing use of incentives such as stock options. Compensation, however, would become much more variable from year to year, and Americans would have to take a much more active role in managing their finances in order to survive short-term hardships. High levels of personal debt could lead to a collapse of the housing market and destroy a significant chunk of the middle class's net worth. The American economy in general would be more prone to booms and busts, although the overall rate of economic growth would be higher than if the government tried to smooth it.

While employment would become more unpredictable, project-oriented, and temporary in nature, for the highly skilled it would likely become more autonomous and flexible as well, as American companies would seek to use the creative and innovative skills of a greater portion of the American workforce. Career paths for intrapreneurs would start to emerge, but many of the best opportunities would be with multinational firms located in Asia. Meanwhile, the success of Chinese firms in low-end markets would drive a wide range of competitors in many developing countries out of business, prompting a huge migration of low-skilled immigrants into the United States. This would drive down the wages for unskilled labor in service industries and increasingly leave semi-skilled American workers with fewer job options, widening the wealth gap between the haves and the have-nots. Meanwhile, the ongoing offshoring of white collar jobs to India would challenge the financial security of college-educated Americans as well, leaving many under-employed.

From a financial perspective, China's insistence on pegging the yuan to a basket of currencies, rather than allowing it to float freely, would lead to continued over-valuation. This would make American imports comparatively expensive and widen the trade gap between the two countries, thus increasing trade displacement and solidifying China's economic power. By 2030, if not sooner, China would overtake the United States as the world's largest economy, having become the worldwide center not only of manufacturing, but of innovation. Right behind it would be India, whose younger population could very well help it to surpass China and become the world's leading economic power a few decades after. Like the Dutch and the British before us, the United States would have to deal with a new world order in which it was no longer the dominant player.

Scenario # 2: The Middle Class Rebellion

While the first scenario describes what might happen if the United States continues to embrace globalization without vigorously supporting innovation, withdrawing from globalization in a fit of protectionism could be just as disastrous. In this scenario, the loss of American jobs from trade displacement and offshoring would start to affect highly skilled white collar workers to such an extent that the middle class revolts in the voting booth. Unwilling to accept the downsides of globalization, it would reject it to the extent that is possible, retreating into economic protectionism and isolationism.

Democrats would embark on revival of the post-war New Deal and tax the wealthy in order to pay for government programs. The intention would be to reduce the wealth gap and promote greater equality, but this would reduce the amount of venture capital and private angel investment available for entrepreneurship and seriously hurt the innovation economy. Underfunded entitlement programs such as Social Security, Medicaid and Medicare would be pushed to the limit as the baby boomers start to retire, eventually forcing broad-based increases in payroll and income taxes. Keynesian-style government spending would be used to dampen the effect of business cycles, but this would result in slower growth over the long run, and lack of fiscal discipline during boom periods would continue to inflate the federal budget deficit.

After decades of ideological devotion to free trade, the new economic consensus would be to establish a trading bloc with other highly developed nations such as Canada, Australia, and New Zealand, perhaps with the inclusion of Mexico and a few Central American countries for the sake of providing limited quantities of cheap labor. While the bloc would be intended to balance the economic power of the European Union and an increasingly powerful and economically integrated Asia, the benefits of free trade on a more global scale would be trumped by the determination to preserve American jobs.

The overall focus on jobs would likely rekindle the power of labor unions, which would once again push for seniority-based, rather than merit-based, compensation systems. Compensation would trend away from variable incentives based on greater sharing of ownership, returning to an emphasis on guaranteed wages and base pay. The government would increasingly vote to restrict the use of stock options and other types of variable pay in order to protect the interests of labor. Without the lure of significant financial gains, talented young people would abandon small entrepreneurial companies and rush to fill positions vacated by the retirement of the baby boomers, shunning the risks of entrepreneurship in favor of stability. The more daring might leave the country entirely to pursue opportunities in more innovation-friendly environments.

Protected from the pressures of foreign competition, corporate America would continue with business as usual, favoring incremental improvements over breakthrough advances. Continually rising costs of business due to health care, insurance, taxes, litigation, and regulatory compliance would lead established corporations to look for ways to cut costs and replace workers through automation, rather than employing technology in ways that would enhance the productivity of labor. Within companies, there would continue to be a distinct separation between the chosen few allowed to make decisions and those who simply carry out orders, as well as a return to more functional specialization and strict hierarchies. As American businesses focused more on cost-cutting than innovation, they would gradually fall behind Asian companies in creating the world's best, most innovative products, eventually resulting in the downgrading of American brands and a tremendous loss of world market share.

A lack of focus on innovation would eventually create a massive loss of well-paying middle class jobs as well. The prevailing sense of insecurity would lead more Americans to attend college than ever before, but their prosperity would depend upon landing well-paying jobs when they graduated. While a rapidly growing economy driven by entrepreneurship demands more highly skilled and educated workers in order to innovate and solve problems, a slowly growing economy offers more routine jobs that can be automated. Without new products and processes, there would be more college graduates than college level-jobs, and the education bubble would burst and drive down wages for white collar professionals.

Meanwhile, the federal budget deficit would eventually reach a crisis, leading the world to abandon the dollar as the currency of choice. The U.S. government would be hard pressed to resist the temptation to print money to pay its debt obligations, which would create serious inflation. The loss of cheap imported products from Asia would also result in a sharp increase in prices domestically, and if combined with oil shortages prompted by increasing demand and variable supply, a repeat of 1970s-style stagflation might result. The combined effect of these negative forces could easily lead to a serious economic depression, which would destroy the net worth of the middle class.

If the worst happened and we did indeed fall into a depression, it would be very difficult to work our way out of it again under the weight of the government's financial obligations. The threat of home-grown terrorism could increase dramatically as young people became dissatisfied with the lack of economic opportunities. The result would be a situation similar to some of the poorer South American countries where the poor view wealthy communities as villages to plunder. Gated communities would proliferate, and Americans would have to spend a lot more on personal safety, as disenfranchised youth turned increasingly to crime. In the end, protectionism and a revival of the New Deal social welfare state could bring about the very effect that the middle class sought to avoid—widespread loss of jobs and a sharp decline in the overall standard of living.

Scenario # 3: International Instability

Another possible scenario is that the health of the economy could take a back seat to other global crises such as terrorism, leading us to ignore our innovation infrastructure as we are distracted by other concerns. This scenario is likely to come into play if there are continued, intermittent terrorist attacks on the homeland, creating an ongoing sense of physical insecurity. It could lead the government to put increasing restrictions on the movement of people as well as goods, capital, and technology, thus inhibiting the global free-market system the United States now relies upon so heavily.

We have already seen in the aftermath of 9/11 that federal funding for non-defense related research has been cut back, and the visa rejection rate for talented foreign students and highly skilled immigrants has increased dramatically. While the scientific community has already started to sound the alarm about the threat this poses to our long-term lead in the innovation race, in a world where terrorism is our primary concern, these protests would fall on deaf ears, countered by the argument that the federal government must not risk letting a terrorist slip into the country on a student or H1 visa. The United States would have a very hard time ramping up a domestic science and technology workforce quickly enough to prevent us from falling behind, and the need to fund a massive defense budget, not to mention the baby boomer retirement, would make significant increases in education spending unlikely.

As the federal government cut back on non-defense related research, the burden of funding basic and early stage commercial applications research would fall increasingly on the private sector. Research funded by private venture capital and industry could lead to the development of sensitive technologies that would be hard for the military to control, resulting in either dissemination of potentially dangerous information or increasingly restrictive regulation by the government. As a result, concerns about security would be likely to produce a strengthening of the Patriot Act and greater infringement on privacy and individual rights. The increasing regulatory burdens would inhibit the competitiveness of small businesses, and the United States would not be the only country affected. Terrorist attacks in Europe and elsewhere would feed into nationalist trends and could produce a widespread retreat from globalization on the part of many countries.

While the attacks on New York, Madrid, and London have brought concerns about terrorism to the forefront, it is far from the only potential issue. Indeed, there are a number of factors besides terrorism that could trigger a political or economic crisis, such as natural disasters, water and energy shortages, financial panics, and pandemics. In 1918, a flu pandemic killed ten times as many Americans as died in action in World War I, and a virus with a similar fatality rate could kill in excess of 50 million in today's global village where people are far more mobile. Currently, there is a full-blown flu epidemic among birds in Asia that has a 100 percent fatality rate in chickens, and if it crossed into the human population, the results could be catastrophic. The resulting panic would almost certainly cause at least a temporary retreat from the extreme interconnectedness of globalization. Unfortunately, the last time the world attempted to reverse economic globalization in the 1920s it brought on a worldwide depression, and the loss of economic opportunities from trade could create another worldwide economic crisis and great political instability.

On the other hand, too much international interdependence would bring dangers as well, and each world region has challenges that could create significant economic problems. Europe is struggling under the legacy burdens of its twentieth century social welfare policies, much of Latin America is politically unstable, and the Middle East is experiencing a population bulge at a time when there are few economic opportunities for young people. Even in China and India, there are many potential problems that could turn their economic miracles into disasters. While both have the ability to keep their economies growing at a rate of an astonishing 8 percent annually, they are going to need that growth to provide jobs for all of the new college graduates they are turning out. An economic slowdown could spell disaster, and could come from a variety of causes. China's banking system is close to insolvent; the red tape in India's bureaucracy is oppressive. Both countries have rampant corruption, serious environmental damage, poor schooling in rural areas, and high rates of HIV infection. Worse, China's increasing tensions with Taiwan, and India's intermittent skirmishes with Pakistan over Kashmir, could boil over into a war at any time.

In a global economy, any sort of turbulence in Asian markets could create global recessions or even depressions. Raw materials shortages would be likely to occur, particularly oil shortages, and while there are potential reserves to meet worldwide demand, they are unproven and would be likely to lag in development. Natural disasters like hurricane Katrina could also cut off supply lines and wreak havoc with the price of oil and other resources. On the other hand, it is possible that instability in China, India, and elsewhere might actually benefit the United States in some ways. This country has long been regarded as the safest place in the world to invest, a fact that has allowed our trade deficit to rise to heights that would be untenable in any other country. If countries such as China and India are seen as politically unstable, the United States might still attract the majority of direct foreign investment, even if economically it is not the most lucrative option.

The fact that our excessive consumption levels drive the world economy, and allow other nations' economies to grow more quickly through exports, also works in our favor. Thus, it is possible that we might be able to fall behind in the innovation race and still maintain world leadership through our reputation for political and economic stability as well as clever strategic partnering. Unfortunately, the federal debt and the trade deficit have grown to such high levels that at some point, the situation will become unsustainable, and the rest of the world will dump American dollars. If that happens, the entire world economy could be thrown into a downward spiral, and it would only take the emergence of one strong, politically stable competitor to lure the majority of investment capital elsewhere, leaving the United States a former world power.

Scenario # 4: Embracing the Future

The best and most hopeful scenario for America is one where we realize that our lead in the innovation race is in jeopardy, and decide to proactively mobilize our resources to make innovation a priority. We would take charge of our own destiny and invest in our innovation infrastructure by increasing spending for federally funded basic research, and strengthening ties between industry and academia. We would revise our immigration policy to allow more highly skilled workers to relocate permanently to America, while discouraging temporary workers who are used merely for their cheap labor. We would reform our public education system to prepare the American workforce for the jobs of the future, encourage entrepreneurship, and work to keep venture capital in the United States by providing attractive investment opportunities. We would find ways to compete in the worldwide economy while allowing American labor to share in the spoils of globalization, and we would remake American companies in a less hierarchical, more flexible mode to tap the innovative potential of the American workforce.

In this version of the future, the information technology revolution would turn out to be the first in a series of revolutionary new technologies that will transform our world, including breakthroughs in areas such as biotechnology, nanotechnology, energy, and space exploration. While the United States would not dominate all of these areas, our continuing commitment to innovation would ensure that we are a leader in enough of them to promote a high level of progress, job creation, and economic growth. There would be a convergence of technologies that create an explosion of innovative activity worldwide, as well as a rapid increase in the overall standard of living and incomes— although the gains would by no means be distributed evenly.

On the world stage, the United States, China, India, the European Union, and other potential future economic powers would compete in a way that spurs greater innovation and growth, rather than devolving into destructive, contentious relationships. As they climbed the economic ladder, China, India, and other emerging nations would cooperate to enforce intellectual property rights more fully, and the United States would draw back from its tendency to act unilaterally in order to cooperatively address overarching global problems such as terrorism, labor and human rights, environmental concerns, and world health issues.

> The best and most hopeful scenario for America is one where we realize that our lead in the innovation race is in jeopardy, and decide to proactively mobilize our resources to make innovation a priority.

At home, breakthrough technologies, particularly in biomedicine, would extend and improve the quality of life while also helping to address energy, water, environmental, and homeland security crises. While Silicon Valley would remain the leader in innovation, other regional hotspots would emerge throughout the country based on partnerships between government, industry, and academia that would help to attract and retain venture capital. American high schools and colleges would embrace the need to revise their teaching methods and curricula in order to address the needs of the knowledge economy, with greater emphasis on problem solving, interactive learning, and the development of specific technical skills. American businesses and universities would also work together to develop a more extensive internship and apprentice system to bridge the gap between school and the working world.

As a result, there would be sufficient growth to offset the effects of automation, consolidation, offshoring, and other sources of job loss. Jobs would be less stable, but more autonomous and flexible as well, and more people would earn their living as self-employed contractors or entrepreneurs. At the same time, American industry would remake itself to focus more intently on innovation, creating opportunities for intrapreneurs in the process. Unions would loosen their hold on American labor to allow for more variable compensation, and the wealth of creative and innovative talent throughout the American workforce would be tapped more fully. While rapid innovation cycles would create jobs unlikely to last for a lifetime, we would have developed safety nets for American workers to negotiate the transition from job to job more easily, such as retraining programs, portable health insurance, and income insurance. For most white collar workers, a greater portion of their earnings would come from equity rather than wages, allowing them to partake more fully in the financial benefits of globalization.

Would it all be smooth sailing in this scenario? Certainly not, for embracing rapid innovation would accelerate the rate of technological and social change even further. Leading the wave of innovation will undoubtedly bring us face-to-face with a myriad of difficult ethical questions as we negotiate the landscape of a highly technological future. While embracing innovation is our best option, it will definitely not be easy. Nevertheless, it is the best chance we have of holding on to the American Dream, and so the next several decades are going to be a critical period for the United States economy. Having stood atop the world podium for many years, our entrepreneurs and intrapreneurs are now running in an innovation race that has more and better competitors than ever before. How we choose to respond to those challengers will do much to determine the course of our future, as well as that of our children and grandchildren.

"A growing majority of people understand we are living in a new world today," says Randall Kempner. "Certainly corporate, university, and labor leaders recognize that they are operating in a new environment, and there are many thousands of people who have lost jobs as a result of non-competitive firms going out of business. We have a chance to do a lot of regional work, and even when we go to small, remote towns, their leaders usually get it. They realize that they're not competing with the rural county next door, they're competing with countries ten thousand miles away. However, there is a lot less clarity about what to do about it."

The question of what America needs to do in response to the challenges of globalization is one we need to answer, and soon. That answer is not to turn our back on globalization—that would be counter-productive, not to mention futile. There is much we have gained from globalization, such as lower prices for a wide variety of consumer products, and the unrelenting pressure to innovate that comes from strong competition. But there must be moderation in all things. Some amount of offshoring makes sense, as it promotes greater efficiency. Going so far as to offshore innovation, however, amounts to outsourcing America's future. We need to decide where to draw the line in order to ensure the best possible outcome.

In a world where a majority of design work is routine and can be done more cheaply in Asia, American companies have a very narrow range of activities that can be done profitably while continuing to create well-paying jobs. Some added value comes from activities that require a high degree of interpersonal interaction, particularly with customers. The rest comes from breakthrough innovation, the kind that is not routine, and thus not easily replicated or outsourced. America needs to recognize and protect its sources of sustainable competitive advantage, and in the final analysis, the most promising source of that advantage is American ingenuity and our entrepreneurial spirit. Leveraging that ingenuity and spirit requires much thought, careful planning, and commitment; American entrepreneurs deserve nothing less than our full support.

"One of the main points that the Council on Competitiveness tries to make is that innovation is an ecosystem in which every player has a role," says Kempner. "It's not a matter of the federal government making a couple of changes and then all of a sudden innovation will stop moving offshore. Every different sector has to come to the table and has to make some changes. Federal legislation alone is not going to make every region in the United States more innovative; change has to happen at the regional level as well. Every place has their own particular challenges and needs to develop and implement particular solutions. Our goal is to galvanize a broad commitment to addressing this issue, and offer some concrete ideas for what to do about it. We need national leaders to focus on innovation as a critical priority."

> America needs to recognize and protect its sources of sustainable competitive advantage, and in the final analysis, the most promising source of that advantage is American ingenuity and our entrepreneurial spirit.

In an increasingly complex world where we are constantly being bombarded by information, commitment to solving any one particular problem—before it becomes critical—is extremely hard to obtain. Yet innovation deserves our attention and commitment, because it has the potential to solve so many of the other potential crises that face us, such as homeland security, global warming, energy shortages, famine, epidemics, and more. Innovation is the wellspring of much of our prosperity, and it holds unlimited potential for the future. The question now is whether we will lose our economic leadership as the British once lost it to us, or create an innovation policy and marshal the resources necessary to rebuild the American Dream.

NOTES

Chapter 1

1. Juan Enriquez, *As the Future Catches You* (New York: Crown Business, 2001), p.16.

2. Janny Scott and David Leonhardt, "Shadowy Lines That Still Divide," *New York Times,* May 15, 2005.

3 J. Bradford DeLong, "Slouching Towards Utopia?: The Economic History of the Twentieth Century," February 1997, http://econ161.berkley.edu/TCEH/Slouch-roaring13.html (accessed September 1, 2005).

4. U.S. Bureau of Economic Analysis, *Table 1.1.5 Gross Domestic Product* (Washington DC: 2005), http://www.bea.gov/bea/dn/nipaweb/index.asp (accessed September 1, 2005).

5. U.S. Bureau of Economic Analysis, *Table 2.1 Personal Income and Its Disposition, Disposable Personal Income Per Capita Current Dollars* (Washington DC: 2005), http://www.bea.gov/bea/dn/nipaweb/SelectTable.asp (accessed September 1, 2005).

6. Griff Witte, "As Income Gap Widens, Uncertainty Spreads: More U.S. Families Struggle to Stay on Track," *Washington Post,* September 20, 2004, p.A1.

7. Ron Hira and Anil Hira, *Outsourcing America* (New York: American Management Association, 2005), p.130.

8. U.S. Bureau of the Census, *Poverty: 2004 Highlights* (Washington DC: 2005), http://www.census.gov/hhes/www/poverty/poverty04/pov04hi.html (accessed September 1, 2005).

9. Edward Luttwak, *Turbo Capitalism* (New York: HarperCollins Publishers, 1999), p.63.

10. Elizabeth Warren and Amelia Warren Tyagi, *The Two-Income Trap* (New York: Basic Books, 2003), pp.15-54.

11. Ibid., pp.50-51.

12. Ibid., pp.22, 24, 39, 42.

13. Ibid., pp.50-51.

14. Richard Wolf, "1.1 Million Americans Joined Ranks of the Poor in 2004," *USA Today,* August 31, 2005.

15. Michael Mandel, "Productivity: Who Wins, Who Loses," *BusinessWeek,* March 22, 2004, p.45.

16 U.S. Bureau of Labor Statistics, *Table 1: Private Sector Gross Job Gains and Job Losses, Seasonally Adjusted* (Washington DC: 2005), http://www.bls.gov/news.release/cewbd.to1.htm (accessed September 1, 2005).

17. James Cooper, "The Price of Efficiency," *BusinessWeek,* March 22, 2004, p.40.

18. Jeremy Rifkin, *The End of Work* (New York: Tarcher, 1994), p.6.

19. Ibid., p.142.

20. Jeremy Rifkin, "Return of a Conundrum," *The Guardian,* March 4, 2004.

21. Bruce Nussbaum, "Where Are the Jobs?" *BusinessWeek,* March 22, 2004, p.37.

22. Jeremy Rifkin, *The End of Work* (New York: Tarcher, 1994), p.5.

23. Office of Advocacy, the U.S. Small Business Administration, *Mergers and Acquisitions in the United States,* 1990-1994 (Washington DC: October 1998), p.3.

24. Aaron Bernstein, "Shaking Up Trade Theory," *BusinessWeek,* December 6, 2004, p.118.

25. Ibid.

26. Bruce Einhorn and Dexter Roberts, "Now College Grads Can't Find a Job," *BusinessWeek,* October 11, 2004, p.63.

27. Edward Wolff, *Changes in Household Wealth in the 1980s and 1990s in the U.S.,* working paper No.407 (New York: Jerome Levy Economics Institute, May 2004), http://www.levy.org/default.asp?view=publications_view&pubID=fca3a440ee (accessed September 1, 2005).

28. Griff Witte, "As Income Gap Widens, Uncertainty Spreads: More U.S. Families Struggle to Stay on Track," *Washington Post,* September 20, 2004, p.A1.

29. U.S. Bureau of Labor Statistics, *Employment Status of the Civilian Non-institutional Population 25 Years and Over by Educational Attainment* (Washington DC: 2005), ftp://ftp.bls.gov/pub/special.requests/lf/aat7.txt (accessed September 1, 2005).

30. U.S. Department of Education, *Outcomes for College Graduates* (Washington DC: 2005), http://www.ed.gov/pubs/CollegeForAll/graduates.html (accessed September 1, 2005).

31. Thomas Friedman, *The World is Flat* (New York: Farrar, Straus and Giroux, 2005), pp.173-200.

32. The Council on Competitiveness, *Innovate America* (Washington DC: December 2004), p.33, http://innovateamerica.org/webscr/report.asp (accessed September 1, 2005).

33. Paul Reynolds and others, *Global Entrepreneurship Monitor: 2003 Executive Report* (Babson Park, Massachusetts: Babson College, the London Business School, and the Kauffman Foundation, 2004), p.9, http://www.gemconsortium.org/document.asp?id=356 (accessed September 1, 2005).

34. Michael J. Mandel, *Rational Exuberance* (New York: HarperBusiness, 2004), p.27.

Chapter 2

1. Paul Reynolds and others, *Global Entrepreneurship Monitor: 2003 Executive Report* (Babson Park, Massachusetts: Babson College, the London Business School, and the Kauffman Foundation, 2004), p.18, http://www.gemconsortium.org/document.asp?id=356 (accessed September 1, 2005).

2. Steve Ballmer, "Microsoft: Dynamic Company, Dynamic Innovation, Optimistic Future" (closing address, Microsoft Financial Analyst Meeting, Redmond, Washington, July 29, 2004), http://www.microsoft.com/msft/speech/FY04/BallmerFAM2004.mspx (accessed September 1, 2005).

3. William Baumol, *The Free-Market Innovation Machine* (Princeton: Princeton University Press, 2002), p.3.

4. The Council on Competitiveness, *Innovate America* (Washington DC: December 2004), p.10, http://innovateamerica.org/webscr/report.asp (accessed September 1, 2005).

5. Price Pritchett, *Culture Shift* (Plano, Texas: Pritchett Rummler-Brache), p.2.

6. Robert Bednarzik, "The Role of Entrepreneurship in U.S. and European Job Growth," *Monthly Labor Review,* July 2000, p.4, http://www.bls.gov/opub/mlr/2000/07/art1full.pdf (accessed February 20, 2004).

7. Steve Ballmer, "Innovation or Stagnation: The Technology Industry at a Crossroads" (keynote address to the Churchill Club, Santa Clara, California, September 15, 2003), http://www.microsoft.com/presspass/exec/steve/2003/09-15churchill.mspx (accessed September 1, 2005).

8. Thomas Friedman, *The Lexus and the Olive Tree* (New York: Farrar, Straus and Giroux, 2000), p.9.

9. John Diamond, "Prediction: India, China will be Economic Giants," *USA Today,* January 14, 2005.

10. Price Pritchett, *New Work Habits* (Plano, Texas: Pritchett Rummler-Brache), pp.20-21.

11. Steve Ballmer, "Innovation or Stagnation: The Technology Industry at a Crossroads" (keynote address to the Churchill Club, Santa Clara, California, September 15, 2003), http://www.microsoft.com/presspass/exec/steve/2003/09-15churchill.mspx (accessed September 1, 2005).

12. Mark Gongloff, "China Not a Locomotive-Yet," *CNN Money,* January 31, 2003, http://money.cnn.com/2003/01/29/news/economy/china/ (accessed September 1, 2005).

13. Harris Nesbitt, *Focus on China* (Montreal: 2004), p.2.

14. Oded Shenkar, *The Chinese Century* (Upper Saddle River, New Jersey: Wharton School Publishing, 2005).

15. Ibid., p.131.

16. Pete Engardio and Dexter Roberts, "The China Price," *BusinessWeek,* December 6, 2004, p.106.

17. Pete Engardio, "A New World Economy," *BusinessWeek,* August 22/29, 2005, pp.52-28.

18. John Carey, "Flying High?" *BusinessWeek,* October 11, 2004, p.117.

19. Paul Reynolds and others, *Global Entrepreneurship Monitor: 2003 Executive Report* (Babson Park, Massachusetts: Babson College, the London Business School, and the Kauffman Foundation, 2004), p.7, http://www.gemconsortium.org/document.asp?id=356 (accessed September 1, 2005).

20. Steve Ballmer, "Microsoft: Dynamic Company, Dynamic Innovation, Optimistic Future" (closing address, Microsoft Financial Analyst Meeting, Redmond, Washington, July 29, 2004), http://www.microsoft.com/msft/speech/FY04/BallmerFAM2004.mspx (accessed September 1, 2005).

21. Steve Ballmer, "Innovation or Stagnation: The Technology Industry at a Crossroads" (keynote address to the Churchill Club, Santa Clara, California, September 15, 2003), http://www.microsoft.com/presspass/exec/steve/2003/09-15churchill.mspx (accessed September 1, 2005).

22. Paul Reynolds and others, *Global Entrepreneurship Monitor: 2003 Executive Report* (Babson Park, Massachusetts: Babson College, the London Business School, and the Kauffman Foundation, 2004), p.16, http://www.gemconsortium.org/document.asp?id=356 (accessed September 1, 2005).

23. The Council on Competitiveness, *Innovate America* (Washington DC: December 2004), p.5, http://innovateamerica.org/webscr/report.asp (accessed September 1, 2005).

Chapter 3

1. Harold Evans, *They Made America* (New York: Little, Brown, and Company, 2004), p.165.

2. Ibid.

3. Ibid., pp.151-171.

4. Richard Florida and Martin Kenney, *The Breakthrough Illusion* (New York: BasicBooks, 1990), p.19.

5. Henry Chesbrough, *Open Innovation* (Boston: Harvard Business School Press, 2003), p.27.

6. Ibid., p.26.

7. Ibid., p.27.

8. Ibid., p.27.

9. The Council on Competitiveness, *Innovate America* (Washington DC: December 2004), p.12, http://innovateamerica.org/webscr/report.asp (accessed September 1, 2005).

10. Pete Engardio, "Scouring the Planet for Brainiacs," *BusinessWeek,* October 11, 2004, p.102.

11. John Carey, "Flying High?" *BusinessWeek,* October 11, 2004, p.117.

12. Jeffrey Garten, "The High-Tech Threat from China," *BusinessWeek,* January 31, 2005, p.22.

13. Office of Advocacy, the U.S. Small Business Administration, "Contribution of Small High-Tech Firms to The New Economy" memorandum, (Washington DC: October 30, 2000), http://www.sba.gov/advo/advo_apptback.pdf (accessed September 1. 2005).

14. Kei Koizumi, *R&D Programs Face Another Rough Year in 2006* (Washington DC: American Association for the Advancement of Science, March 9, 2005), p.1, http://www.aaas.org/spp/rd (accessed September 1, 2005).

15. Ibid., table 1.

16. John Carey, "Flying High?" *BusinessWeek,* October 11, 2004, p.118.

17. Richard Florida and Martin Kenney, *The Breakthrough Illusion* (New York: Basic Books, 1990), p.32.

18. Kei Koizumi, *R&D Programs Face Another Rough Year in 2006* (Washington DC: American Association for the Advancement of Science, March 9, 2005), p.6, http://www.aaas.org/spp/rd (accessed September 1, 2005).

19. The Council on Competitiveness, *Innovate America* (Washington DC: December 2004), p.23, http://innovateamerica.org/webscr/report.asp (accessed September 1, 2005).

20. Ibid., p.25.

21. Ibid., p.19.

22. John Carey, "Flying High," *BusinessWeek,* October 11, 2004, p.117.

23. Pete Engardio, "Scouring the Planet for Brainiacs," *BusinessWeek,* October 11, 2004, p.100.

24. Raymond Wolfe, *Research and Development in Industry: 2001* (Arlington, VA: National Science Foundation, Division of Science Resources Statistics, 2005), NSF 05-305.

25. Pete Engardio and Bruce Einhorn, "Outsourcing Innovation," *BusinessWeek,* March 21, 2005, p.88.

Chapter 4
1. Thomas Stanley and William Danko, *The Millionaire Next Door* (Atlanta: Longstreet Press, 1996), p.165.
2. Timothy Bates, "Entrepreneur Human Capital Inputs and Small Business Longevity," *The Review of Economics and Statistics,* November 1990, p.551.
3. Margaret Fletcher, "Promoting Entrepreneurship As a Career Option: The Graduate Enterprise Programme," *Journal of European Industrial Training,* Vol.23, Issue 3, 1999, p.127.
4. "Millions Dream of Millions," *CollegeBoundNews.com,* Vol. 16, No.7, March 2002, www.collegeboundnews.com/01-02issues/mar02.html (accessed September 1, 2005).
5. Cynthia Georges, "Entrepreneurial Pursuits," *Olin Gateway,* Vol. 3, No.5, Summer 2004, http://www.olin.wustl.edu/discovery/feature.cfm?sid=301&i=16&pg=7 (accessed September 1, 2005).
6. Sarah Jack and Alistair Anderson, "Entrepreneurship Education within the Enterprise Culture: Producing Reflective Practitioners," *International Journal of Entrepreneurial Behaviour & Research,* Vol. 5, Issue 3, 1999, p.110.
7. Jennifer Merritt, "The Best B-Schools," *BusinessWeek,* October 18, 2004, pp.64-65; David Newton and Mark Henricks, "Can Entrepreneurship Be Taught?" *Entrepreneur,* April 2003, pp.68-69.
8. "Academic Shortcomings," *CollegeBoundNews.com,* Vol. 16, No.7, March 2002, www.collegeboundnews.com/01-02issues/mar02.html (accessed September 1, 2005).
9. Jennifer Merritt, "Hatching Success," *BusinessWeek Online,* October 2, 2002, http://www.businessweek.com:/2000/00_40/b3701020.htm (accessed July 7, 2003).
10. David Newton and Mark Henricks, "Can Entrepreneurship Be Taught?" *Entrepreneur,* April 2003, p.70.

Chapter 5
1. Harold Evans, *They Made America* (New York: Little, Brown and Company, 2004), p.304.
2. Ibid., pp.302-307.
3. National Venture Capital Association, *Frequently Asked Questions,* http://www.nvca.org/faqs.html (accessed September 1, 2005).
4. The South Sea Bubble was the result of speculation in the South Sea Company, which was formed to take over all of England's public debts by converting government fixed-interest annuities into lower-yield bonds. This created the largest financial bubble in history.
5. John Micklethwait and Adrian Wooldridge, *The Company* (New York: The Modern Library, 2003), p.xxi.
6. Susan Preston, *Angel Investment Groups, Networks, and Funds* (Kauffman Foundation: August 2004), p.5.
7. Ibid., p.3.
8. The MoneyTree™ Survey by PricewaterhouseCoopers, Thomson Venture Economics, and the National Venture Capital Association, *Venture Capital Investing Rises to $21 Billion in 2004 After Three Years of Decline* (Washington DC: January 24, 2004), http://www.nvca.org/pdf/Moneytreeq404final.pdf.

9. Carol Cain, "Budding Entrepreneurs Owe Thanks to Angels for Investments and Guidance." *Detroit Free Press,* Monday, April 18, 2005.

10. Jeff Sohl, "Angel Groups in Action: Funding Early Stage Innovation" (presentation before the MIT Enterprise Forum, Boston, June 1, 2005), http://enterpriseforum.mit.edu/network/broadcasts/200506/index.html (accessed September 1, 2005).

11. The Council on Competitiveness, *Innovate America* (Washington DC: December 2004), p.36, http://innovateamerica.org/webscr/report.asp (accessed September 1, 2005).

12. Cora Daniels, "Minority Rule," *Fortune Small Business,* December 2003, p.65.

13. The National Women's Business Council, *Best Practices in Supporting Women's Entrepreneurship* (Washington DC: June 2004), http://www.nwbc.gov/documents/Best-practices-brief.pdf (accessed September 1, 2005).

14. Cora Daniels, "Minority Rule," *Fortune Small Business,* December 2003, p.66.

15. Patricia Abaroa, *The International Investment Position of the United States at Yearend 2003* (Washington DC: Bureau of Economic Analysis, July 2004), http://www.bea.doc.gov/bea/newsrel/intinvnewsrelease.html (accessed September 1, 2005).

16. South Centre, *The Emergence of Foreign Portfolio Investment as a Primary Channel for Capital Flows to Developing Countries,* http://southcentre.org/papers/finance/jones/fondad-03.htm (accessed September 1, 2005).

17. Patricia Abaroa, *The International Investment Position of the United States at Yearend 2003* (Washington DC: Bureau of Economic Analysis, July 2004), http://www.bea.doc.gov/bea/newsrel/intinvnewsrelease.html (accessed September 1, 2005).

18. Jim Hopkins, "To Start Up Here, Companies Hire Over There," *USA Today,* February 11, 2005, B1.

19. Deloitte & Touche and the National Venture Capital Association, *U.S. VCs to Expand Global Investments; China and India Named as Top Global Targets* (San Jose, California: June 22, 2005), http://www.nvca.org/pdf/VC%20Survey%20PR%20FINAL%206-22-05.pdf (accessed September 1, 2005).

20. Zoltan Acs and others, *Global Entrepreneurship Monitor: 2004 Executive Report* (Babson Park: Massachusetts: Babson College and the London Business School, 2005), p.20, http://www.gemconsortium.org/document.asp?id=364 (accessed September 1, 2005).

Chapter 6

1. Jeremy Rifkin, *The End of Work* (New York: Tarcher, 1994), p.175.

2. Ladas & Parry LLP, *A Brief History of the Patent Law of the Untied States,* http://www.ladas.com/patents/USpatenthistory.html (accessed September 1, 2005).

3. Ibid.

4. Thomas DiBacco, *Made in the USA* (New York: Harper and Row, 1987), p. 140.

5. U.S. Immigration and Customs Enforcement, *Fact Sheet: Strategy Targeting Organized Piracy* (Washington DC: October 4, 2004), http://www.ice.gov/graphics/news/factsheets/STOP_FS100404.htm (accessed September 15, 2005).

6. John Micklethwait and Adrian Wooldridge, *The Company* (New York: The Modern Library, 2003), p. 131.

7. Eric Smith, "Piracy of Intellectual Property," (written statement before the Subcommittee on Intellectual Property Senate Judiciary Committee, Washington DC, May 25, 2005) http://www.iipa.com/rbi/2005_May25_China_Russia_Testimony.pdf (accessed September 1, 2005).

8. International Intellectual Property Alliance, *USTR 2005: Special 301 Decisions* (Washington DC: 2005), http://www.iipa.com/rbc/2005SPE301PRCrev.pdf (accessed September 1, 2005).

9. Tom Davis, "Intellectual Property Piracy: Are We Doing Enough to Protect U.S. Innovation Abroad?" (opening statement to the U.S. House of Representatives Committee on Government Reform, Washington DC, September 23, 2004), http://reform.house.gov/UploadedFiles/TMD%20IP%20Piracy%20Opener.pdf (accessed September 21, 2005).

10. Frederik Balfour, "Fakes," *BusinessWeek,* February 7, 2005, p.56.

11. Tom Davis, "Intellectual Property Piracy: Are We Doing Enough to Protect U.S. Innovation Abroad?" (opening statement to the U.S. House of Representatives Committee on Government Reform, Washington DC, September 23, 2004), http://reform.house.gov/UploadedFiles/TMD%20IP%20Piracy%20Opener.pdf (accessed September 21, 2005).

12. E.M. Swift and Don Yaeger, "Pssst... Wanna Buy Some Clubs?" *Time,* July 21, 2003.

13. International Intellectual Property Alliance, *USTR 2005: Special 301 Decisions* (Washington DC: 2005), http://www.iipa.com/rbc/2005SPE301PRCrev.pdf (accessed September 1, 2005).

14. Eric Smith, "Piracy of Intellectual Property," (written statement before the Subcommittee on Intellectual Property Senate Judiciary Committee, Washington DC, May 25, 2005), http://www.iipa.com/rbi/2005_May25_China_Russia_Testimony.pdf (accessed September 1. 2005).

15. U.S. Immigration and Customs Enforcement, *Fact Sheet: Strategy Targeting Organized Piracy* (Washington DC: October 4, 2004), http://www.ice.gov/graphics/news/factsheets/STOP_FS100404.htm (accessed September 15, 2005).

16. Seth Schulman, *Owning the Future* (Boston: Houghton Mifflin Company, 1999), p.115.

17. Pearl Patent Enforcement and Royalties, *Patent Infringement Lawsuits: By the Numbers,* http://www.pearlltd.com/content/pat_inf_law.html (accessed September 1, 2005).

18. Stephen Merrill and others, editors. *A Patent System for the 21st Century* (Washington DC: The National Academies Press, 2001), p.74.

19. United States Patent and Trademark Office, *21st Century Strategic Plan* (Washington DC: February 3, 2003), http://www.uspto.gov/web/offices/com/strat21/ (accessed September 1, 2005).

20. Seth Schulman, *Owning the Future* (Boston: Houghton Mifflin Company, 1999), p.11.

21. Samantha Grover, *Intellectual Property Owners Association Supports Patent and Trademark Fee Modernization Provision of the COMPETE Act* (Washington DC: Intellectual Property Owners Association, May 13, 2005), http://www.ipo.org/Template.cfm?Section=Home&Template=/ContentManagement/ContentDisplay.cfm&ContentID=18368 (accessed September 1, 2005).

22. Michael Meurer, *Controlling Opportunistic and Anti-Competitive Intellectual Property Litigation,* http://www.bc.edu/schools/law/lawreviews/meta-elements/journals/bclawr/44_2/07_TXT.htm (accessed September 1, 2005).

Chapter 7

1. Thomas Stanley and William Danko, *The Millionaire Next Door* (Atlanta: Longstreet Press, 1996), p.8. Matthew Miller and Peter Newcomb, ed., "The Forbes 400: The Top Ten," *Forbes,* October 10, 2005, pp.90-100.

2. Steven Birmingham, *America's Secret Aristocracy* (Boston: Little, Brown & Co., 1987), pp.204-205.

3. Michael Klepper and Robert Guenther, *The Wealthy 100* (Secaucus, New Jersey: Carol Publishing Group, 1996), p.xi.

4. Daniel Gross, "Cash of the Titans," *Robb Report,* April 2002, pp.123-127.

5. Data for CEO compensation from *BusinessWeek* annual executive pay surveys. Data for S&P 500 Index from Standard and Poor's Corporation. Data for corporate Profits from the Bureau of Economic Analysis, "National Income." Data for average worker pay from the Bureau of Labor Statistics, "Average Weekly Earnings of Production Workers, Total Private Sector." Data for inflation from the Bureau of Labor Statistics, "Consumer Price Index, All Urban Consumers."

6. James Clifton, "The Emotional Economy of the Workplace," (presentation to the Society of Human Resource Managers Foundation, Fourth Annual Thought Leaders Retreat, May, 2003).

7. Ibid.

8. Jason Hoody, *Primer: Recent History of Employee Stock Options* (Washington DC: Financial Policy Forum Derivatives Study Center, 2005), http://www.financialpolicy.org/dscprimerstockoption2a.htm, (accessed September 1, 2005).

9. John Micklethwait and Adrian Wooldridge, *The Company* (New York: The Modern Library, 2003), p.144.

10. Michael Mandel, "Productivity: Who Wins, Who Loses," *BusinessWeek,* March 22, 2004, p.45.

11. Monique Morrissey, "Background Report: Employee Stock Options," *Financial Market Center,* 2000.

Chapter 8

1. John F. Kennedy (address at Rice University on the nation's space effort, Houston, September 12, 1962), http://www/jfklibrary.org/speeches.htm (accessed September 1, 2005).

2. William Burrows, *This New Ocean* (New York: Random House, 1998).

3. Paul Reynolds and others, *Global Entrepreneurship Monitor: 2003 Executive Report* (Babson Park, Massachusetts: Babson College, the London Business School, and the Kauffman Foundation, 2004), p.18, http://www.gemconsortium.org/document.asp?id=356 (accessed September 1, 2005).

4. Zoltan Acs and others, *Global Entrepreneurship Monitor 2004 Executive Report* (Babson Park: Massachusetts: Babson College and the London Business School, 2005), p.14, http://www.gemconsortium.org/document.asp?id=364 (accessed September 1, 2005).

5. John Micklethwait and Adrian Wooldridge, *The Company* (New York: The Modern Library, 2003), pp.130-131.

6. White House, *Fact Sheet: Supporting America's Small Businesses* (Washington DC: 2005), http://www.whitehouse.gov/infocus/smallbusiness/ (accessed September 1, 2005).

7. Clayton Christensen, *The Innovator's Dilemma* (Boston: Harvard Business School Press, 1997), pp.42-48.

8. Small Business Administration, *Contribution of Small High-Tech Firms to the New Economy* memorandum, (Washington DC: 2004), http://www.sba.gov/advo/ advo_apptback.pdf (accessed September 1, 2005).

9. Art Kleiner, "Professor Chandler's Revolution," *Strategy+Business,* Issue 27, p.90.

10. Paul Reynolds and others, *Global Entrepreneurship Monitor: 2003 Executive Report* (Babson Park, Massachusetts: Babson College, the London Business School, and the Kauffman Foundation, 2004), p.10, http://www.gemconsortium. org/document.asp?id=356 (accessed September 1, 2005). The authors of the report note that, "There is substantial variation among countries, although differences between most adjacent countries are not statistically significant. The major factor that affects the confidence intervals is the number of respondents reporting that they were owner-managers of large firms. Larger numbers of owner-managers may result from large samples or higher prevalence rates in the population. It is clear from this presentation that while Chile may be higher than other countries on this measure, there is clearly something unique about this extreme value. It seems to reflect a distinctive use of the survey items related to perceived market impact of the business, one of the indicators used to identify entrepreneurial firms; Chile is unlikely to be three times the country average."

11. Ibid., p.13.

12. Gifford Pinchot, "The Five People of Innovation," *Innovation & Intrapreneuring,* http://www.pinchot.com/MainPages/BooksArticles/InnovationInt rapreneuring/FivePeople.html.

13. Gifford Pinchot, *Intrapreneuring* (New York, Harper and Row, 1985).

14. Ibid., p.6.

15. The Council on Competitiveness' National Innovation Initiative, *Innovate America* (Washington DC: Council on Competitiveness, December 2004), p.17, http://innovateamerica.org/webscr/report.asp (accessed September 1, 2005).

16. Ibid., p.18.

17. David Mowery and others, *Ivory Tower and Industrial Revolution,* (Stanford: Stanford Business Books, 2004), p.23.

Chapter 9

1. Kevin Philips, *Boiling Point* (New York: Random House, 1993), p.199.

2. Ibid.

3. National Center for Education Statistics (2001). "The Nation's Report Card: Mathematics 2000." Washington, D.C.: U.S. Government Printing Office (NCES 2001-517).

BIBLIOGRAPHY

Acs, Zoltan, and Pai Arenius, Michael Hay, Maria Minniti and others. *Global Entrepreneurship Monitor: 2004 Executive Report*. Babson Park, Massachusetts: Babson College and the London Business School, 2005. http://www.gemconsortium.org/document.asp?id=364 (accessed September 1, 2005).

Balfour, Frederik. "Fakes," *BusinessWeek*, February 7, 2005.

Baumol, William. *The Free-Market Innovation Machine: Analyzing the Growth Miracle of Capitalism*. Princeton: Princeton University Press, 2002.

Bernstein, Aaron. "Shaking Up Trade Theory," *BusinessWeek*, December 6, 2004.

Burrows, William. *This New Ocean: The Story of the First Space Age*. New York: Random House, 1998.

Carey, John. "Flying High?" *BusinessWeek*, October 11, 2004.

Chesbrough, Henry. *Open Innovation: The New Imperative for Creating and Profiting from Technology*. Boston: Harvard Business School Press, 2003.

Christensen, Clayton. *The Innovator's Dilemma: When New Technologies Cause Great Firms to Fail*. Boston: Harvard Business School Press, 1997.

Cooper, James. "The Price of Efficiency," *BusinessWeek*, March 22, 2004.

The Council on Competitiveness. *Innovate America*. Washington DC: December 2004. http://innovateamerica.org/webscr/report.asp (accessed September 1, 2005).

Daniels, Cora. "Minority Rule," *Fortune Small Business*, December 2003.

DeSoto, Hernando. *The Mystery of Capital: Why Capitalism Triumphs in the West and Fails Everywhere Else*. New York: Basic Books, 2000.

Diamond, John. "Prediction: India, China will be Economic Giants," *USA Today*, January 14, 2005.

DiBacco, Thomas. *Made in the U.S.A.: The History of American Business*. New York: Harper and Row, 1987.

Drucker, Peter. *Innovation and Entrepreneurship: Practice and Principles*. New York: Harper and Row, 1985.

Einhorn, Bruce, and Dexter Roberts. "Now College Grads Can't Find a Job," *BusinessWeek*, October 11, 2004.

Engardio, Pete, and Dexter Roberts. "The China Price," *BusinessWeek,* December 6, 2004.

Engardio, Pete. "A New World Economy," *BusinessWeek,* August 22/29, 2005.

Engardio, Pete, and Bruce Einhorn. "Outsourcing Innovation," *BusinessWeek,* March 21, 2005.

Engardio, Pete. "Scouring the Planet for Brainiacs," *BusinessWeek,* October 11, 2004.

Enriquez, Juan. *As the Future Catches You: How Genomics & Other Forces are Changing Your Life, Work, Health & Wealth.* New York: Crown Business, 2001.

Evans, Harold. *They Made America: Two Centuries of Innovators from the Steam Engine to the Search Engine.* New York: Little, Brown and Company, 2004.

Fletcher, Margaret. "Promoting Entrepreneurship As a Career Option: The Graduate Enterprise Programme," *Journal of European Industrial Training,* Vol.23, Issue 3, 1999.

Florida, Richard. *The Rise of the Creative Class: And How It's Transforming Work, Leisure, Community, and Everyday Life.* New York: Basic Books, 2002.

Florida, Richard, and Martin Kenney. *The Breakthrough Illusion.* New York: BasicBooks, 1990.

Friedman, Thomas. *The Lexus and the Olive Tree: Understanding Globalization.* New York: Farrar, Straus and Giroux, 2000.

Friedman, Thomas. *The World is Flat: A Brief History of the Twenty-first Century.* New York: Farrar, Straus and Giroux, 2005.

Garten, Jeffrey. "The High-Tech Threat from China," *BusinessWeek,* January 31, 2005.

Gross, Daniel. "Cash of the Titans," *Robb Report,* April 2002.

Hagadorn, Andrew. *How Breakthroughs Happen: The Surprising Truth About How Companies Innovate.* Boston: Harvard Business School Press, 2003.

Hira, Ron, and Anil Hira, *Outsourcing America: What's Behind Our National Crisis and How We Can Reclaim American Jobs.* New York: AMACOM American Management Association, 2005.

Hopkins, Jim. "To Start Up Here, Companies Hire Over There," *USA Today,* February 11, 2005, B1.

Jack, Sarah, and Alistair Anderson. "Entrepreneurship Education within the Enterprise Culture: Producing Reflective Practitioners," *International Journal of Entrepreneurial Behaviour & Research,* Vol. 5, Issue 3, 1999.

Klepper, Michael, and Robert Guenther. *The Wealthy 100: From Benjamin Franklin to Bill Gates—A Ranking of the Richest Americans, Past and Present.* Secaucus, New Jersey: Carol Publishing Group, 1996.

Koizumi, Kei. *R&D Programs Face Another Rough Year in 2006: Cuts for Many, Gains for Space and Homeland Security.* Washington DC: American Association for the Advancement of Science, March 9, 2005. http://www.aaas.org/spp/rd (accessed September 1, 2005).

Luttwak, Edward. *Turbo Capitalism: Winners and Losers in the Global Economy.* New York: HarperCollins Publishers, 1999.

Mandel, Michael. "Productivity: Who Wins, Who Loses," *BusinessWeek,* March 22, 2004.

Mandel, Michael. *Rational Exuberance: Silencing the Enemies of Growth.* New York: HarperBusiness, 2004.

Merrill, Stephen, and Richard Levin, Mark Meyers, editors. *A Patent System for the 21st Century.* Washington DC: The National Academies Press, 2001.

Merritt, Jennifer. "Hatching Success," *BusinessWeek Online,* October 2, 2002, http://www.businessweek.com:/2000/00_40/b3701020.htm (accessed July 7, 2003).

Meurer, Michael. "Controlling Opportunistic and Anti-Competitive Intellectual Property Litigation," http://www.bc.edu/schools/law/lawreviews/meta-elements/journals/bclawr/44_2/07_TXT.htm (accessed September 1, 2005).

Miller, Matthew, and Peter Newcomb, ed. "The Forbes 400: The Top Ten," *Forbes,* October 10, 2005.

Micklethwait, John, and Adrian Wooldridge, *The Company: A Short History of a Revolutionary Idea.* New York: The Modern Library, 2003.

Morrissey, Monique. "Background Report: Employee Stock Options," *Financial Market Center,* 2000.

Mowery, David, and Richard Nelson, Bhaven Sampat and Arvids Ziedonis. *Ivory Tower and Industrial Revolution.* Stanford: Stanford Business Books, 2004.

The National Women's Business Council. *Best Practices in Supporting Women's Entrepreneurship.* Washington DC: The National Women's Business Council, June 2004. http://www.nwbc.gov/documents/Best-practices-brief.pdf (accessed September 1, 2005).

Newman, Kathleen. *Declining Fortunes: The Withering of the American Dream.* New York: Basic Books, 1994.

Newton, David and Mark Henricks, "Can Entrepreneurship Be Taught?" *Entrepreneur,* April 2003.

Nussbaum, Bruce. "Where Are the Jobs?" *BusinessWeek,* March 22, 2004.

Office of Advocacy, the U.S. Small Business Administration. *Mergers and Acquisitions in the United States, 1990-1994.* Washington DC: Office of Advocacy, U.S. Small Business Administration, October 1998.

Philips, Kevin. *Boiling Point: Democrats, Republicans, and the Decline of Middle-Class Prosperity.* New York: Random House, 1993.

Pinchot, Gifford. *Intrapreneuring: Why You Don't Have to Leave the Corporation to Become an Entrepreneur.* New York, Harper and Row, 1985.

Preston, Susan. *Angel Investment Groups, Networks, and Funds.* Kansas City, Missouri: Kauffman Foundation, August 2004.

Prestowitz, Clyde. *Three Billion New Capitalists: The Great Shift of Wealth and Power to the East.* New York: Basic Books, 2005.

Pritchett, Price. *Culture Shift.* Plano, Texas: Pritchett Rummler-Brache.

Pritchett, Price. *New Work Habits.* Plano, Texas: Pritchett Rummler-Brache.

Reynolds, Paul, William Bygrave, Erkko Autio and others. *Global Entrepreneurship Monitor: 2003 Executive Report.* Babson Park, Massachusetts: Babson College, the London Business School, and the Kauffman Foundation, 2004. http://www.gemconsortium.org/document.asp?id=356 (accessed September 1, 2005).

Rifkin, Jeremy. *The End of Work: The Decline of the Global Labor Force and the Dawn of the Post-Market Era.* New York: Tarcher, 1994.

Rifkin, Jeremy. "Return of a Conundrum," *The Guardian,* March 4, 2004.

Schulman, Seth. *Owning the Future: Inside the Battles to Control the New Assets-Genes, Software, Databases, and Technological Know-How-That Make Up the Lifeblood of the New Economy.* Boston: Houghton Mifflin Company, 1999.

Shenkar, Oded. *The Chinese Century: The Rising Chinese Economy and Its Impact on the Global Economy, the Balance of Power, and Your Job.* Upper Saddle River, New Jersey: Wharton School Publishing, 2005.

Stanley, Thomas, and William Danko. *The Millionaire Next Door: The Surprising Secrets of America's Wealthy.* Atlanta: Longstreet Press, 1996.

Surowiecki, James. *The Wisdom of Crowds: Why the Many Are Smarter Than the Few and How Collective Wisdom Shapes Business, Economies, Societies, and Nations.* New York: Doubleday, 2004.

Warren, Elizabeth, and Amelia Warren Tyagi. *The Two-Income Trap: Why Middle-Class Parents Are Going Broke.* New York: Basic Books, 2003.

Witte, Griff. "As Income Gap Widens, Uncertainty Spreads: More U.S. Families Struggle to Stay on Track." *Washington Post,* September 20, 2004. http://www.washingtonpost.com/wp-dyn/articles/A34235-2004Sep19.html (accessed September 1, 2005).

Wolf, Richard. "1.1 Million Americans Joined Ranks of the Poor in 2004," *USA Today,* August 31, 2005.

Wolff, Edward. "Changes in Household Wealth in the 1980s and 1990s in the U.S.," Jerome Levy Economics Institute, May 2004.

INDEX